Graduate Admissions Essays

Graduate Admissions Essays

WRITE YOUR WAY
INTO THE GRADUATE SCHOOL
OF YOUR CHOICE

THIRD EDITION

DONALD ASHER

TEN SPEED PRESS
Berkeley | Toronto

TEN SPEED PRESS
PO Box 7123
Berkeley CA 94707
www.tenspeed.com

Distributed in Australia by Simon and Schuster Australia, in Canada by Ten Speed Press Canada, in New Zealand by Southern Publishers Group, in South Africa by Real Books, and in the United Kingdom and Europe by Publishers Group UK.

Cover design by Laura Milton
Book design and composition by Chris Hall/Ampersand

Library of Congress Cataloging-in-Publication Data
Asher, Donald.
   Graduate admissions essays : write your way into the graduate school of your choice / Donald Asher. —
3rd ed.
      p. cm.
   Includes bibliographical references and indexes.
   ISBN-13: 978-1-58008-872-5 (alk. paper)
   ISBN-10: 1-58008-872-4 (alk. paper)
   1. College applications—United States. 2. Universities and
colleges—United States—Graduate work—Admission. 3. Exposition (Rhetoric) 4. Essay—Authorship.
I. Title.
   LB2351.52.U6A74 2008
   808'.066378—dc22

                          2007049830

Printed in the United States of America

First printing, 2008

1 2 3 4 5 6 7 8 9 10 — 12 11 10 09 08

Contents

A great professor of history can make the French Revolution come alive so that you can see the barricades in the streets of Paris and hear the swish of the guillotine's blade as it descends. Likewise, a Shakespearean scholar can help you feel the anguish of the protagonists in the tragedies and can show you the contemporary nature of the humor in the Bard's comedies. But how do you excite and entertain an audience when talking about getting into graduate school? Well, Donald Asher does exactly that . . . you'll find you not only enjoy yourself, but you'll also learn a great deal about tactics and strategies that will help you increase the odds of getting into the graduate or professional program of your choice. Donald is uniquely qualified to present this program. He's met with admissions officers all across the country and spoken at dozens of colleges and universities. . . . His book, *Graduate Admissions Essays,* has been a huge seller, and he's written a variety of other books and articles. . . . I'm proud to introduce . . . Donald Asher.

—Dr. Robert Greenberg, NACE fellow and host of
the National Teleconference on Graduate Admissions

Acknowledgments

I owe special thanks to:

Dr. Orlando Taylor, Dean of the Graduate School, Howard University; Dr. Judith L. Kuipers, President, Fielding Graduate University; Dr. David Payne, Executive Director, GRE ; Charles Johnson, Director, Master's & Executive Programs, Krannert School of Management, Purdue University; Alan D. Ferrell, Director, Graduate Career Services, Krannert School of Management, Purdue University; Geri Weilacher, Director, Penn State TRIO Training Institute; Dr. Thomas Rochon, Executive Vice-President and Chief Academic Officer, University of St. Thomas-Minnesota; Mary L. Gonzalez, Assistant Vice President, Division of Special Programs, Texas A&M University-Kingsville; Cherryl Arnold, Director, Educational Opportunity & TRIO Programs, Georgia State University; Michael L. Jeffries, Associate Dean and Director of Minority Student Affairs, University of Illinois at Urbana-Champaign, and Founder, McNair Scholars National Conference; Dr. Priscilla J. Fortier, Assistant Dean of Students, University of Illinois at Urbana-Champaign; Colin Diver, President, Reed College; Dr. Ruby Ausbrooks, Educational Consultant, Gerlach, Nevada; Dr. Carolyn Herman, Pre-Med Advisor and Dean, College of Arts & Sciences, Washington University in St. Louis; Dr. Jennifer Vega La Serna, Dean of Arts and Letters, College of the Sequoias; Julie Kern Smith, Career Services-Experiential Learning, Reed College; Dr. George B. Robbins, Associate Director of Graduate Academic & Enrollment Services, Rensselaer Polytechnic Institute; Samuel T. Lindquist, Director of Admissions, The Amos Tuck School of Business Administration; Dr. Gerald Foster, Director of Admissions, Harvard Medical School; Richard Badger, Dean of Admissions, The Law School of the University of Chicago; Kathleen Plessas, Director of Admissions, School of Medicine, University of California, San Francisco; Louise Goldsmith, Graduate Assistant Admissions Coordinator, U.C.L.A.-Architecture; Judy Colwell, Assistant Director of Admissions, Stanford University School of Medicine; Dr. Robert Greenberg, NACE Fellow, University of Tennessee, Knoxville; Dr. Cathi L. Eagan, Assistant Dean, Research and the University Graduate School, Director, McNair Scholars Program, Associate Director, MEDIC-B Program, Indiana University; Dr. Barbara A. Herman Center, University of Wisconsin-Madison Medical School; Dr. Linda Arbuckle, Graduate Coordinator, University of Florida, Gainesville; Dr. Judy Jones, Executive Director, Pond Mountain Lodge & Retreat-Eureka Springs; Dr. Manuel Febres, Programa McNair, Universidad de Puerto Rico-San Juan; Dr. Michelle Sparacino, Director of Recruitment & Admissions, School of Public Health and Health Services, George Washington University; Dr. Kay Reed, The Graduate School of the University of Tennessee, Knoxville; Bertha Thomas, Director, McNair Scholars Program, Truman State University; Dr. Vicki M. Curby, Director, McNair Scholars Program, University of Missouri-Columbia; Dr. Steven M. Ehrlich, Assistant Dean, College of Arts & Sciences, Washington University; Jeffrey Johnson, NAGAP Membership Director and Director of Admissions, Tulane School of Public Health and Tropical Medicine; Dr. Janet Goebel, Rhodes Adviser and Director of the Robert E. Cook Honors College, Indiana University of Pennsylvania; Nick Ewold, Director, McNair Scholars

Program, Beloit College; DeVon Wilson, Assistant Dean, University of Wisconsin–Madison; Linda Vivian, Coordinator of Special Projects for the Graduate School of the University of Florida; Dr. Larry Duffy, Chair, Pre-Medical Advising Committee, The University of Alaska, Fairbanks; John Garic, Esq., Pre-Law & Graduate School Advising, Franklin & Marshall College; Dr. Mary E. Kirtley, Office for Graduate and Professional Studies, Dickinson College; James A. Marino, Director, Career Center, Rutgers-Camden; Katherine K. Nobles, Director, Career Services, Oglethorpe University; Dr. Thomas Q. Reefe, Director, Career Development Center, University of California, Santa Cruz; Tom Francis, Director (Ret.) Career Services, Swarthmore College; Dr. Robert C. Pebworth, Jr., Director, Career Planning & Placement, Wabash College; Saul Reyes, Director, Career Center, Jacksonville University; Dr. Edward Zovinka, Chemistry Department, St. Francis College-Loretto; John Adams, Director, Career Services, Davidson College; Tony Butchello, Associate Director, Career Services, Davidson College; Gar Cropser, Associate Director, Career Services, University of California, Irvine; Tom R. Cath, Director, Career Center, DePauw University; Carla Mollins Rinde, Director, Career Center, Ursinus College; Lisa B. Dickter, Associate Director, Career Services, Carnegie Mellon University; Judy L. Fisher, Director, Career Center, Harvey Mudd College; Pamela S. Backes, Associate Director, Career Services, Keene State College; Patricia M. Campbell, Director, Career Services, Keene State College; Dr. Rebecca A. Emery, Director, Career Services, Salisbury State University; Stephanie Paramore, Assistant Director, Priscilla A. Scotlan Career Services Center, University of San Francisco; Amy Wilms, Director, Career Services, University of Redlands; Dr. Tariq Shakoor, Director, Career Center, Emory University; Yolanda M. Manora, Associate Director, Pre-Professional Advising, Emory University; Katherine Harper, Director, Career Center, Western Oregon University; Patrick D. Mullane, Director, Career Development Services, Dickinson College; Rob Felton, Public Affairs Officer, George Fox University; Seth L. Smythe, Willamette University; Nancy Norton, Director, Career Center, Willamette University; Anne Hardin Ballard, Director, Career Development Services, Linfield College; Peter S. Van Houten and Mary Blakeslee, Pre-Professional/Pre-Graduate Advising, University of California, Berkeley; Dr. Dandré Desandies, Associate Director, Career Development, Stanford University; Toinette Menashe, Director, Master of Arts in Liberal Studies Program, Reed College; Dr. Walter Englert, Chair, Classics Department, Reed College; Lisa Garb, Director of Public Relations, Peterson's Guides; Ricky L. Parham, Applicant Relations, American Association of Medical Colleges; Brian P. O'Driscoll, Director, Career Services, Pacific University; Dr. Jason Morris, Director, Master's Program in Higher Education, Abilene Christain University; Jennifer Tucker, Associate Director, Field and Career Office, Beloit College; Nancy B. Karpinski, Director, Career Development Services, Wells College; Maureen Daly, Kilian Kerwin, Mohamed Yunus Rafiq, Michelle Levy, Fang-Yuan Chang, Rob Saldin, Gerrad Jones, Damian Madan, Brian T. Powers, Rachel Elizabeth Anderson, Erin E. Bonuso, Yung-Hsiang Hsu, Jonathan Doti, Manny Mora, Juana Gatson, Senetta Bancroft, Catherine Glew Hylands, Todd Hobler, Adam N. Green, Flay Rogers, Margie Lariviere, Andrea J. Morgan, Brad Wurtz, Meyer M. Speary, H. Glickman, Bob Muldoon, Victor F. Simonyi, Kevin Kelleher, Gennine Zinner, R.D., Jennifer Ferenstein, Lisa Kemmerer, Linda C. Saremi, Gretchen Craft, Wendy Richardson, Tod Cochran, Molly Stenzel, Deborah E. Gallant, Brian Boyl, Sabrina Gee, Dr. Anastasia Pinoris, David Lawrence Conlin, David Coleman, Dr. Bruce Johnson, Kevan Shokat, Dr. John R. Vasquez, Debbie Redd, Shane Whittington, Rebecca Weller, Dr. Majid Tavakkolijou, Dr. Arturo F. Muñoz, Robert Fallon, Paul F. Laubscher, Ranessa L. Cooper, Jeffrey P. Henkle, Jennifer Drayton Sohn, Mills College, Jennifer Nagy, Charles Kosan, and of course, anonymous.

I owe special thanks also to Phil Wood and Lorena Jones of Ten Speed Press for their continued support of this book. Special thanks also to my in-house editor Veronica Randall and to designer Chris Hall of Ampersand for their work on the third edition. And continuing debt to George Young, Mariah Bear, and Becky Lemov for their guidance on the first edition. The errors are all mine, but many, many people have contributed to the success of this book. Thank you all.

Many of the names, dates, schools, firm names, and other specific details in these essays were changed at the request of the contributors, and others were changed at the discretion of the editors. No particular individual named in these essays should be presumed to be any particular actual individual, and any such assumption would be unwarranted.

Some of the colleges and universities where Donald Asher has lectured:

East: Brown, University of Pennsylvania, Penn State, NYU, Babson, Carnegie Mellon, Swarthmore, Case Western Reserve, University of Maryland, Middlebury, Haverford, Bryn Mawr, University of Pittsburgh, Albright, Indiana University of Pennsylvania, Millersville, Hillsdale, Grove City College, Villanova, Ithaca, Keene State, New England College, Wells, Cedar Crest, Muhlenberg, St. Francis, Rosemont, Dickinson, Rutgers, Gettysburg, Franklin & Marshall, Washington & Jefferson, Westminster (Penn.), Villa Julie, SUNY Institute of Technology, SUNY Geneseo, SUNY Fredonia, SUNY Stony Brook, SUNY Pottsdam, SUNY Purchase, Post, Providence College, Cayuga Community College, Buffalo State, University at Buffalo, CUNY-Hunter College, Mercy College (New York), Daemen, Arcadia, Niagara, Ursinus, Skidmore, Lafayette, Moravian, Baldwin-Wallace, Hiram, Ohio University, St. John's (Annapolis), Michigan State, Ferris State, Lyndon State, St. Vincent (Penn.), Medaille, Macomb Community College, University of Tennessee-Knoxville, University of Tennessee-Chattanooga, Davidson, University of North Carolina-Chapel Hill, University of North Carolina-Greensboro, University of Puerto Rico-San Juan, *and more.*

West: Stanford, Reed, Caltech, Harvey Mudd, Scripps, U.C. Berkeley, U.C. Irvine, U.C. San Diego, U.C. Santa Cruz, Cal State-Dominguez Hills, Lewis & Clark, Linfield, Linfield-Portland, University of Santa Clara, Claremont Graduate University, Academy of Art (San Francisco), Azusa Pacific, University of Arizona, University of New Mexico, Portland State, University of Portland, University of Redlands, Occidental, George Fox, University of Colorado, University of Denver, University of Northern Colorado, Colorado School of Mines, Central Washington University, Eastern Washington University, Westminster (Utah), Carroll, University of Alaska-Fairbanks, University of Alaska-Anchorage, Baylor, University of Texas-Arlington, Abilene Christian University, Our Lady of the Lake, St. Edwards, University of San Francisco, Biola, San Francisco State, Mills, University of Oregon, Oregon State University, Western Oregon, Albertson, Willamette, Pacific University, Eastern Oregon, Walla Walla, Whitman, Westmont, University of Nevada, Brigham Young University-Hawaii, *and more.*

Midwest/South: University of Chicago, Tulane, Purdue, Indiana University, Washington University in St. Louis, Virginia Tech, Rose-Hulman, Marquette, University of Wisconsin-Madison, Beloit, St. Norbert, Creighton, IUPUI, Concordia (Minn.), North Dakota State, Minnesota State-Moorhead, University of Missouri, University of South Carolina, Babcock, Rhodes, Hendrix, University of Arkansas, University of Arkansas-Little Rock, University of Arkansas-Pine Bluff, Henderson State, Oglethorpe, Earlham, DePauw, DePaul, Wabash, Truman State, Kansas State, Principia, Marian (Indianapolis), Knox, Albion, Hanover, University of Oklahoma, Fairmont, Concord State, Harding, Emory, S.M.U., TAMUK, Centre, Transylvania, Murray State, Berea, University of Indianapolis, New College, Florida International University, University of Central Florida, Rockford, Franklin, East Central University (Oklahoma), Jacksonville University, University of Alabama, University of the South (Sewanee), *and more.*

To arrange speaking engagements on graduate admissions or career development issues, at graduate or undergraduate levels, contact Asher Associates, San Francisco, 415-543-7130; email don@donaldasher.com.

Introduction

How to Use This Book

The best way to use this book is to read it in its entirety, even the sections that do not apply to you directly. Then start over, completing each assignment before you go on to the next. Plan on rewriting your essay several times. Whatever you do, do not write a word until you have done the personal assessments in chapter 5, "Getting Ready to Write."

If you have procrastinated until the last minute, the first thing you need to do is *relax*. You can still finish a great essay by tomorrow morning. Just take out a pad of paper and a pen, or fire up your computer; read chapters 4, 5, 6, and 7, in order; and follow the assignments as you come across them. Do not read ahead. If any sections don't apply to your particular case, just skip them.

This book makes only one assumption about you, the reader. Readers in general tend to be much smarter than the average human; given this book's topic, it is probably safe to assume that you are much smarter than the average reader. Incidentally, after years of having college professors focus on your errors and shortcomings, you are probably a lot smarter than *you* think. It is a luxury for an author to be able to write for such an audience.

This book presents a variety of techniques that students use to gain admission to highly competitive graduate programs. Some are so competitive that only 2 percent of applicants are accepted; for every fifty students who apply, only one will be entering the program. Even if your targeted schools are relatively easy to get into, these techniques should be of interest to you in winning scholarships, assistantships, and other valuable considerations. Pay particular attention to the strategies for contacting professors and overcoming liabilities in your background, and you'll be able to gain admission to more competitive programs than you otherwise might.

One of the unique features of this book is its inclusion of a full chapter on letters of recommendation (chapter 9). Letters of recommendation are a critical component of your application process, and they deserve full and separate consideration. In addition to providing a plan for selecting and motivating writers of these letters, the chapter provides a handout you can give them—"Better Letters of Recommendation"—to guide them through the process.

Another unique feature is the inclusion of scholarship, residency, fellowship, postgraduate, and postdoctoral essays. This information was available in no other book at the time this edition went to press. As one proceeds up the ivory tower, essays become more precise, more specific, and less personal, in a seamless continuum. Reading these samples will help you see your own in the larger context of academic essay and proposal writing.

SO HOW'S COLLEGE, SON?

UHH... DAD, I JOINED THE MOONIES.

SON, DON'T WASTE YOUR TIME ON ASTRONOMY— GOTTA GET INTO GRAD SCHOOL!

"REVEREND WHO?"

Copyright 1991 John Grimes. Used with permission.

This book's goal is to take all of the mystery and most of the stress out of the graduate applications process and guide you through drafting a compelling graduate admissions essay. This is also a resource book, with recommendations for supplementary reading, Web sites, and other materials throughout the text. I have included information on financial aid, graduate admissions testing, and other aspects of the graduate admissions process to give you a clearer picture of the graduate essay as an integral part of the entire application process. You should also seek the advice of other guides that focus exclusively on these topics.

This book is not intended to replace the advice of professors, college career counselors, and undergraduate advising officers. On the contrary, this guide is meant to encourage you to *visit them as early as possible*, and with more knowledge than you would otherwise have possessed, so that you can be a more intelligent user of their services. Spend time learning the mechanics from this book, and you can devote more of your time with advisers to true counseling.

Over the years students have made two complaints about the early editions of this book: Too many of the examples are from people with unusual backgrounds, and I advocate that the student do too much work to apply to graduate school (surely, they plead, there must be an easier way). For example, one grad applicant wrote:

The purpose of your book should be to help the graduate student who isn't from Russia and taking theoretical physics, hasn't set up an educational program at Yale, hasn't overcome severe hardships because he's from Vietnam, etc. If I had something like this, I probably wouldn't need your book. Please keep in mind, for your next edition, the essays of the more ordinary students like me. We can't all run away with the carnival.

In response, I have included more essay samples from regular students; that is, students of traditional graduate school age, with traditional academic experience. Nevertheless, you will note that these too are unusual students: They are unusually well prepared, unusually thoughtful, unusually well directed, unusually well read in their chosen fields. Further, it is my contention that all students are unusual in one way or another; the prewriting exercises in chapter 5 will help you discover how you differ from the background noise of common applicants.

As to the amount of work involved, it is important to remember that this is a book about gaining admission to *highly competitive graduate programs.* It has been my goal to find out what the students who are admitted to these programs do differently from the students who are not admitted. This book is the answer.

As you read, remember that this is, to some extent, a study of the ideal way to apply. You needn't do all this if you are not applying to highly competitive programs, or you have some safety schools on your list, or you have a backup plan, or you're just too darn busy. Take the tips and pointers that you can, that make sense to you, and don't worry about the rest. This is a guide, not a recipe that you must slavishly follow. Adjust it to suit your particular needs, and let it improve the job you do in applying to graduate school.

While you cannot change who you are and what you have done with your life so far, you *can* make a good graduate application. Students tend to underestimate, rather than overestimate, their academic value. The number of students fully qualified for graduate study far exceeds the number who actually apply. To the extent that this book facilitates your application and contributes to the realization of your potential, so let it be judged.

Should You Go to Grad School, and How Are You Going to Pay for This?

Before launching the application process, it seems prudent to consider whether you should go to graduate school at all.

Good reasons to go to grad school

1. You have a passionate interest in a narrow topic or an unusual combination of topics.

2. You have a vocational interest that carries a graduate degree credential as an entrance requirement.

3. You want to earn more money than you otherwise would have.

4. You want to ensure continued career advancement.

5. You seek a richer and more satisfying life.

6. You like to do research.

7. School is easy for you and you like it.

The single best reason to go to graduate school is because you have a passionate interest in a subject area. There is some molecular process that just fascinates you, or some nineteenth-century French feminist poet whose words wake you in the night with a start. Graduate school offers a chance to advance your understanding of those topics that have fascinated you as an undergraduate. Graduate school is often also a place where you can combine disciplines that are not combinable in undergraduate studies, such as chemistry and art history, or acoustics and marine biology. You could be the one to discover a fail-safe method for dating and authenticating oil paintings, or you could discover once and for all how to communicate with dolphins. These interdisciplinary inquiries offer some of the most exciting opportunities for study at the graduate level.

Many students are motivated not only by the study itself but also by the desire to pursue a profession that requires a graduate degree as a credential. To become an attorney, doctor, dentist, scientist, veterinarian, architect, psychologist, or college professor, you must successfully complete one *or several* graduate degree programs. There may be some rare exceptions, but certainly the overwhelming majority of practitioners in these fields will possess the normal academic credentials.

If you are interested in becoming a college professor, you need to know that the competition is fierce at this time, with many more highly qualified candidates completing their preparation each year than there are available slots. For more on this, follow the ongoing debate in the *Chronicle of Higher Education* and the newsletter for the Modern Language Association. Being willing to move anywhere increases your chances, but a prudent person will also have a backup career goal.

Perhaps you are interested in earning more money over the span of your career. The Bureau of Labor Statistics has studied high-income individuals for decades and found that high-income people have more education than lower-income people. As a matter of fact, there is a lock-step relationship between education and income (see diagram).

As you can see, after completing your bachelor's degree, you are making a $1,300,000 decision whether to pursue the doctorate, and a $2,300,000 decision whether to pursue a professional degree. These are not decisions to make without considering the lifetime income implications. Even a master's degree will give you a $400,000 boost in lifetime earnings, which will certainly allow you to pay back any loans you take out along the way. In the top earning category, a recent study found that primary-care medical doctors average $162,000 in annual income. In addition to the strong positive impact on income, higher education has a strong negative impact on unemployment. For example, the unemployment rate for Ph.D.s runs around 1% or 2%. (There is a myth that Ph.D.s are unemployed and underpaid; the exact opposite is true.) Further, those Ph.D.s who don't find academic jobs earn even more outside of academic life.

Median Lifetime Earnings for Workers
Ranked by Education

Professional degree*	$4,400,000
Doctorate	$3,400,000
Master's degree	$2,500,000
Bachelor's degree	$2,100,000
High-school graduate	$1,200,000

*M.D., D.D.S., D.V.M., J.D..

Source: Bureau of Labor Statistics Population Survey

Graduate school is probably the second best investment you'll ever make in your life, after your bachelor's degree. And remember, the beautiful thing about investing in education is that it cannot be repossessed.

Also, if you're interested in continued career advancement throughout your working life, plan on graduate school sooner or later. We're entering an era that touts and believes in continuous learning. It's becoming hard to find a senior executive *without* a graduate degree—whether in business, nonprofit, or government. The trend toward higher education for all senior managers is compounded by the trend to work for more and more employers over the span of a career. The latest business school data suggest that current graduates will work for *six to fifteen employers* between graduate school and retirement. This means that even if you are an outstanding performer, you will need to prove yourself to others who are not personally acquainted with you. Credentials are essential for smooth and continuous career advancement.

Money and career advancement aside, graduate education contributes to a rich and full quality of life. If you are an engineer and you drive under a bridge, you see more than a bridge; you see stress dynamics. Everything you see, do, touch, or think about will be influenced by your graduate education. At least one longitudinal study of college-educated workers found a lockstep relationship between education and reports of satisfaction with life (not just work life, but all aspects of life: work, family, social, financial, and so on). Plato's dialogue, *Philebus,* amounts to an elaborate argument in favor of the intellectual life. Don't trust me; trust Socrates as quoted by Plato.

If you like to do research, then graduate school is an opportunity to pursue that passion without regard to any immediate industrial or economic benefit. If you enjoy designing methodologies that will prove or disprove hypotheses and you can live with the results either way, then you're truly a candidate for graduate school. Even if you eventually pursue a career in industrial research, you may forever think back fondly to the intellectual freedom of your academic years.

If you just enjoy going to school and you're naturally good at it, going to grad school is certainly a better use of your time than whiling away a few years in an entry-level job. For those who find the academic life easier than, say, learning how to sell insurance by phone, pursuing graduate education is a logical endeavor.

Finally, it has been proved that with each year of graduate study your IQ will go up, and that people with higher IQs have more sex than people with lower IQs. (There's another study that says graduate students have a below-average frequency of sex, so this may be a delayed benefit.)

So if you are going to have more satisfaction, more money, and more sex, why *wouldn't* you go to grad school?

Reasons *not* to go to grad school right now

Three warning signs concerning your graduate school plans:

1. You're going to grad school to please someone else.

2. You're clueless about a subject to study.

3. You're secretly trying to avoid the job market.

If your primary motivation for going to graduate school is to please someone outside yourself, then you had better rethink the whole endeavor. If your father thinks you *have* to be an attorney or your mother thinks you *have* to be a doctor, and that's your main motivation for pursuing these goals, then you're in trouble. One study of unhappy attorneys showed that a significant proportion of them went to law school in the first place to please a close family member. You need strong *internal* motivation to thrive in graduate school. If you and your mother agree on your academic plans, fine, but if you disagree, better think twice before making a move not in alignment with your own interests.

If you're not at all sure what you want to pursue at the graduate level, that is a milder warning sign. You may need to seek more academic and career counseling; discuss your plans with mentors, parents, and other people you admire; take some career aptitude tests; take a few more classes in the subjects that interest you; and otherwise explore your options. Some schools will admit you as an unspecified-major graduate student and allow you to take graduate courses in one or more disciplines for a year or two while you decide. Even some outstanding students find themselves unsure of their next academic step.

Finally, some students seek to avoid a bad job market by hiding out in graduate school. This is okay as a general rule, as long as hiding out in graduate school does not take the place of prudent career planning. In other words, if you choose a graduate degree program that will enhance your career goals later, then fine, but if you're just passing time and running up loans—that is, if you're just *delaying* confronting your career problem—then you'd be a lot better off facing your career issues now. Interestingly enough, the skills required to get into a highly competitive graduate program are the same ones that would allow you to seek and obtain desirable, career-launching employment right now.

If you're unsure of your academic and career plans, answer these questions: When were you the most excited about your studies as an undergraduate, and what were you doing that caused all that excitement? What would you do for a living if money were no object—or, taking this to the logical limit, what career would you be willing to pay someone else to let you do? What have you fantasized about doing for a living? Think of several people you deeply admire. What do *they* do for a living?

Many, if not most, graduate applicants are somewhat vague about their career plans, but you certainly should have some plan for utilizing your education in a career, no matter how tenuous that plan may be and how many times you change that plan later.

One of the worst reasons *not* to go to grad school is that you don't know how you're going to pay for it. If you want to go, you can find a way to pay for it.

Getting financing for grad school

There may be no more confusing and illogical thing in the world than graduate school financing:

1.   You cannot tell how much it will cost until you apply *and are admitted.*

2.   It's often cheaper to go to an expensive school.

3.   It's often cheaper to pursue the Ph.D. than the master's.

4.   It's often cheaper to borrow the money and go full time than to work your way through part time.

5.   Even if you're wealthy, you should apply for financial aid.

Suppose you wanted to buy a car, and you went down to the car lot and asked the salesperson, "How much for this beautiful red convertible?" Further suppose that the salesperson then said, "Well, I dunno. You need to apply for the car, and if we decide to sell it to you at all, it's either going to cost you $50,000 *or we'll pay you to drive it home.* First, you have to fill out all this paperwork, pay a nonrefundable deposit, give us three references, and wait for months."

That's a nutty way to do business, you might think, but that's exactly how graduate financial aid works. You simply cannot tell how much it will cost until you apply and are admitted. The sticker price on that car and the sticker price on graduate education are often meaningless.

It's often cheaper to go to an expensive school because those schools have deeper resources for aid. At some schools, in some departments, no one has paid a dime to attend the program in decades. The tuition is offset by grants, foundation monies, and various endowed funding mechanisms; the schools continue to publish tuition rates because other departments may be actually collecting tuition (for example, the chemistry department is well funded and nobody pays, while the theatre department collects full tuition).

"JENNIFER, I'M QUITTING MY JOB AND GOING TO GRADUATE SCHOOL. WILL YOU CARRY ME?"

Sometimes students are forced to make a decision on which graduate school to attend *before* they receive a financial award. A close friend of mine received a letter from a Harvard graduate program that started out like this:

> We are happy to extend an offer of admission to you for the fall incoming class. It is absolutely imperative that you respond by April 15th or your seat will be offered to another . . .

The letter was dated April 17th. It didn't say one word about a financial award. So he crafted a quick and clever response:

"I am honored to be offered a position in the fall incoming class. I am slightly confused by the fact that I have not received a financial aid package. However, since I know as esteemed an institution as Harvard would not make such an offer in jest and, as you know all my financial particulars in my application, I assume the award, when it does eventually come, will be sufficient to allow me to participate in this wonderful opportunity. So, I am delighted to accept." (Incidentally, this weird practice is hardly unique to Harvard.)

It's often cheaper to pursue the Ph.D. because Ph.D. candidates are better funded than master's candidates. Even while they're taking the same classes and sitting side by side, Ph.D. candidates may be paid to attend class, while master's candidates pay for the privilege. Don't let financial fears keep you from pursuing the degree you want. For more on these issues, visit the Web site for the Council of Graduate Schools, www.cgsnet.org, and the National Center for Education Statistics, www.nces.ed.gov.

By the way, never pursue the Ph.D. unless you want the terminal degree; in other words, don't apply for a Ph.D. when you really want a master's just because the Ph.D. funding is better. The "bailout master's" is not counted the same in industry or academe as the master's you intentionally obtain; you will be seen as someone who "dropped out of a Ph.D. program." If you're unsure, pursue the master's degree first. Many people have a master's in one topic and a career in another field, or have two master's degrees in unrelated topics, but getting a Ph.D. is like getting married in a Catholic church in a Latin American country. It's a real commitment.

In general, it is cheaper to go to school full time rather than part time for two reasons. First, the money you borrow to go full time is repaid after you graduate, when you should have a much higher rate of earnings. Even considering the accrued interest on the loans, it will probably cost you less overall. Second, students who go to school part time frequently do not get the career boost that comes from completing a full-time degree program. The big reward for those students who go to school part time is frequently a card of congratulations from their employer. So what? If you end up having to change jobs to achieve the market rate for your education, what have you gained by working your way through?

Many college graduates seek an employer who will pay for their graduate education. Is this smart? Maybe not. Employers place many restrictions on these programs, including a period of time after completion during which, if you leave your employer, you must repay their investment in your education. A basic understanding of economics indicates that they believe they are paying you below market rate for your salary *or they wouldn't do it*. If the employer you already have and are happy with is willing to pay your education expenses, fine. However, you should not choose an employer based solely on this factor. Whether you're choosing an employer who may fund your education or considering whether to take advantage of your current employer's funding, be sure to run the numbers yourself before you think you're getting something for nothing. Usually your greatest boost in salary will come from going to school full time, with the goal of aggressively seeking a full-time career position *that requires your new education.*

Even if you have the means to pay for your entire graduate education, it is often advisable to apply for financial aid. Much financial aid at the graduate level is merit-based, and failing to pursue these awards will leave you without the necessary credentials to obtain postgraduate employment and other appointments. In particular, if you eventually want to be a college professor or a university-based research scientist, you almost have to be a teaching or research assistant while in graduate school. Although these assignments are most often run as aid programs, you should consider their other benefits.

Here are the most typical aid sources:

- Teaching assistantships

- Research assistantships

- Fellowships

- Grants

- Tuition waivers

- Loans

Teaching assistantships require you to teach undergraduate courses or labs. You will probably have your tuition waived, and usually receive a stipend (which varies widely from school to school). Having a teaching assistantship is very prestigious; if you plan to become a college professor, it's an impressive addition to your credentials. However, the workload can be severe, with all your preparation and grading effort in addition to your class time each week. Whatever your estimate of the time commitment, your first semester you should expect it to be almost double.

Consult IRS Publication 970 and Tax Topic 421 for tax rules governing scholarships.

Warning

Assistantship applications often have very early deadlines—sometimes months before the deadline to apply to the graduate program—and often require another essay and a different set of letters of recommendation. Visiting the department can greatly increase your chances of being selected for an assistantship.

You get teaching assistantships by applying to the department you will be in as a graduate student. You need grades good enough to impress everyone in the department. It also helps to have done some teaching, tutoring, or proctoring as an undergraduate. Sometimes students get assistantships in other departments to offset their educational expenses. For example, I interviewed one student, a native speaker of French, who got an assistantship teaching first-year French even though he was studying something else at graduate school. You can also supplement your income with less well-known, assistantship-like assignments elsewhere in the university system; for example, you could serve as a residence hall adviser or a career counselor, especially if you're studying any kind of psychology, counseling, business, or higher education administration.

You get research assistantships by applying to a specific professor or laboratory at the graduate school. These are much easier to get, in that you don't have to impress a whole department to win an assignment. The best way to earn an assignment like this is to learn as much as you can about the research going on in the lab, then let the laboratory chief know of your desire to participate in that research. It's a big plus if you have a great respect for the concept of integrity in original research, have conducted original research as an undergraduate, or have already been published. You do not need perfect grades to earn these jobs; I spoke with one dean who funded a research assistant whose GPA was 2.85 (but it is important to note that his GPA in math, physics, and fluid dynamics was 3.85, and this was a fluid dynamics lab).

To see how your stipend stacks up, go to http://gradschool.binghampton.edu/stipendsurvey.

If you cannot get a research or teaching assistantship with your department, look for other part-time jobs with the department that could gain you both exposure to professors and savvy in how the department operates. This can cut down on your time to complete the degree program and help solve any problems you may run into as a graduate student.

Fellowships are large awards that come with no strings attached; that is, the student doesn't have to perform any work to earn the award. They are reserved for those students whose academic promise is so great that they shouldn't be distracted at all from their studies—or, more rarely, for underrepresented students the program has a great desire to recruit. Fellowships come in two flavors: internal and external. You learn about internal fellowships from the graduate school or department to which you're applying. You learn about external fellowships (the same as a scholarship, really) by researching them yourself. Two good Web sites are finaid.org and fastweb.com.

Three sample books on this subject are *The Yale Daily News Guide to Fellowships and Grants*, *The Higher Education MoneyBook for Women and Minorities: A Directory of Scholarships, Fellowships, Internships, Grants and Loans*, by Doris M. Young and William C. Young, and Laurie Blum's *Free Money for Graduate School: A Guide to More Than 1,000 Grants For Graduate Study*. Your academic or career development adviser can point you to more. It is your job to do the research. For example, the EPA offers a generous fellowship including research-related expenses for graduate students in environmentally-related fields of study. The Gertrude Fogelson Cultural and Creative Arts Award was created to encourage and honor mothers who demonstrate talent in visual arts, creative writing, or vocal music. The Paul and Daisy Soros Fellowships provide stipends and tuition for "new Americans" who hold Green cards or are naturalized citizens, or who are the children of two parents who are both naturalized citizens.

Grants are just smaller fellowships, ranging from a few hundred to a few thousand dollars, and they work exactly the same way; you can find them by using your fellowship research resources. With a little effort and experimentation, you may find extra money available to you because you graduated from high school in Iowa, or your father works for a telephone company, or you're left-handed, or a felon. No kidding. The money's out there. You just have to go seek it.

Tuition waivers are extremely common for Ph.D. candidates and for all candidates in the laboratory sciences. They are less common for master's degree candidates in the humanities and for most students in preprofessional programs such as business, law, medicine, architecture, and so on. As mentioned above, many programs list tuition in their bulletins and literature, even though no one has paid that tuition in years.

When all else fails, you can fund the gap between what you need and what you can get granted or waived with education loans. If you have a pulse, are a United States citizen, and have not ruined your credit rating entirely, you can borrow $22,500 each and every year you are in graduate school (based on the maximum of Stafford and Perkins loans). Learn about the standard loan programs at finaid.org, fastweb.com, and salliemae.com. Plan on preparing a FAFSA (Free Application for Federal Student Aid) and/or forms from the Graduate and Professional School Financial Aid Service (GAPSFAS), available from any graduate or undergraduate financial aid office, or by printout from finaid.org.

Warning

Some schools have begun front-end loading their aid to win students in open competition with other schools. This means that you may find a decreasing award over time, or no support during research phases when you critically need it. Ask pointed questions, such as: "How reliable is your financial aid year to year? Is the first-year offer always sustained, given attainment of academic goals?"

Normally, your undergraduate student loans will be deferred while you're in graduate school. On some loans the interest accrual is arrested during graduate school. Inquire at the financial aid office of your undergraduate institution, and at the graduate school to which you're applying, for more details on your particular loan portfolio.

By the way, borrowing is generally the primary way to finance graduate study in professional schools (business, law, medicine, especially), even though there is a hidden assistantship at business and law schools: working for the career placement office. Inquire about how to apply for these coveted slots before you attend. Otherwise, plan on borrowing a lot. You will get the payback if you complete the program in a timely manner and launch a career with average success.

A student did ask me once if she should borrow $30,000 to study dance in Manhattan. I asked her to explain to me her plan for ever being able to repay this money. She decided not to borrow the money. Though the program very strongly encouraged her to take on this large debt, even they couldn't tell her how she would be able to earn enough as a dancer to pay it back.

Student debt is not to be taken lightly. Even though it is almost always a good investment, you need to watch your total indebtedness. There's an old saying in law school: "Live like a attorney while you're in law school and you'll live like a law student when you're an attorney."

Remember, your first source for financial aid information of all types is the program to which you are applying, but *you may not find out how much it will cost until you've applied and been accepted.* Even after you've gotten a financial offer, however, there may be room to play. Some schools are responsive to appeals based on need (married with children, long distance to relocate, medical needs, and so on); others have responded to appeals based on competing offers. I know one student who was offered admission to Harvard and Stanford, but only got a support offer from Harvard. He took Harvard's written support offer to Stanford and said, "I have this offer from Harvard. I think your program is better, but of course I'd be crazy to turn down this stipend." Stanford came up with a slightly higher award. Some deans have told me that they try never to do this—adjust an offer on request or match another school's offer—but students tell me it happens frequently. Especially when the difference is small, say $5,000 or less, going back to a program to ask again may result in a matching offer. It can't hurt to ask, especially if you explain that you're only asking because you think their program would be a better match for you.

Finally, on the whole topic of paying for your grad school education by assistantships and fellowships, you need to know about *Getting What You Came For*, by Robert L. Peters. This outstanding book goes into greater depth on different funding sources, the benefits of assistantships, selecting an adviser, departmental politics, and other important matters. I could not recommend this book more strongly for anyone pursuing an academic master's or Ph.D. For example, if you read it and pay attention, it can shave a full year off the time to complete your Ph.D. How's that for an endorsement?

Other books to check out:

Financing Graduate School: How to Get Money for Your Master's or Ph.D., Patricia McWade.

Foundation Grants to Individuals, Foundation Center.

Scholarships, Fellowships, and Loans, Gale Research.

Dan Cassidy's Worldwide Graduate Scholarship Directory: Thousands of Top Scholarships Throughout the U.S. and Around the World, Daniel J. Cassidy.

Peterson's Grants for Graduate & Postdoctoral Studies.

Annual Register of Grant Support: A Directory of Funding Sources, R. R. Bowker, ed.

Harvard College Guide to Grants, Lisa M. Muto.

Financial Aids for Higher Education, Judy K. Santamaria and Oreon Keeslar.

Paying the Piper: Productivity, Incentives, and Financing in U.S. Higher Educucation, Michael S. McPherson, Morton Owen Shapiro, and Gordon C. Winston.

Free Money for Graduate School, H. Holt and Co.

Directory of Financial Aids for Minorities, Gail Ann Schlachter.

Directory of Financial Aids for Women, Gail Ann Schlachter.

The Higher Education Moneybook for Women & Minorities: A Directory of Scholarships, Fellowships, Internships, Grants and Loans, Doris M. Young and William C. Young.

Financial Resources for International Study: A Guide for U.S. Students and Professionals, Institute of International Education.

Financial Aid for Study and Training Abroad, R. David Weber and Gail Ann Schlachter.

Funding for United States Study: A Guide for International Students and Professionals, Marie O'Sullivan, ed., Sara Steen.

Official Guide to Financing Your MBA, Bart Astor.

The Graduate Student's Complete Scholarship Book, Student Services, Inc.

The following pages list some of the most prestigious scholarships in the world. To win these, undergraduates typically work with the scholarship committee on their undergraduate campus, and *early planning is absolutely critical.* The application processes typically require essays, recommendations, and personal interviews. Some applications are regional, which may give an advantage to those applying from less competitive regions.

Warning

Be sure to apply to graduate school at the same time. No one should be so confident as to assume she will win one of these elite scholarships. In any case, any graduate program will grant you a deferral if you are selected for one of these scholarships. Ask your academic adviser or scholarship committee chair for more information.

—TOP SCHOLARSHIPS—

Rhodes Two- or three-year graduate scholarships, with generous living allowance, to attend the University of Oxford, England. Funded by Cecil Rhodes, an Oxford alumnus and South African colonialist; he was the first to consolidate the De Beers mines (at one time in control of 90 percent of the world's known diamond reserves), and eventually had a country named after him: Rhodesia, now Zimbabwe. The applicant must be an unmarried United States citizen between eighteen and twenty-four, and have a commitment to public service and athletics (physical vigor is an explicit requirement, even though Rhodes was a sickly child). This is arguably the most prestigious scholarship in the world. You will forever be a Rhodes Scholar. Most successful candidates work closely with advisers toward this goal from the sophomore year.

Fulbright One-year grants for postgraduate study abroad, with extensions possible. Host country language skills are required. Emphasis on promoting better understanding among differing cultures. Highly prestigious. Most Fulbright scholars return to complete their graduate programs at top-ranked U.S. universities.

Marshall Similar to the Rhodes. Applicants must be under twenty-six at the time they apply, but there is no athletics requirement. According to the scholarship's own material, "In short, the programme looks for tomorrow's leader: for high intelligence and academic achievement; for social commitment and responsibility; for leadership potential; and for originality and flair." Go for it.

Rotary This program is similar to the Fulbright: a full-ride year abroad to advance cross-cultural human understanding; in fact, Rotarians will call you a Rotary Ambassador. The odd thing about the Rotary International Fellowship for Graduate Study Abroad is that if you have any close relationship to a Rotarian, you're ineligible. Contact your local Rotary Club to learn how to apply. One candidate I interviewed read thirty years of the *Rotarian Magazine.* "I may not have been the best candidate that year, but I knew more about the Rotary Club than anybody, including the selection committee," he told me. He was selected.

Watson The Watson favors travelers and adventurers, with "an initial postgraduate year of independent study and travel abroad." The foundation "hopes to provide Fellows an opportunity for a focused and disciplined Wanderjahr of their own devising." A good independent study plan is *de rigueur,* but prior experience abroad is not required.

Mellon For seniors or recent graduates interested in pursuing the Ph.D. in the humanities at an institution in the United States or Canada, who have *not yet applied nor been* *admitted to* a program of graduate study. Apply directly to The Woodrow Wilson National Fellowship Foundation, Mellon Fellowships, Humanities, Princeton, New Jersey.

Also consider:
  The Winston Churchill Foundation Scholarship to Churchill College,
    Cambridge University
  Keasbey Fellowships to United Kingdom universities
  St. Andrews Society of New York Scholarship for Graduate Study in Scotland
  OAS Fellowship for Graduate Study in Latin America
  Luce Scholars Program (Asia)
  Abraham Lincoln Scholarship for Graduate Study in Mexico
  Alliance Française de New York Scholarship for Graduate Study in France
  The American Scandinavian Foundation Award for Study in Scandinavia
  Wallenberg Scholarship for Hebrew University, Jerusalem
  National Science Foundation Graduate Fellowships
  National Science Foundation Minority Graduate Fellowships
  The Whitaker Graduate Fellowship Program for Biomedical Engineering
  The Roothbert Fund for Persons Motivated by Spiritual Values
  The Carnegie Endowment for International Peace Junior Fellows Program
  The African-American Graduate Fellowship for Doctoral Study
  The Ford Foundation Fellowship for Minority Students
  The Jacob K. Javits Fellowship for Doctoral Studies
  National Defense Science and Engineering Graduate Fellowship Program
  Howard Hughes Predoctoral Fellowship in Biological Sciences

and many, many more you can learn about by doing a little research.

There is a Rhodes essay on page 173, a Fulbright on page 145, and a Watson on page 197 of this book; your college or university scholarship committee can provide you with more examples.

Warning

Do not even think about modeling your essay too closely on someone else's example; essays in this book are provided so that you may learn how to write the best statement for your own unique background.

2

Choosing a School or Program

The biggest mistake you can make in selecting a graduate program is to blindly choose "the best program I can get into." Annual magazine rankings notwithstanding, there is no one criterion, no single hierarchy of good-better-best on which to base such a decision. You must consider several criteria and develop your own standards for evaluation.

If your choice is good, there will be a good fit between you and the program; you will enjoy your studies, you will find friends among faculty and fellow students, and your education will further your career goals both directly and indirectly. If your choice is poor, the opposite will be true.

This chapter will guide you through the process of compiling and ranking a list of the good-better-best programs *for you,* and the following chapters will tell you how to get in.

Build a list of possible schools

First, you need to build a list of possible schools. I recommend that you find a minimum of twenty (don't worry—you won't have to apply to all twenty schools).

Be sure to search nationally, for two good reasons. First, the market for students in higher education is national, so if you don't look nationally, you're putting yourself at a competitive disadvantage. Second, graduate programs are concerned with a concept called "reach," as evidenced by statements in their viewbooks, such as this one: "Our program draws students from twenty-one states and three Canadian provinces." If your application represents a twenty-second state, and you are genuinely interested in the program, you have an advantage. Most students err in looking for a graduate program only within an four-hour drive of their current home. What if a school on the other side of the country would *pay you* or *pay you more* to pursue graduate study? Consider expanding your horizons.

Tap these resources to find out about graduate programs:

- Professors

- Alumni

- Peterson's guides

- Specialty guides

- Your parents, your friends' parents, your parents' friends

- Practicing professionals

- Academic journals, including citations

- *The Real Guide to Grad School: What You Better Know Before You Choose Humanities & Social Sciences,* Robert E. Clark and John Palatella, eds.

- *Accounting to Zoology: Graduate Fields Defined,* Amy J. Goldstein, ed.

- *Research-Doctorate Programs in the United States: Continuity and Change,* Marvin L. Goldberger, ed.

- *Educational Rankings Annual: Over 4700 Rankings and Lists on Education,* Lynne C. Hattendorf Westney, ed.

- *The Gourman Report: A Rating of Graduate and Professional Programs in American and International Universities,* Jack Gorman.

- Annual business magazine rankings

- www.ulinks.com

- www.allaboutgradschool.com

- www.gradschools.com

- www.gradadmissions.about.com

- Go to www.donaldasher.com/gradschool for more links.

Your first stop for all your grad school planning should be a visit to your academic adviser's office. She knows graduate schools from coast to coast in her own area of expertise, although she may be a little weak outside that specialty. Next, identify faculty in other departments who may know about your chosen field. It doesn't matter whether you've ever taken classes from them; just call them up, introduce yourself, and ask for advice. Even if you graduated from college ten years ago, or even twenty, professors at your alma mater will help you learn about graduate programs.

Next, identify alumni of your alma mater who are currently enrolled in graduate programs in your subject area. Your career planning center and alumni office can guide you to graduates currently in graduate school in any given topic. Currently enrolled graduate students can often give you long discourses on the differences between graduate programs: who's hot, who's overrated, who has this emphasis or that approach, which one lost its superstar faculty, and so on.

Don't be shy. Poll *all* your personal contacts for recommendations of good graduate programs in your area of interest.

All the resources just described will give you the bulk of the twenty-plus list of schools that are appropriate for you, with heavy emphasis on the types of programs in which prior alumni, with backgrounds similar to yours, have had success. Next, turn to Peterson's guides, available in book form or online. The book versions have exponentially more information, so go to the library! The Peterson's guides in book format are:

Peterson's Guide to Graduate & Professional Programs: An Overview

Peterson's Guide to Graduate Programs in Business, Education, Health, Information Studies, Law, & Social Work

Peterson's Guide to Graduate Programs in the Humanities, Arts, & Social Sciences

Peterson's Guide to Graduate Programs in the Physical Sciences, Mathematics, & Agricultural Sciences.

Peterson's Guide to Graduate Programs in the Biological Sciences

Peterson's Guide to Graduate Programs in Engineering and Applied Sciences

If you can imagine the offspring of an unholy union between the Manhattan telephone directory and a thesaurus, you'd get the flavor of these guides. However, they do contain every accredited graduate program in the United States, and for that reason they are invaluable, especially for filling your mandate to look for graduate programs nationally and for discovering programs that match obscure interests.

There are hundreds of other specialized guides for programs in fine arts, geography, marine sciences, neurosciences, film, environmental engineering, dance, teaching English as a second language, art therapy, religion, business, women's studies, and so on, ad infinitum. No field is too obscure to have its own guide; here's a typical example: The American College of Sports Medicine's *Directory of Graduate Programs in Sports Medicine and Exercise Science.* There are also affinity guides, such as *National Science Foundation Alliance: Graduate School Opportunities,* to assist you in discovering elite programs.

There are many ways to find out about these guides. Your academic advisers can make sure you don't miss any major ones; for example, you'd be nuts to even think about applying to medical school without using the Association of American Medical College's *Medical School Admission Requirements: United States and Canada.*

If you're long out of college, or your undergraduate advising center is nonexistent or parochial, then, unfortunately, the full burden of research falls upon you. Peterson's guides can be found in almost all major libraries, but the other, lesser-known guides may not be. Try the subject search engines at Amazon.com or other online bookstores and on the *Books in Print* database at your nearest bookstore. The *Encyclopedia of Associations* is a great resource; for example, you may discover that there is an American Speech-Language Hearing Association, call them (their number is provided right there in the encyclopedia), and find that they publish a *Guide to Graduate Education in Speech-Language Pathology & Audiology.*

In addition to seeking out guides, remember to pursue word-of-mouth advice. Poll your parents, your parents' friends, and your friends' parents for recommendations. Survey your entire network of acquaintances. Visit the alumni office to identify practicing professionals in your chosen field. Call them up and ask them for general advice on getting into the field, as well as grad program recommendations. Here are some suggested questions:

1. How did you get into this field?

2. What education or credentials are required for *continued* advancement in this field?

3. What was different than what you expected? Any myths you want to shatter for me?

4. What advice would you have for a young person interested in this field?

5. Should I go to grad school right away or work for a year or two first? If work, what kind of experiences would be best?

6. Which grad schools do you think are best in this field? Why?

7. Do you know any professors that I should contact?

If you are shy, use email to ask the same questions.

Research-Doctorate Programs in the United States: subject areas

Aerospace Engineering	Economics	Music
Anthropology	Electrical Engineering	Neurosciences
Art History	English Language and Literature	Oceanography
Astrophysics and Astronomy	French Language and Literature	Pharmacology
Biochemistry and Molecular Biology	Geography	Philosophy
Biomedical Engineering	Geosciences	Physics
Cell and Developmental Biology	German Language and Literature	Physiology
Chemical Engineering	History	Political Science
Chemistry	Industrial Engineering	Psychology
Civil Engineering	Linguistics	Religion
Classics	Materials Science	Sociology
Comparative Literature	Mathematics	Spanish and Portuguese Language and Literature
Computer Sciences	Mechanical Engineering	Statistics and Biostatistics
Ecology, Evolution, and Behavior	Molecular and General Genetics	

Savvy students, with the drive and preparation to get into the most highly competitive graduate programs, get their grad school leads straight from the academic journals for their fields. This is doubly smart because not only are the programs generating the most recent articles on the cutting edge in their fields, but their articles also give the student a good idea of the type of work coming out of those programs. Seek out articles in popular and specialty academic journals, find out where the authors teach and do research, and you'll have an "A" list of graduate programs in your field. Read the citations, too—they can lead you to brilliant professors who might not write a lot, but are highly respected. If you want help with identifying appropriate journals and learning how to track down professors based on articles about their research, see your academic adviser.

The bible of information on graduate programs is *Research-Doctorate Programs in the United States*, published by the National Research Council. This book is not easy to understand and lumps some large areas together (for example, clinical psychology with programs emphasizing research), it is delightful in its detail, covering forty-one different subject areas on dozens of criteria. (See opposite page.)

Research-Doctorate Programs in the United States evaluates graduate programs using such criteria as overall reputation, percentage of faculty publishing, number of publications per faculty member, number of faculty, gender balance of degree recipients, total R&D budgets, and one of the most fascinating data measures you'll find anywhere: median time to complete the Ph.D. It's not a perfect book, but it offers unbiased information you'll find nowhere else. An updated study has been released on the Web, so look for it.

The business and news magazines have gotten into the habit of writing annual graduate school guides. They are a decent source for learning about graduate programs, but you should not give much credence to their ranking systems. They are most useful when focusing on a narrow, unusual topic, such as "Best Business Schools for Entrepreneurs," and not so useful when ranking programs in which they have no editorial expertise.

One of the fastest ways to find graduate programs is do to an advanced Google search on obscure terminology that will be unique to your area of interest. Restrict the search to .edu domains, and then search for "Egyptian mathematics," or "pollen morphologies," or "Bas van Fraassen," or whatever, and you will find faculty members with the same interests as you. This technique is quick and easy, and produces very high-quality contacts.

With all these resources available to you, you should have no problem identifying twenty programs that have what you want. Basically, if you have a heartbeat and a bachelor's degree, there's a grad school out there for you. There are more options for graduate education than you can imagine. You can go full time, part time, nights, Saturdays only, or one weekend a month to study anything from engineering to nuclear medicine to recreation to general liberal studies. At the low end of the scale in terms of time commitment, there are more one-year master's programs than ever before. At the high end, there are more part-time doctoral programs and more postdoctorate research fellowships than ever before, extending your educational options into the multiple decades. If you want to go to school, whatever your motivations and whatever your goals, there's a grad school out there for you. Go find it.

How to explore your options

The process of selecting a graduate program involves balancing at least five main components:

- The academics
- The people (faculty, students, administration)
- The locale
- The cost
- Admissibility

The academics

The academics can be thought of as the intellectual feast. What are you going to learn? It should certainly be something you want to learn. Read the journals in your field. Read the writings of the faculty at targeted programs. Ask your professors to evaluate the schools on your short list, and be sure to ask them to suggest particular professors, writers, and researchers who could further your academic interests. Professors are your number-one source of really useful information about graduate programs—talk to them often.

As mentioned in the handout on the next two pages, you should write to prospective programs for more specific information on what they teach, what they research, and how they operate their programs. Here is another email to consider as a model:

Dear Dr. Russell:

I am a senior biology major at Truman State University. Because I have taken almost every biology course offered at Truman, I will graduate in May with an unusual double degree: a bachelor of arts in biology and a bachelor of science in biology. I also have a French minor, and have taught myself to read the excellent research published in French from institutions in France, Quebec, and Africa.

Since the beginning of my sophomore year, I have been conducting research under the guidance of Dr. Jeffrey M. Osborn. For the past two years, I have been studying pollen and anther morphology in the Callitrichaceae, a family of aquatic flowering plants. During the course of this project, I have learned a variety of laboratory techniques, written research proposals, and delivered oral presentations of my findings. I have enclosed a copy of my curriculum vitae to give you an indication of my research experience and educational background to date.

For the past two summers, I have been funded to do full-time research. I very much enjoyed the opportunity to participate in these programs without the added responsibilities of coursework. I am looking forward to focusing more on research at the graduate level.

Due to my interest in pursuing the doctoral degree in structural/developmental botany, I have discovered your laboratory and read some of your more recent articles. I would appreciate it if you could send me information about your current research projects, or let me know how to find out more about them on my own. Can you also let me know if you will be accepting a graduate student next fall for your laboratory? I have also written to the graduate studies chair of your department for relevant application materials and general information about graduate study at the University of Oklahoma, so you needn't track down basic materials for me. If you could please just share with me information about your own projects and your laboratory, I would be most appreciative.

Thank you for your assistance, and I look forward to hearing from you via mail or email at your earliest convenience.

Sincerely,

Vanessa Raye Adkins

If you are evaluating preprofessional schools—business, law, medicine, architecture, and so on—it is somewhat more difficult to discern the differences between programs. Nevertheless, these schools are each quite distinct, and understanding this not only increases your chances of finding the right one for you, it also increases your chances of developing a compelling application and gaining admission to your first-choice schools.

For example, some medical schools have an emphasis on public health built into the regular medical school curriculum, others offer a special combined M.D./M.P.H. program, and some have both. Some teaching medical centers are located in the heart of decayed urban centers, taking pride in serving disadvantaged patient populations, while others are famous for their cardiology units or their pediatric hospitals. Some architecture schools are known worldwide for their concern with handicapped access and social issues, while others remain devotees of the International Style of Mies van der Rohe. Failing to research such differences between programs is akin to going to the lake and diving headfirst into unknown waters. Obviously, if you are applying to thirty medical schools you cannot take a year off and research every one of them, but you should have a very well-defined impression of your top three to five choices.

Be careful of confusing reputation with academics. A school's reputation is certainly a consideration, but what you are going to learn is far more important. If reputation is highly important to you, you need to evaluate this factor carefully. Since reputations lag behind current conditions by three to five years, a school's current reputation may reflect circumstances that have passed. A school's reputation in five to ten years will be more important to your career than its reputation at the moment you matriculate. So you should analyze and project long-term trends and not fixate on any one year's rankings. Is the school investing in infrastructure, faculty salaries, and new programs that would indicate it has a commitment to continued excellence? Or has it not implemented a new idea in ten years? Resources providing information on the reputation

Warning

At the graduate level, schools as a whole do not have reputations—only programs do. There are outstanding programs nestled in otherwise undistinguished institutions, and there are paralyzed-from-the-neck-up, we-don't-care-we-got-tenure-twenty-years-ago graduate departments ensconced in some of the most elite universities on the continent. You want information on the reputation of specific departments, not institutions as a whole.

—HOW TO APPROACH A GRADUATE SCHOOL—
(ideally)

Using the Internet, go from

The University Home Page

↓

The Department Home Page

↓

Specific Labs or Subdepartmental Specialty Areas

↓

Individual Faculty Home Pages

↓

Advisees, i.e., Currently Enrolled Grad Students

Identify one to four faculty members who have the potential to be future mentors to you. Look for faculty who publish, who have ongoing research projects directly related to your interests, and who win grants, honors, and awards. You can often read writings by that faculty member by linking directly from faculty home pages to research summaries, abstracts, or academic journals.

Write to faculty by email and/or snail mail

1. **Ask for some clarification of the program**. Keep your query as specific as possible: "I noticed on the departmental home page that you are the expert in microdynamics. Does your lab have any plans to pursue projects in nanomachinery?" Or, "I am interested in cultural anthropology of Native Americans in urban settings post-1945. Who would be the most appropriate faculty member to contact about this interest?"

   If you have access to writings about the professor's work, by the professor or others, read them well and offer some thoughtful comments. Don't be afraid to state your own views, but exercise caution when it comes to outright disagreement. If you point out: "On page three of your proof in the most recent edition of *Mathmatica,* I noticed a fatal error in logic . . ." you'd better be sure you are right.

2. **Propose a study topic, if it is directly related to their research specialty.** Be sure to follow Asher's Law (see page 41). Here is an example of such an email:

Dear Dr. Herrick:

I am interested in continuing my graduate work in history at SUNY Binghamton. I recently completed my master's project at NYU under the direction of Dr. T.L.I. Fitzsimons (see attached c.v.), and I will be receiving my degree this February. After a brief hiatus, I hope to return to my studies next fall with the intent of pursing a program of study culminating in the doctoral degree.

My area of interest within the Binghamton History Department is U.S. social history. I am particularly intrigued by the history of the New Left in the United States and did my research project on student movements of the late 1960s and early 1970s. In the course of my research, I came across your name often. I would appreciate the opportunity to further explore and analyze this topic, as I believe that we all have much more to learn about the American New Left and its shifting place in history.

My current interest is an analysis of the schism between . . .

If a professor doesn't write back, *do not be discouraged.* Professors get tons of unsolicited mail. They are used to skimming and delaying response to a lot of it. If you really want to reach them, email them and wait a day or two at most; if there's no response, email them again, with this added to the top, "I'm not sure you received my recent email. Here's what I emailed before." If there's still no response, print it out and snail-mail it to them, with this added at the top: "Perhaps I don't have an accurate email address for you. Here's my query printed out. I hope to hear from you by email or regular mail at your convenience. Thank you so much." If they *still* don't respond, it's probably just as well to leave them alone. Even if they never respond, it doesn't mean they're not with a good graduate program. They may be out of the country or have another perfectly good rationale for not being able to get back to you.

Write to others who can help you decide if this program is a good match

Do not hesitate to make contact with a school at multiple levels: the graduate school office, the departmental office, key faculty members, student associations you would like to join after admission, and perhaps even friends of your family who are prominent alumni.

If you're really interested in a program, be sure to email currently enrolled graduate students. Ask: Is this a good program? Which professors would you recommend? How long do you think it will take you to complete the degree program? Any hot tips for a prospective student? Then be sure to ask them about their studies and research projects.

Warning

The reputation of your graduate program is important for one reason. If you want to be a college professor, you need to know about The Law of Descending Prestige. According to this law, in general, you will teach at an institution with less prestige than the one that granted your highest degree. There will be exceptions, but an investigation of any random group of higher education hiring decisions will prove that the law is in effect for the overwhelming majority of cases. Also, be aware of the strong competition for academic positions in general. For example, as this book goes to press, the number of Ph.D.s being granted in the humanities is roughly twice the number of all announced teaching positions. At least half of those degree recipients will need some other career option, like it or not.

of graduate programs are *The Gourman Report, Educational Rankings, Research-Doctorate Programs in the United Sates*, and the Faculty Scholarly Productivity Index.

Gossip may actually be the best way to rank graduate programs. Faculty and currently enrolled graduate students have the latest and best information about whether program A is better than program B, or whether program X is improving or waning. So ask around. A student can design her own ranking system, by looking at the per-capita number of peer-reviewed articles produced by faculty at any given school, and by seeing if authors from school A are citing authors from school B, *or are cited by* authors from school B. This is not easy, but then again, neither is graduate school. Check out the "most cited researchers" tab at www.esi-topics.com/index.html. Graduate students themselves have occasionally ranked their own programs; see the web site for the National Association of Graduate and Professional Students, www.NAGPS.org. There are well established ranking systems for business, law, and medicine, and your advisor can guide you to them. Also, for more links and books on rankings and reputation, see www.donaldasher.com/gradschool.

My personal recommendation is to ignore reputation and concentrate on what the program can offer you. Learning nothing of use to you and being miserable at the Number-One School of Business is probably not as good for your career as being really excited about the entrepreneurial program at the Number-Thirty School of Business. Think about it.

The people

All other things being equal, people are the most important component of your graduate education. This means the faculty and fellow students with whom you will live and work closely for the next two to six years, or more. You want to be sure that you can work with them and that they can work with you. If you've attended a large university, you may not have spent more than twenty hours in your entire undergraduate career in the presence of a full professor; now you will work hand in glove with them on research they will monitor closely. If the best place in the world to study fractals is a program dominated by tyrannical gargoyles, you might want to take a look at the other schools on your list.

Similarly, if you have just spent four years fighting every day for the creation of a major in feminist political theory, do yourself a favor and find a graduate program with that established focus. Graduate school is not a good place to pioneer a new topic or to study without guidance. Although forging a new path is not impossible, studying in a program that aligns with your interests will probably be more gratifying and productive. When you choose a school whose program closely matches your interests, and your application essay explains this clearly, your essay can vault you further than your grades and test scores ever could.

The locale

The school's physical locale will be important to some applicants and totally irrelevant to others. If you are committed to your studies, you will not be too concerned with the weather or the proximity of ocean beaches. However, if you truly believe that you will be miserable in New York City, or Iowa City for that matter, then that has to be a factor in your decision. Wherever you attend graduate school, you are likely to make many friends and contacts you will wish to keep for a lifetime—this will prolong your relationship with the location of your school. You should also consider the benefits of studying in a city where you would like to be employed after graduation. Be mindful, too, of the "spouse factor." If you fail to consider the needs of your spouse, you may find yourself in need of a new one.

The cost

The cost of living in the area around the school will have a direct bearing on the cost of your graduate education, but students are usually quite creative at controlling overhead. Even if you have been living the good life between college and graduate school, you can return to a frugal lifestyle more easily than you might think. Remember, all your colleagues will be in the same boat. Cost of living is considered in all financial aid arrangements. In general, cost of living by itself should not be a determining factor in your selection.

On the other hand, the cost of the programs themselves can be quite daunting. As related in the prior chapter, that cost is often difficult or impossible to estimate before you apply and are accepted.

Warning

Be wary of choosing a graduate program because of just one professor. Professors move, go on sabbatical, fail to win tenure, serve as guest lecturers and scholars in residence at other institutions, die, lose favor in their departments, and change their beliefs. In each program you consider, try to identify two or three professors who have something to offer you.

A formula for selecting schools to apply to

First, rank all the graduate programs you have been investigating in order of interest to you, from most attractive overall to least attractive overall.

Then, *in a completely separate list,* divide your schools into three categories:

1. Those schools to which you are pretty sure you can get admitted, namely, safety schools.

2. Those schools to which you probably, *maybe* can get admitted.

3. Those schools to which it would be a reach for you to be admitted, perhaps even a miracle.

You can assign these categories based on what you have learned of the schools to date, combined with hard data, such as the percentage of applicants admitted, available from the Peterson's guides, *The Gourman Report*, and *Research-Doctorate Programs in the United States*. Most professors can handicap your chances with particular schools in their own field.

Applying to a European Graduate School?

If you're applying offshore, you might want to reconsider the tone of your documents. United States' citizens are notorious for bragging, whereas in Europe the norm would be to be a little more circumspect. Thus, in the U.S. we might say, "I conducted an experiment . . ." in Europe one would more likely say, "I was fortunate enough to be selected the junior member of a team doing some rather exciting work . . ."

Secondly, I know from interviews and information from my correspondents that European schools almost always read all of every portfolio, even the students they summarily reject. This changes the dynamic. You can trust the readers a bit more than in the U.S., where you sometimes have to speak up—shout if you will—in order to be sure that readers notice your best parts.

Thirdly, European educators in particular find "To Whom It May Concern" letters of recommendation to be insulting, both to themselves and to the student being recommended. Although they are an accepted part of the process in the U.S., be sure your recommenders write individualized letters for each program outside the U.S.

Finally, European faculty and admissions officers tend to respond to inquiries promptly and personally, whereas in the U.S. it is common for even very good schools to ignore student queries unless and until the applicant is actually admitted.

Next, going back to your ranking of schools from most desirable to least desirable, choose the *first two* "reach" schools, the *first two* "probably/maybe" schools, and the *first two* "safety" schools. This leaves you with a list of six schools—a reasonable number of graduate programs to apply to—and with a statistically high probability of getting admitted overall. If you are a borderline student or need maximum funding, you'll need to apply to more schools. However, and this is a very important point: **You must customize every application.** If you do not customize your applications, your "safe" schools are no longer safe. Failure to customize is the biggest mistake that graduate applicants make, and this is true across the board, from medicine to exobiology.

The best students often overestimate their admissibility and omit safety schools, while students with less-than-perfect portfolios often self-select out of graduate programs that would have been happy to have them. Don't fear rejection. If you do this correctly you'll be rejected by about half the places you apply. You may choose another methodology for selecting schools if you wish, but this formula is prudent for all applicants.

I once interviewed a student who applied to 34 medical schools. A little strategy on his part could have saved him considerably on application fees. I have interviewed hundreds of students who applied only to top schools and were rejected by all of them. One student provided the most interesting probability analysis I have ever heard: "I applied to Harvard, Princeton, Yale, and Stanford. I figured I had a twenty-five percent chance, since that's four schools." Deconstruct that logic if you can. I know of one student who graduated with a 4.0 and won a $24,000 fellowship applicable at any accredited graduate program, yet she was rejected by every one of the top ten programs in her field. Unfortunately, those were the only ten programs she applied to.

The dean of enrollment at a graduate school of business told me about rejecting a student with a perfect GMAT score. "He was arrogant," the dean said. "We didn't think he'd be a welcome addition to our student body." On the other hand, I've interviewed numerous students in medical school with an undergraduate GPA right around 3.0. I interviewed a dean who gave full funding to a student with a 2.85 when the school's target minimum GPA was 3.5. Another student told me that when she first contacted her graduate program they actually told her she'd never get in, yet she did.

For perspective, you should know that students applying to competitive programs typically apply to between four and fifteen schools. The national average number of applications per medical school aspirant is twelve. For most non-medical school students, a strategically chosen six is prudent. If you have questions about this strategy, be sure to discuss it with your faculty and advisers.

Why would you need two safety schools if a safety school is, by definition, safe? There are two good reasons. First, things go wrong; second, one might give you generous funding while the other offers none. Applicants want to believe that the graduate admissions process is fair and scientific, but in practice it's a mixture of science, art, and accident. Graduate admissions professionals work very hard to choose an incoming class and, believe me, they agonize over the borderline applicants. Nevertheless, the outcome is not always as it should be. Here are some actual cases:

- One student was rejected because her portfolio was "accidentally placed on the wrong pile." The graduate school discovered its mistake later in the season, but had already sent the student a rejection letter. Rather than admit what had happened, they let the decision stand.

- A student applying for a Ph.D. in philosophy received a letter from a major university rejecting his application for a Ph.D. in Germanic languages.

- A student was rejected by an internationally acclaimed architecture program after his portfolio was reviewed by Prof. X. When he called to inquire about the status of his application, Prof. Y picked up his portfolio, glanced through it while the student was on hold, and reversed the decision of Prof X. Thus was he admitted.

- One professor forgot to mail a wonderful letter of recommendation he had written for his favorite advisee, and she was rejected.

- Another professor was not granted tenure, and stopped performing all duties whatsoever that were not contractually required. This included writing letters of recommendation *that he had already agreed to write.* At least one of his advisees was not admitted to a graduate program because of this. The student never knew what happened.

- A student failed to send original transcripts from a community college she had attended while in high school. The transfer grades from the community college appeared on her regular college transcript but, through a bizarre chain of events, an overzealous student employee and a 50-cent library fine from six years prior conspired to keep her out of graduate school.

- A student had a wonderful exchange of letters with a department chair, some of which included such statements as, "We're so delighted that you will be joining us next year." Nevertheless, she was rejected by the graduate school office, which had more authority than the department.

As you narrow down your choices, resist the temptation to apply for two different programs at the same institution. Applying to multiple programs (at different schools) is expected; applying to multiple *different* programs is a warning flag to faculty about the depth of your commitment. If you truly have divergent interests and decide to apply for graduate programs in history and mathematics, for example, apply to mathematics programs at some institutions and history programs at others.

On the other hand, applying to combined degree programs, such as the M.D./Ph.D. or M.B.A./J.D., has no negative implications. Processes vary from institution to institution, so inquire at the targeted programs for more information.

Finally, as a strategic hedge, some Ph.D.-bound students will apply to a mix of Ph.D. and master's degree programs (of course, not at the same institution). This way, if they don't get into a Ph.D. program of their choice, they can continue their studies uninterruptedly and apply again when they are near to completing the intermediate degree. By the way, getting an intermediate degree is a good way to improve your chances of getting into some highly coveted graduate programs, including medical school and clinical psychology, among others.

First-choice school?

It is perhaps human nature to have a first-choice school on your list, but smart students avoid locking in on any one school or program. Select a wide range of schools, make your best application to each of the schools on your list, and let the process take its course. Besides, you learn constantly about programs by the very act of preparing to apply, applying, talking to faculty and friends, and watching how the schools treat you as the process unfolds. You may discover that your first-choice school has gargoyles for faculty, has zero funding for you, is famous for the work of several key professors who are about to retire, and so on, while a school you thought was not really a match turns up to have "hot" professors doing cutting-edge research, or is about to launch a new lab or research initiative focusing on your favorite topic. Or maybe they're just super nice and convince you you'd thrive there. Or you can always use the selection criterion of a student I interviewed at Oxford: "It's really quite easy to select programs. I apply for a lot of funding and awards, and I consistently find that the opportunities that come through with the most money attached are in fact the most interesting." (It sounds very logical in a British accent.)

• • •

In subsequent chapters, I assume that you have selected and ranked a group of viable graduate programs; from this point on the focus of the material is entirely on how to get in. There is no one formula that all successful applicants have followed, but applicants who are consistently successful, who win scholarships and grants and admission to several of their top-ranked schools, tend to use most of the strategies and follow most of the guidelines presented to you in the following chapters.

Again, this book's main focus is to present the *ideal* way to apply to *highly competitive* programs. If you've already selected a program that you're pretty sure you can get into and just want help writing a good essay, feel free to skip ahead to chapter 5, "Getting Ready to Write."

3

Planning and Managing Your Application Process

Applying to a graduate program requires more than typing up the application and writing an interesting essay. You must successfully orchestrate a number of independent assignments in order to complete them all ahead of the application deadline. Some of the major steps of your application process are:

1. Opening and managing online application accounts with each school,

2. drafting, rewriting, and polishing a compelling essay, statement of purpose, and/or autobiography,

3. taking the appropriate standardized graduate admissions test(s),

4. getting the test scores forwarded to your schools of interest,

5. obtaining multiple letters of recommendation from faculty members and other busy people,

6. obtaining original transcripts from all your schools of record,

7. sending any paper-based materials to your target schools via a guaranteed carrier,

8. entering data on forms, finalizing your essays, and hitting "submit,"

9. verifying that your application is complete.

Throughout the process, you must be sure to double-check every step that depends on other people's actions.

deadline **1 :** a clearly marked line around prisoner-of-war camps at which an escaping prisoner would be shot to death, orig. U.S. Civil War
2 a: a date or time after which a story cannot be accepted for publication or broadcast **b:** the worst possible time to turn in your application to graduate school

As you get catalogs and application packets in the mail or print out application instructions from university home pages, write each program's application deadline in big, scary letters on your appointment calendar.

Oddly enough, if students are given four years to apply to graduate school, 50 percent of them will apply in the last ten days anyway. Whatever you do, strive to apply at least 30 days early! (If you are a premedical student, you need to know that most premed advisers are now trying to get all their students to complete their applications by the end of the summer between the junior and senior year.)

There are two good reasons to turn in your materials early. First, it gives you more time to make a mistake. You can send another request for documents lost in the mail, motivate any slow-moving recommendation writers, and fix any disasters. It is always the student's responsibility to make sure that every document requested by the admissions committee is in her file before the deadline. This is reason enough to plan on submitting your application months ahead of schedule.

The second reason to apply early has to do with the other end of the admissions process and what happens to your application when it arrives. Almost all admissions officers use some form of three-tiered ranking system for applicants: (1) those students they definitely want to admit, (2) those they are not sure about, and (3) those they will reject. If the school uses a rolling admissions process, admissions staff read and evaluate applications as they arrive. The closer you get to the deadline, the greater the number of outstanding candidates already admitted and the longer the wait list will be.

If the school uses a fixed-date system instead of rolling admissions, the essays may or may not be read all at one time. Most often, admissions staff will read the applications as they arrive or in periodic batches ahead of the deadline, hoping to lighten the crush of work that follows. The earlier your application arrives, the greater its chances of being favorably reviewed by an alert, intelligent, compassionate admissions representative. The later it arrives, the more likely it is to receive a cursory examination by an overworked admissions representative who has already reviewed a large number of outstanding candidates and compiled a sizable wait list.

I once asked the dean of an elite graduate school what she did with the applications that came in late. "Confidentially?" she asked. "Strictly background," I assured her. "We cash the checks," she replied.

All of this should be taken with a grain of salt, however. I have interviewed students who applied late, whose applications were incomplete, and so on, who were admitted to graduate programs. If you are applying to an obscure program that is not swamped with applicants, if you are an outstanding or unusual candidate, or if you have made several contacts with the program and they are expecting your application, then you need not worry overmuch about turning in your application several weeks ahead of the deadline. If you are applying to a highly competitive program, however, timing is simply too important a factor to ignore. For the most competitive programs in the nation, my recommendation is to apply two or more months early. If you are unsure of the best time to apply for the type of programs you have targeted, be sure to discuss it with your adviser.

• • •

Take time to really read online program information, faculty home pages, and the application forms. Then prepare your activity log and timeline. Start with your first-choice school. Re-read the materials with a magnifying glass in one hand and fine-toothed comb in the other. Break down the application process into a series of smaller assignments, like the list that starts this chapter. Then, arrange these assignments in the order in which you plan to complete them. Put a target date next to each assignment, and check off each one when it is finished. See pages 30–31 for an example of how one student managed her deadline in an Excel speedsheet.

After you have prepared a detailed activity log and timeline for your first-choice school, make activity logs and timelines for all the other schools you plan to apply to, but keep your first-choice schools first in mind. If you miss an interim deadline for your first-choice school because you were chasing down an obscure community college transcript for your last-choice school, you are not prioritizing your tasks wisely.

There are two basic models for managing the graduate application process: the traditional model and the self-managed application. Under the traditional application model, the school will open a file on you either when they have a clear indication from you that you are going to apply, or as soon as you submit your online application forms. Any correspondence you may have with the school, and any notes that the recruiter may have made from meeting you, will accumulate in this file. Transcripts, letters of recommendation, your application forms and essays, and supporting materials from diverse sources will all land in this file, which is often still a paper file.

The trouble is, at those schools that don't open a file for you until they receive your online application and fee, any items that come in ahead of your application are at risk of being lost or misdirected. Under the self-managed application model, the student collects any paper-based materials and submits them in a packet she has assembled herself. Confidentiality is assured through different methods, most commonly by the senders of paper letters and transcripts signing their names or placing an official stamp across the envelope's seal. It is the student's responsibility to be sure the application file is complete and that all rules have been followed, although

Warning

Approach your letter-of-recommendation writers at the earliest possible moment. Be sure to read the instructions on pages 36–37 and in chapter 9.

schools will sometimes wait for a straggling letter or late-arriving test scores. It is your responsibility to discover each graduate school's preferred procedures and to comply.

A word about fees: Application fees usually run from $40 to $150 per school, which can get expensive for your typical poverty-stricken undergraduate. *Do not scrimp on application fees.* Remember, whether you get in and whether you get funding are determined by applying to a reasonable, strategically chosen number of schools. This is a very large financial decision you are making, ultimately worth tens of thousands of dollars. Do not make this decision based on an application fee of a few tens of dollars. Some schools will waive fees if you apply early and submit a letter from your undergraduate financial aid officer (or in some cases, your adviser) explaining your financial need. Your financial aid officer is accustomed to writing these letters and knows exactly what to say. Letters from students, no matter the circumstances described, are usually

Target List for Madison Allbrecht

Program →	Mega U.	Northern U.	Wassamatta U.	Outback U.	Closeto U.	Safe U.
size of department	23	4	16	8	6	5
# of faculty with my interest	3	1	?	2	1.5	0
ranking, if known	tops	very good	so so	very good, but mostly for bioinformatics	so so	okay
Ph.D. or master's	Ph.D.	Ph.D.	Ph.D.	Ph.D.	start w/ master's	terminal master's
deadline to apply	Jan 1	Feb 10	Feb 1	Feb 15	Mar 15	Apr 1
deadline for support	Nov 15	Feb 10	Jan 15	Feb. 1	Mar 1	Apr 1
date application verified as complete						
waiver of app. Fees	yes	never	yes	yes	yes	yes
app fee	75	80	early only 45	45	90	45 for online
fellowship or assistantship	all admitted students get first-year fellowship	minority fellowship teaching & research assistantships	"We select students for fellowship and assistantship funding in March or April. Not all admitted students receive these types of funding."	all admitted are funded one way or another	no	"maybe"
GRE requirements	yes, plus subject test 1000 combined minimum	yes, but "not very important"	optional for students with 3.5+ subject test is also optional	yes, plus subject test 600+ on quant.. is "recommended" subject test "recommended"	yes, but "there is no minimum score, we look at each candidate as a whole"	no
are they nice to me?	not really	yes, very	so far	yes	yes	yes

ineffective. Some schools will not waive application fees under any circumstances. Finally, just to confuse the matter totally, some schools that claim they never waive fees have been known to do so when the student is an outstanding applicant and has made a personal and direct appeal to the right administrator.

Testing

Proper preparation for the graduate admissions exams requires extensive lead time. Fall break is a good time to take the exams, as is the summer before your senior year. Students often pick one of the worst times—the end of the fall semester. Students don't mean to take the exams then; they just fail to take them sooner, and then that's what time it is.

On the following pages are some of the more common exams and resources for learning more about them.

Program →	Mega U.	Northern U.	Wassamatta U.	Outback U.	Closeto U.	Safe U.
minimum or target GPA	no	3.0 minimum	web site says "students with less than 3.5 are not usually successful, but are not discouraged from applying" whatever that means...	3.0	no	no
faculty connections	Dr. S. Smithers Dr. L. Joss Dr. R. Massey	Dr. J. Watkins have very encouraging letter from Dr. Watkins	need to find	Dr. W. Moss Dr. V. Martin Also, spoke with the chair of the dept. at national meeting in Chicago last year, Dr. Stossen	Dr. Wilson	Dr. P. Ling
admissions contacts, the "official" contact	admis@noru.edu no other contact provided	Melissa Martel (202) 555-1894 mmadmin@mega.edu	dir@adm.wassa.edu also: "each department directly"	Lynda Granger (412) 555-5928 apply@obu.edu	Grad office: Lawrence Millhouse A&S@closeto.edu Department: Maria Menendez mm@bio.closeto.edu (513) 555-3959 (she's very nice)	It's all on the web site portal www.admissions.safeu.edu Dr. Ling said call her about anything
Notes	19% admit rate submitting a research sample is "recommended"	separate applications for research and teaching assistantships!	need to do further research re mentors Dr. Wilson knows somebody at this school; email her soon re this	need to read some abstracts of Dr. Martin to be sure of fit	admit is only to the master's program, can go directly on to their Ph.D. if they like you NO FUNDING first two years	terminal master's but claims high transfer rate to Ph.D. programs, need to find out what "high" means...
Accepted? Rejected? Wait listed?						
Deadline to respond?						

Warning

There is a rumor floating around university campuses that you can take the GRE on computer and see if you like the score before accepting the test as official. This is absolutely false. Once you push the button to compute the final score, your record is *automatically and immediately official*. That score is tied to your social security number and stays on record for five years. Never take an official test for practice.

Graduate Record Examination (GRE), ETS
   P.O. Box 6000, Princeton, NJ 08541-6000
   phone (609) 771-7670
   GRE Information Bulletin (free)
   Practicing to Take the GRE General Test. 9th ed.
   Practicing to Take the {subject name here} Test
   www.gre.org

Miller Analogies Test (MAT)
   The Psychological Corp.
   555 Academic Court, San Antonio, Texas 78204-3956
   phone (800) 622-3231 or (512) 921-8800
   MAT Candidate Information Booklet
   www.hbtpc.com/mat/index.html

Graduate Management Admissions Test (GMAT), ETS
   P.O. Box 6103, Princeton, NJ 08541-6103
   phone (609) 771-7330
   GMAT Bulletin of Information (free)
   The Official Guide for GMAT Review
   The Official Software for GMAT Review
   www.gmat.org

Law School Admission Test (LSAT)
   Law School Admissions Service
   P.O. Box 2000, Newtown, PA 18940-0998
   phone (215) 968-1100
   Law Services Information Book (free)
   www.lsac.org/lsat.htm

Medical College Admission Test (MCAT)
   Association of American Medical Colleges
   Attn: Membership & Publication Orders
   One Dupont Circle NW, Suite 200, Washington, D.C. 20036
   phone (202) 828-0416, program office phone (510) 654-1200
   MCAT Student Manual
   Medical School Admissions Requirements
   www.aamc.org

Dental Admission Test (DAT)
   American Dental Association
   211 E. Chicago Avenue, Chicago, Illinois 60611
   phone (312) 440-2689
   www.ada.org/prac/careers/dat-01.html

Veterinary College Admission Test (VCAT)

   The Psychological Corp.

   555 Academic Court, San Antonio, Texas 78204-2498

   phone (800) 622-3231 or (210) 921-8861

Optometry College Admission Test (OCAT)

   The Psychological Corp.

   555 Academic Court, San Antonio, Texas 78204-2498

   phone (800) 622-3231 or (210) 921-8861

Pharmacy College Admission Test (PCAT)

   The Psychological Corp.

   555 Academic Court, San Antonio, Texas 78204-2498

   phone (800) 622-3231 or (210) 921-8861

   www.tpcweb.com/pse/g-contso.htm

Other test-related web sites

www.ets.org

www.petersons.com

www.review.com

www.kaplan.com

www.lsac.org

www.gmat.org

www.test.com

www.vocabulary.com

www.donaldasher.com/gradschool

Note that some dental programs will accept an MCAT score, and some graduate schools will accept the MAT in place of the GRE, even if they don't reveal this in their application materials. Call them and ask.

Most academic graduate programs expect you to take the GRE, or Graduate Record Exam. This test has three sections: verbal, analytical writing, and quantitative. This test is not unlike the tests you took to get into college, but how long has it been, really, since you saw a question like this: "Six young people are standing on the edge of a river. They have two large sea kayaks, one of which is freshly painted a bright blue. They have no life vests, and two can't swim. It is four o'clock in the afternoon, and the sun is 15 degrees above the horizon, obscured by clouds. Where are these people, what are they doing, and which one is pregnant?" Think you need some practice? Yes, you do.

Top students sometimes make the mistake of going in to take these tests cold, without any preparation at all. Let there be no doubt: You should study for any graduate admissions test; studying *will* result in a better score. Take a test preparation class or buy test preparation booklets. Study in those areas in which you have forgotten basic material. Brush up on your math. Play logic games. Specific questions will vary, but the types of questions and the material covered stay the same year to year. Remember, these tests cover a set of basic knowledge and concepts, so you need not worry about truly in-depth or obscure

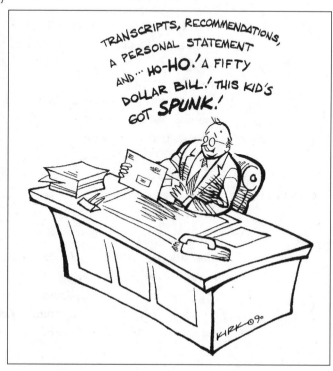

Warning

Some poets want to believe that their math scores don't matter (and some English departments might agree with them), but in spite of the extracts on this page from *GRE: Guide to the Use of Scores,* the graduate schools often have minimum scores that students must exceed before their folios can be forwarded to the department for final consideration. No one can afford to totally bomb any part of the GRE. If you want to avoid mathematical testing, see if your graduate school will accept the MAT in place of the GRE. Some will.

knowledge (the exception to this is the GRE subject tests, which can be rather exhaustive). Be sure to take as many practice tests as you can get your hands on. Most study booklets and software packets have at least one sample test.

By the way, if you are interested in taking the GRE on paper, it can still be done—in Sub-Saharan Africa. Good luck.

For descriptions of the other tests, see their study guides. In addition to the orientation guides available from the various test administrators listed above and in the references section, or from your nearest university career planning office, there are many, many study guides available. Your college bookstore probably carries hundreds of titles, almost all of them very good, so just take your pick. It's a good idea to get at least three different guides and run through them all. Look particularly for at least one with a CD study aid and practice test so that you can get the actual feel of the exam on computer.

Studying a couple of hours a day for thirty days before the test is more than sufficient. The study preparation courses are expensive, but they are effective. Some regional test preparation companies are significantly less expensive.

Here are some interesting observations from a recent edition of *GRE: Guide to the Use of Scores,* a publication available from the Graduate Record Examinations Board of the Educational Testing Service (also see www.ets.org or www.gre.org):

> GRE scores should not be used in isolation. Use of multiple criteria is particularly important when using GRE scores to assess the abilities of educationally disadvantaged students, students whose primary language is not English, and students who are returning to school after an extended absence . . .
>
> GRE scores, like those on similar standardized tests, cannot completely represent the potential of any person, nor can they alone reflect an individual's chances of long-term success in an academic environment . . .
>
> Special care is required in interpreting the GRE scores of students who may have had an educational and cultural experience somewhat different from that of the traditional majority . . .
>
> A cutoff score below which every applicant is categorically rejected without consideration of any other information should not be used . . .
>
> A low score may be the result of a lack of exposure to an area rather than a lack of mastery.

You may wish to obtain and review this booklet yourself, and perhaps even quote some of these observations in your essay.

Again, you must read the application requirements carefully, and read the test manuals carefully as well. Do not rely on the advice of others. Talented faculty, deans, and even the test preparation companies have, occasionally, gotten basic facts wrong about the tests. *It is your job to read the official bulletins!*

Long-term preparation to be an outstanding candidate

As you may have realized by now, time is one of the most important factors in your application process. Some of the best techniques require extensive lead time. For example, it is much easier to get into a summer program at a top-tier school than it is to get admitted to a regular degree program at the same school. Some medical and dental schools even offer auxiliary summer premedical classes open to undergraduates. You must plan to attend such a program as much as a full year before you intend to apply to a graduate program, but the advantages are immense. If you study hard and make high grades, you will have demonstrated that you can perform at the level the school demands. Besides, the experience looks great on your transcript wherever you go.

If you get into *any* summer program at a highly selective institution, you can walk over to the department you are interested in for graduate studies and make friends. This should not be difficult. Just walk over and say, "Hi, I'm Andrea Tipton and I'm interested in graduate studies in cultural anthropology. What is your program emphasis here?" Be friendly. This edge, and the names you can weave into your essay later, can cinch your admittance. I met one American student who got admitted to Oxford by taking a summer enrichment program and impressing the professor. Finally, I'll let you in on a little-known secret: At some of the most elite universities on the continent, there are no admissions requirements for summer school. If your check is good, you're in.

Similarly, you can take internships or gain employment in your field of interest. This demonstrates commitment to your career goal and reassures admissions counselors that your interest is not a passing fancy. If you intend to study law or medicine, it is a real plus to prove that you know what the daily life of an attorney or a physician is really like. Applications for summer internships are typically accepted the winter before, and by March most programs will be full. You can obtain a summer job later, but it is a good idea to start making contacts one to three months before summer break.

Here are some specific tips to up your chances with law, medical, or business schools. Anyone planning to attend law school should read *Double Billing: A Young Lawyer's Tale of Greed, Sex, Lies, and the Pursuit of a Swivel Chair* by Cameron Stracher; *Full Disclosure: Do You Really Want to Be a Lawyer* compiled by Susan J. Bell for The Young Lawyers Division of the ABA; and *Running from the Law: Why Good Lawyers Are Getting Out of the Legal Profession* by Deborah L. Arron. What law schools love to see: exposure to real lawyers doing real lawyering in place of idealistic fantasies about the law (or, even worse, anything you might have picked up from watching glamorous and powerful lawyers on television and in the movies). For example, litigators are only in court about 5 percent of the time. Did you know that? Well, every single attorney in North America does know that. Attorneys spend very little time doing what most people imagine they do.

Anyone planning to attend medical school should read *Medical School Admissions: The Insider's Guide* by J. Zebala, D. Jones, and S. Jones; and the Association of American Medical College's *Medical School Admission Requirements: United States and Canada*. What medical schools love to see: exposure to medical procedures, especially those involving bodily fluids, rather than the more common "feel-good" internships in nonclinical medical settings. A solid 3.5 student with extensive exposure to medical procedures is more desirable than a 4.0 student who has never been outside the confines of a chemistry lab. (Again, work closely with your institution's premedical advisers; they know how this works and can offer sound advice.)

What business schools love to see: two to four years of experience with a large organization, *with rapid advancement* and a high salary for your age. More experience than that is not really necessary. If you have several significant internships, high grades, proven drive and ambition, and a clear vision of what you want to do after you graduate, you shouldn't hesitate to apply right out of college. Be sure to read these MBA guides: *Case in Point, The Wharton MBA Case Interview Study Guide* vols. I and II, *Ace Your Case!*, and *15 Questions: More Practice to Help Ace Your Consulting Case.*

Volunteer to gain related experience. Volunteering in public service areas demonstrates social commitment, in addition to whatever skills and maturity you may gain from the experience itself.

—GETTING FANTASTIC LETTERS OF RECOMMENDATION—

You shouldn't just suddenly appear in a professor's doorway and ask for a letter of recommendation. Instead, visit your professors often during your undergraduate years. Show them your list of targeted schools, and discuss your motivations. Usually, the professors will bring up the question of letters of recommendation themselves.

1. Take these materials to the meeting:

    a) your printed transcript (which is available online) or a list of your most important classes with grades for each class,

    b) a paper or a lab showing some of your best work,

    c) a resume or a C.V., especially if the professor doesn't know about some of your work or internship experiences,

    d) a list of your activities,

    e) copies of all correspondence you have had with targeted graduate programs,

    f) a copy of the latest draft of your statement of purpose,

    g) a list of the other professors you plan to ask for letters,

    h) all the stamps, envelopes, and forms your professor might need, all filled out and ready to go,

    i) suggested "talking points," especially if this professor is not in your primary discipline. For example, ask your theatre professor to comment on whether your acting ability would be useful to you in teaching an introductory biology class for undergraduates, or ask your adviser to comment on your independent study project, or

Volunteering is also a way of creating your own business internships. Students have volunteered at such venues as television stations and architectural studios to gain experience and explore their interest in a particular field of graduate study.

If you are applying to competitive programs, your activities and honors can sometimes be a deciding factor between admission and rejection. However, students tend to overestimate the value of activities. As a rough guess, activities are worth one quarter of a grade point; maybe a half point in truly extraordinary cases. It is better to devote yourself to your studies than to explain your weak grade-point average with a fistful of activities. In general, quality counts over quantity. It is preferable to be an officer of one organization than a member of five or six.

---

your tutoring of other students, or your service as a test proctor for a class or lab. Help professors think of beneficial things to say about you, but remember: *The professor will write about whatever she wants.* You can only offer suggestions.

2. Ask this question: "Dr. Johnson, would you be comfortable making a strong recommendation for me for graduate study in _____?" If the answer is less than enthusiastic, consider your other options.

3. Ask this question: "Dr. Johnson, what will you be able to say about me?" This is a tough question to ask, but when do you want to find out? Before or after your first-choice graduate school does?

4. Always stress the date when you're going to apply, as in "Dr. Lee, I'll be applying by November 5. Will you be able to have the letter ready by then?" Never talk about the deadline. Avoid needing a letter just before or after the end of the term. Allow a professor two to six weeks to write your letter. Otherwise, it may start out like this: "Paul, from what I can remember, was usually prompt, and had good handwriting . . ." This is even worse if your name is not Paul.

5. Check in with your professor every Thursday to see if the letter is done. Be nice about it, but don't fall off the radar screen.

6. Be sure to give each professor a warm and sincere thank-you card once the letter has been submitted on your behalf.

For much more on letters of recommendation, see chapter 9, "Letters of Recommendation."

Warning

Do not ever make up even the smallest item on your application. It is patently immoral, and ultimately it may ruin your life. Schools routinely request supporting material whenever they get an application that seems unlikely, and they all subscribe to the same listserv to alert one another to fraudulent applicants. News item:

> A federal judge in Hartford, Conn., threw out the defamation lawsuit against Princeton University filed by disgruntled, would-be medical student Rommel Nobay, who claimed that Princeton's having bad-mouthed him for lying on his application discouraged other schools from accepting him. Nobay admitted to fudging his class standing, SAT score, and other things that applicants sometimes exaggerate; however, attracting more attention were his personal statements, in which Nobay wrote that a family of lepers in Kenya had so much faith in him that they had donated "half their beggings" to help him with his education. (News of the Weird)

Graduate admissions professionals consistently mention the following three activities as most persuasive to them:

- serving as a research assistant on original research while you're still an undergraduate, especially working in a laboratory where original research is underway;

- serving as an instructional assistant to a professor, which can mean serving as a test proctor, grader, teaching lab assistant, tutor, or similar; and

- serving as a residence hall adviser.

The most impressive academic activity, according to graduate admissions professionals, is any kind of extended, independent research project. However, even the relatively mundane task of verifying citations in student bibliographies qualifies as a highly regarded activity. Professors pick students for these jobs who are reliable, extremely thorough, and mature; these are qualities that graduate programs value highly. Deans usually pick residence hall advisers; these students go through formal training, and their behavior goes under a microscope for at least a year, so they are also regarded as mature and reliable. I know of one department chair who admitted a student to graduate school because he had been a house sitter for his undergraduate adviser, and the adviser had mentioned it in his letter of recommendation. "That's trust," said the chair.

Student government is also highly regarded. I know of one medical school applicant who got in a year early, before completing his premed program—and *before he even applied*—because of an odd confluence of events. To begin with, he had been a management consultant before returning to school to complete his undergraduate degree in a premed program. He got elected to student government, and at the same time started volunteering eight hours a week at the local hospital emergency room. The university had just launched a strategic planning phase involving considerable financial planning and, because the applicant was the only member of student government with heavy-duty financial skills, he was appointed to serve as the student member of the board of trustees. He did a great job, which also involved occasionally working with top officers of the university's medical school. He then heard about something called a "dean's admit," whereby, in very rare cases, the dean of the medical school could admit students directly. Since he knew the dean from his work as a trustee, it was easy to ask him for a dean's admit. The dean reviewed his background and admitted him, subject to a good MCAT. The applicant aced the MCAT and went to medical school a year early *without ever having applied and with no undergraduate degree.* This is, admittedly, an unusual and very talented student—but the point is that instead of trudging through his premed curriculum, he chose to get involved. It paid off handsomely.

Completely off-campus, nonacademic endeavors also count, sometimes more than the routine college-sponsored activities. For example, if you are a nationally ranked horseback rider in dressage, your commitment to excellence in this outside arena will be highly regarded by admissions readers. Any enduring outside passion is usually seen as positive, unless you reveal that you are unsure whether to become a professional soccer player or go on to medical school. If you are confused about your true priorities, your avocation or pastime could threaten your future vocation.

True commitment over a length of time to any charitable organization will make a favorable impression on reviewers. Do not overlook opportunities to make unusual contributions; students have helped launch soup kitchens, performed as puppeteers and clowns at daycare centers, and volunteered for whole summers at wildlife rehabilitation facilities located in the middle of nowhere.

Having your own work published is a recognized sign of intellectual and academic promise, and is somewhat easier than most undergraduates think. (It's impossible, of course, if you never prepare and submit an article for publication.) If you are working closely with a professor on research work that will be submitted for publication, you should brazenly ask to be included as a co-author. The worst that can happen is that the answer will be no. On the other hand, if it's yes, the result *could* be even worse: a massive increase in your responsibilities on the project. This is often the price of one's early publications.

Most major universities and many smaller institutions have some sort of undergraduate research journal, in which student research is published in the standardized style for that field. The main purpose of these journals is not so much to disseminate the fascinating research of undergraduates as it is to teach students the publication formats and practices that will be required for success later in their academic careers. If there is no journal appropriate for your submission, start your own. Do a good job of it, because it is very likely the admissions committee will ask to see a copy.

Don't neglect the many undergraduate research meetings throughout the country, such as the McNair program for undergraduate research. These are outstanding opportunities for you to present your research as table topics or in brief presentations to a usually friendly audience. These experiences go in your application, too. An example of a table presentation submitted as part of an application to graduate school begins on page 161.

Stress your memberships in academic societies, but don't oversell social sororities and fraternities. If you are an officer or a committee chair, then stress these leadership roles. (If you are chair of the social committee of a fraternity, don't even mention it. That's tantamount to bragging that you are an expert—and an evangelist to others—in the fine art of drinking beer.)

Many students start their own activities, demonstrating initiative as well as organizational and interpersonal skills. It's never too late to found Students for the Elimination of Xeronisus. There are dozens of organizations waiting for your participation, so help them out while strengthening your own candidacy.

Although the example shown in the sidebar on the opposite page is extreme, there are routine notices on the listserv about falsified credentials and inflated claims, such as this one:

Alert: We have received an application from a student from _____ by the name of _____.
The certified translation of his transcript does not match the original transcripts provided

by _____. The English-speaking reference for his class ranking has been discovered to be his wife. The letter of recommendation from his professor has been verified by that professor as forged. If you need additional information please call _____ at _____.

This message recently went out to every graduate admissions professional in North America. Don't be the subject of a notice like this!

The three most immediate ways to stand out

It's nice to develop yourself as a candidate from the time you are a junior in college, but suppose you are a senior or a graduate, and you've got to apply now. What are the best ways to stand out in the application process?

- Write to the professors.
- Visit the graduate program.
- Submit an outstanding work sample.

You can write to the professors and currently enrolled students using the techniques recommended on page 20. This approach is recommended more for academic and research programs than for business, law, or medical schools, although with tact you should feel comfortable using it anywhere. Remember, the first goal is to establish whether this program is a good match for your interests, level of academic preparation, and work ethic. It is only a secondary benefit that this makes you stand out from the overwhelming majority of applicants who will not have established direct bonds with the program. (A very few schools actually request that you name a faculty sponsor as part of your application process.)

You should visit your top-choice schools if you can. Although compulsory interviews have all but disappeared, almost all schools welcome visits from prospective students. A personal interview makes a deep impression on faculty and admissions counselors, much deeper than an essay and a file full of two-dimensional application materials. However, a personal visit is a risky endeavor, as you may reveal more about yourself than you intend. A successful visit requires planning and due consideration of protocol.

First of all, it helps to look the part—that is, to look like somebody who belongs at the graduate school you're visiting. In some departments, students and professors will be wearing shorts and Birkenstocks, while at others, they'll look like they understand the phrase "sophisticated casual." (One grad student told me he wore a Hawaiian shirt to every interview, to stand out in interviewers' minds and to let them know he had a sense of humor. It must have worked; he got a very good assignment in a world-class lab.) My recommendation is to look clean, healthy, sane, and comfortable, without pretending to be someone you're not. Jewelry should be kept to a minimum; avoid scents entirely; new clothes look better than old clothes. Try not to look fabulously wealthy or magazine glamorous.

Never, never, never just "show up" on campus and expect to be shown around. Call the departmental office or the admissions office well in advance of your visit, tell them you are very

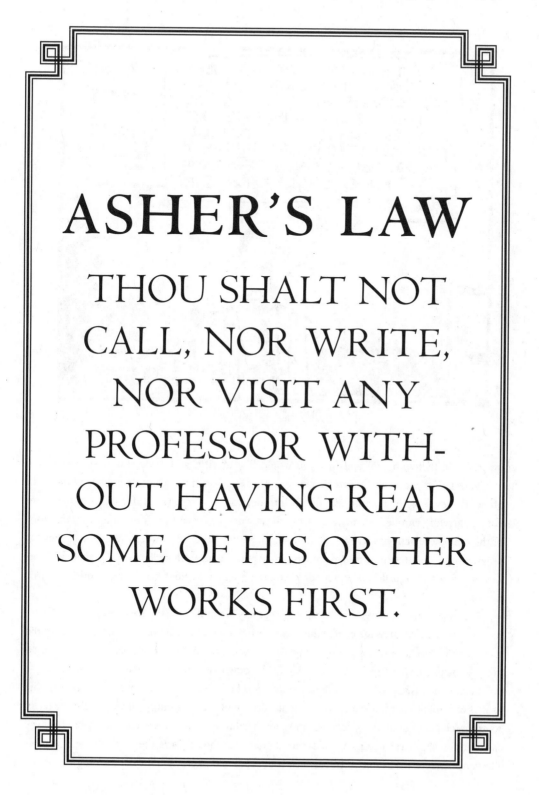

ASHER'S LAW

THOU SHALT NOT CALL, NOR WRITE, NOR VISIT ANY PROFESSOR WITHOUT HAVING READ SOME OF HIS OR HER WORKS FIRST.

DAN BLOWS HIS INTERVIEW.

interested in their program and that you would like to visit, and respectfully ask if someone could meet with you while you are on campus. Always broaden your objectives beyond the main office. For example, you could ask for an introduction to a specific professor, or ask to meet with a currently enrolled graduate student whose work you've admired, or inquire about a tour of their famous electron microscopy laboratory, or some other special feature of the campus or program. In general, expect to make your own appointments with professors. Remember *Asher's Law:* Thou shalt not call, nor write, nor visit any professor without having read some of his or her works first.

A few days before your visit, call and confirm every appointment. You needn't reach your party; just leave a voicemail message confirming the date and time. This little act of courtesy is one of the most overlooked, and most appreciated, of polite gestures. It demonstrates consideration and maturity, and also helps ensure that you do not wait outside somebody's office for hours to no avail.

Before you visit, you should prepare yourself to be articulate about your choice of graduate studies and about your interest in the particular school you are visiting. You should also be ready to ask intelligent questions about their program, facilities, faculty, research, and so on. (See the questions on pages 43 and 44.) If you cannot do this, you should forgo the visit entirely. If you act like you are interested in a good fit between your needs and interests and what the program offers, you will make a more favorable impression than if you seem like a supplicant begging for any spot on next year's roster. Some applicants even ask admissions counselors or currently enrolled students to rank and discuss the *other* programs the applicant is considering, but I am not convinced that this is such a great idea. No one is going to enjoy saying, "Yes, their program is better than ours."

These are the types of questions you can expect:

- So, have you read any good books lately?

- Which theorists or thought leaders do you admire in our field?

- What can you tell me that's not in your formal application materials?

- So, why do you want to be a _____?

- What do you know about our research topic and methodologies?

- Can you tell me about your undergraduate adviser?

- What do you do with your leisure time?

- Could you describe how you study? What is your routine?

- Could you tell me about a major failure in your life and how you dealt with it?

- What are your career plans and how does our particular program fit in with them?

- What other programs are you applying to now?

- What will you do if you don't get in?

- Why should we admit you over the many other fine and highly qualified candidates we have this year?

- What makes you different?

The best advice is to be well prepared, and then just be yourself. Remember your interviewer's name, sit up straight and lean slightly forward in your chair, and pay attention. Do not be afraid to say those three magic words, "I don't know."

Ideally, you should show up a day or at least several hours early and walk through the campus to find the office and get a feel for the atmosphere. (Of course you will resist the temptation to "just pop in for a moment" prior to your scheduled appointment.) Show up for all scheduled meetings exactly five minutes early. Always have a pen and tablet with you in case you need to take notes, but don't let your note-taking interfere with natural conversation.

If you are a little different, in any way, interviewing can give you the edge you need. I know of an outstanding candidate who came from a small college in a rural area. He applied to top programs all over the country. He took note of the fact that he was admitted at every program he visited and rejected by every program where he did not. I know of another candidate who wanted a coveted slot in a museum studies program, but had a spotty background. She called the departmental office but was told that she did not "meet the profile" of a successful candidate. She was interested in a particular curator who was a professor in the program and called him at his museum. He agreed to meet with her "briefly" as a courtesy, so she buried herself in the library to read up on his specialty

—QUESTIONS TO ASK ANY GRADUATE PROGRAM—

1. What do you teach here?

2. What is the largest and the most typical class size for a graduate class? Are classes restricted to graduate students? To majors?

3. What would be the advantages and disadvantages to going to grad school immediately after completing an undergraduate degree? The advantages and disadvantages of waiting a few years? The best use of the interim time?

4. What are the criteria and process for selecting TAs, RAs, and Fellows?

5. Will I get to develop my own topics, or will I be expected to work on a professor's ongoing research?

6. What facilities are available for graduate students? Are there any restrictions on access?

7. What is the mean time to complete (a) classwork, (b) research, (c) thesis or dissertation? (That is, what is the mean time to complete the master's or Ph.D.?) Ask about the program as a whole, but perhaps more importantly, by professor.

8. What is your attrition rate? Of those who don't finish, what are their reasons?

9. What kind of student thrives in your program?

10. How reliable is your financial support year to year? Is the first-year offer always sustained, given attainment of academic goals?

11. What are the age range, gender balance, ratio of married/single, and geographical origins of graduate students in the program?

12. Can you tell me who is launching new projects? Which professors have won awards and grants lately? (These presumably need graduate assistants.)

13. Can you tell me about your placement rates and types of jobs obtained by recent graduates? (Avoid relying on testimonials and anecdotal evidence.)

14. May I meet some currently enrolled students? (In person, or later via phone or email; be sure to ask about their research topics and be sure to take notes on specific professors mentioned.)

15. How can I be a strong candidate for a program like this?

before the visit. They had a three-hour meeting, leading to an offer from him to serve as her mentor. "I may not be able to get in," she said. "Oh, I can get you in," he said, and he certainly did. If you admire a particular professor, go meet with her.

Another way to stand out at the application phase is to submit a work sample. Some programs ask for them, but most don't. There are two rules for submitting a work sample:

1. It should be very directly related to the graduate topic.

2. It must be very, very good.

The best work sample to submit is a graded thesis, paper, or lab on the same subject you want to work on in graduate school, on which

Warning

If you choose to submit a video or film, it had better be very good right away. Any visual media should be submitted in the most universal and accessible format: standard DVD for moving pictures, prints instead of slides for photographs. (Some art and architecture programs require submission of a portfolio; read the application carefully and submit your work in the format specified.)

a professor has written, "A+. Julie, you're a genius. I never fully realized it until I read this. If you don't become a research scientist it will be a loss for all humankind." Obviously, submitting your award-winning poetry would be the kiss of death in applying to a Lit Crit program, but some academic faux pas are so subtle that an undergraduate may miss them. In general, avoid submitting any work sample without running it past a faculty adviser.

Some students take the time to further improve a class project before submitting it as part of their graduate application. Ask an adviser, "Is this paper good enough to submit as a work sample, or can you make some specific recommendations for improvement?" It's certainly within the bounds of propriety to submit published articles that relate directly to the program of interest.

Again, let quality take precedence over quantity. Admissions counselors have only so much time to devote to each application, so a smart applicant will, for instance, send in her *best* article and list the others on a bibliography. I know of one applicant for a theater MFA program who enclosed a copy of a play he had written. The head of the department picked up the play for a quick look and ended up reading it straight through in one sitting. He was so excited about this applicant that he called the candidate and basically admitted him over the phone. Now *that's* a good work sample.

In this same vein, an applicant to architectural school might submit a rendering, applicants to film school might submit a short, and so on. All students should consider submitting some sort of projects summary or research summary, such as the one described on page 61, *Sample Undergraduate Research Projects*. Note also the table topic work sample beginning on page 161.

Also, do not substitute any unusual item for something officially requested. Follow the directions. If the admissions packet calls for a 2½-inch by 2½-inch color photo, then provide one; a self-portrait in pastels would be an egregious error. Some admissions people are amused by such shenanigans, but far more are annoyed by them.

What Happens to Your Application

Online applications have vastly improved a candidate's ability to manage the application process. On most of these systems, you start by opening an account, for free. All you need is an email address. Then you have as much time as you want to draft and redraft your essays, upload information onto the forms, and peruse the workings of the site.

Once you hit "submit" however, you can't change another thing. It's game over, and the waiting begins.

Before we get to what happens on the other side of this process, let's really understand what you are supposed to be submitting, and how. First of all, whenever you are offered the option of an online process or a paper-based process, my recommendation is to opt for the online route. The whole paper vs. electronic debate is over, and electronic won. There are a few small programs still working with paper, but I predict that even they are planning to migrate to an e-system soon. I recently ran a survey of graduate programs on this issue, and *not one grad program in the country* indicated that they preferred a paper application. Not one. Some offer the option to apply either with a paper application or online, but many don't even accept paper applications anymore (although they may accept other materials submitted on paper).

Essays are submitted online either as an attachment or by filling in a window, and some programs allow either method. Forms are filled in online, from name to activities and honors and awards. Resumes and CVs and writing samples can be submitted, usually as attachments, although occasionally you have to send them in on paper because there is no established methodology to handle them electronically. Be sure to follow the instructions for each program, as there is so far no standardization of these processes.

Even letters of recommendation are, increasingly, submitted online, which has had the ironic consequence of increasing the workload for letter writers. Once upon a time faculty could just scribble "see attached letter of recommendation" on forms, and use a "To whom it may concern" salutation and Bam! a little work at the copier, an original signature on each, and the process was done. The online systems actually create more work per letter on the part of faculty, and a higher expectation of customization

The only part of the process that is so far resistant to electronic submission is transcripts. There is no national norm for transcript design, layout, or content. There is not even an agreement regarding the size or color of paper that a transcript will be printed on. So transcripts are the last paper link in this process. I am sure that American Association of Collegiate Registrars and Admissions Officers will soon resolve this issue, although students with old transcripts may have trouble for many years to come.

Online applications are a boon because they reduce snail mail, with all its famously frustrating delivery failures, and because they create online check-off systems that are much more reliable and resistant to human error. Also, online systems reduce phone calls about missing material, which was (and is) the most hated communication in any admissions office. Finally, they virtually eliminate data entry, which exponentially increases error into any system.

Warning

Just because a school says your materials are complete doesn't mean that they really are. I interviewed a student who was told by two different schools that her materials were complete, but a professor had failed to send in a letter of recommendation. In both cases she was denied admission.

Here are some things to watch out for: If you are submitting an essay by filling in a window, my advice is to draft it in another program and then copy and paste only your final draft onto the forms. Although it is unlikely that an admissions person would have the time or inclination to observe your drafts, I have discovered that in most of these programs, they easily can if they decide to do so. Think about that.

Second, some of these programs have character- or word-count features. If you write overlong, the bottom part of your essay may simply disappear. Verify that the entire essay is readable in the submission window.

Also, not all of these programs are fully compatible with even the most common word processing programs. So watch for apostrophes, quote marks, dashes, or scientific notations that become something very different when pasted into application windows. If you cannot get the appearance you want, in particular with scientific or technical materials, you may have to send it in as an attachment—or even send in a paper essay—with an explanation of the problem.

What if you want to submit writing samples or research papers or even copies of publications? This gets really sticky. If there are instructions on how to submit this material, then follow them, but often there is simply no clear way to submit extra material, requested or not. As mentioned elsewhere, your awesome work sample can be a clincher for admission, so this really matters. Paper, MS Word, or in the case of some materials, a .pdf file may be the best choice. I am a big fan of sending it in both electronic and paper formats. This increases the chances that someone will actually see this material. And if you have identified or corresponded with a particular professor, you can send her a copy as well.

Also, if you are seeking a waiver of an application fee, you will need to know how that works online, which varies from school to school, and almost always adds some layers of communication and delays in time. Some programs still require those seeking a waiver to apply on paper, some offer a code to use in place of a credit card, and so on. When in doubt, call them and ask.

Then what happens?

Once you submit your application, what happens to it? Maybe nothing at all. If your application is not complete, most programs will not distribute it to reviewers. If you are missing a letter of recommendation or a transcript, or you left a required field blank or, heaven forfend, your credit card was denied, you will fall into limbo. It is critical that you check the online check-off system to see if all your expected materials have been received and logged. Many programs will notify you via postcard or email, or both, once your file is complete.

Most organizations are still printing out everything you have submitted and creating paper applicant files, just like in the old days. Some are scanning everything you send on paper, so they have completely redundant records, an e-version and a paper version.

Reviewers can access your online submission from anywhere, but your paper submissions, if any, may be invisible to remote viewers. This is why it is a good idea to send materials to anyone you think may be serving on the admission committee, or interested in the decision whether to admit *you*.

Where the decision is made

A graduate program may expect you to meet several different sets of criteria. The regents of a major university may set general guidelines for graduate admissions. The specific graduate school—as a hypothetical example, The Graduate School of the College of Arts and Sciences—may develop another set of criteria. Finally, a department may set its own standards. When you apply, you are really applying to different constituencies, at least to the graduate school and the department. These are distinctly separate entities.

There are two models for making admissions decisions: a strong graduate school with a weak department, or a weak graduate school with a strong department. Under the weak graduate school model, the graduate school office serves more as an administrative office: processing application files, making sure everything is in order, and forwarding applicant folios to the departments. The departments are in charge; the decision is made in the departments. Harvard is a classic institution with strong departments.

Under the other model, the graduate school is strong, and may set standards that are higher than, or just different from, what some departments may want. When conflict arises, the graduate school has the final say. Duke is, more or less, an example of an institution with a strong graduate school.

In professional schools such as those for business, law, and medicine, the authority is usually held entirely by the admissions staff, which almost always includes a good percentage of faculty. Faculty, and even currently enrolled students, will rotate through admissions assignments lasting a season or two.

To further complicate the matter, most programs reserve a small percentage of their admissions for people with special circumstances, who meet some but not all of their admissions requirements.

If you are trying to imagine what's going on with your application, keep these structures in mind.

Admit dances and wait lists

When all your materials are ready, hit the submit button and mail in any paper-based materials via registered mail, return receipt requested, or by courier. This way you know for sure when those materials arrive. If it is anywhere near the deadline, even remotely near it, use an overnight courier. You should not trust any time-sensitive or vitally important documents to regular first-class mail. Most programs will send you an email or send you a postcard alerting you to missing materials, or confirming your complete application. If you do not receive such confirmation, call the program and verify whether your application is complete.

Remember, the mail room may be all the way on the other side of campus, and the on-campus mail delivery person may be a closet marijuana smoker. You need to verify with the office itself.

Be very nice to the person who answers the phone. Get to know this person, as you may be calling her again. Say, "May I have your name, please?" Write it down on your activity log for that program. While you have this person on the line, ask when you should expect to hear about the admission decision. Be prepared to be interrupted and to be put on hold for long stretches of time. (See the story on page 25 of a student who was admitted while he waited patiently on hold.) Be considerate, be compassionate, and be sure not to alienate this communications resource. Many applicants underestimate the power wielded by academic receptionists and office managers. They are usually highly intelligent individuals who could make a lot more money working somewhere else. You may never actually succeed in speaking with the department head or the admissions director, but these people do every day. They can be your allies or your enemies in the admissions process; the choice is yours. (Incidentally, in smaller programs the departmental secretary often does the initial screening of graduate applications.)

Larger programs hate it when students call repeatedly without waiting for the process to work itself out. Call only when something seems amiss. Smaller programs are generally more receptive to calls, but any time you become a pest it will sink your candidacy. Some programs with rolling admission will notify you within a few weeks. Some programs announce all admissions and rejections for the year on a single day, leaving you to bite your nails and wait along with everybody else. Most try to complete the process well before the official decision date of April 15.

Warning

Avoid sending anything gratuitous or weird. Many years ago an applicant gave a ship in a bottle to the Stanford Graduate School of Business. It was a very good ship, but it was not directly related to graduate business education. More recently a student applying to law school included with her application a six-foot-long cookie that she had baked in a pizza oven. Her note said, "Please take a break to enjoy this cookie when you review my application." Another student used his AMCAS essay to write some kind of country-and-western song about his desire to be a doctor. A law school once received an extra letter of recommendation for one applicant: a crayon drawing from the applicant's baby sister, stating "Please admit my big sister." All of these applicants were rejected.

• • •

According to the Council of Graduate Schools, no CGS-member program can make you declare your intentions before April 15. Unfortunately, more and more programs are ignoring this rule. Admissions seem to be running earlier every year, and in some cases students are receiving admissions, and pressure to decide, before the deadline to *apply* has arrived. Science and engineering tend to run early, and social science and humanities tend to run a bit later. Nevertheless, you should be prepared for a little admissions dance, and that dance has everything to do with yield and funding allocations. Yield is the percentage of candidates who are offered admission who actually accept. The ideal yield is 100 percent. Every program wants maximum yield: it's more efficient, makes the program look more exclusive, and allows for more precise planning of aid allocation. So, you may have department chairs calling you up and asking questions like this: "We're intrigued by your candidacy. If we were to offer admission to you, do you think you'll decide to attend our program?" To which you say, "I'm intrigued by your program but, of course, it would depend on the specific aid package you might offer, and the ones that I anticipate from other programs. I think you have a wonderful program, or I wouldn't have applied, but I do need to make a decision based on all the data. What aid offer did you have in mind?" And so on. (Schools try to get first-round aid offers formalized by April 1, at the latest, but some will run late.)

Get faculty counsel on how to deal with these queries. These calls are designed to identify the applicants most likely to accept if admitted. You need to be honest, but protect your options until you know what your options actually are. Again, it cannot be overstressed: *Get faculty advice on how to handle these calls.*

No news is not necessarily the worst news; it may mean that you have been "wait listed." There are at least two common kinds of wait lists. First, there is the "maybe" list that every program collects at the first sort. This maybe list turns into an informal wait list, and it can last for months, as the clearly outstanding are admitted and the clearly unprepared are rejected. This informal wait list can even go well past April 15, which is exactly why the friend I mentioned earlier got that letter on April 17 that began, "We are happy to extend an offer of admission to you for the fall incoming class. It is absolutely imperative that you respond by April 15th or your seat will be offered to another." He, obviously, was one of the "anothers." If you have confirmed that you applied properly, and you don't hear by April 15, you are in all likelihood on this type of wait list.

The other type of wait list is a formal wait list. You will receive a letter informing you that you are on the wait list—due, no doubt, to the unusually strong candidate pool this year, yada, yada, yada. These wait lists are bad, as they sometimes require you to wait around until the first week of classes to discover your status. Interestingly enough, you will probably have to provide another school with confirmation and a deposit.

If you are called up from the wait list, you face a dilemma. You have confirmed at one school, yet another is asking you to renege. *Relax.* No school wants a graduate student who is unhappy from day one. The first school also has a wait list, and they'll call someone up from it if you decide to jump. (Although they may not tell you this, and your deposit is a goner.) Your bigger problem is you have two offers, possibly from schools with very different reputations, and usually the better school is coming up with the worse aid offer. On top of that, everybody wants you to decide *right now.* You simply have to weigh your options and make your best choice. Call your adviser, talk to your peers, discuss it with representatives of both schools, and make a decision.

Be very diplomatic and professional in declining offers. You may later do a postdoc, or need a faculty job, or be on a research project involving people from the institution. Academia is a small world, with a very long memory.

If you have any reason to believe that you have been wait-listed, do something! Send another letter of recommendation, send your mid-year grades, get a professor to call and rave about your potential, get a family member to contact one of her friends at the target school. Above all, remind them of your interest in *their* program. One student I interviewed for this book was told that he was wait-listed at a top business school. They told him there was nothing he could do about it, and that he should not call, but just wait and see how the year's applicant pool shaped up. "When they said not to call, I thought that meant 'don't call more than once a week,'" he told me. He not only called fairly often to restate his interest in the program, he also drafted the following letter to update the admissions committee on his activities:

Dear Ladies and Gentlemen of the Committee:

I am writing to supplement my application to Stanford's Graduate School of Business.

Currently, I am on the waiting list for entrance for the fall incoming class. Because the scope of my consulting duties at Halperin-Smythe Associates has expanded considerably in recent months, I would like to make the admissions committee aware of some of my new responsibilities. Also, please find included four recommendations from my superiors at Halperin-Smythe.

The most important project I worked on at Halperin-Smythe was our poison-pill impact study (copy included), which shows that companies protected by shareholder rights plans (poison pills) receive significantly higher takeover premiums than unprotected companies. As a result of the study, we received an enormous amount of media exposure, including a write-up as the subject of a Heard on the Street column in *The Wall Street Journal*, a first for Halperin-Smythe Associates. Our findings have been used by companies with poison-pill recision proposals on the agendas of their annual meetings to combat these proposals and have contributed to a number of proxy victories. Our study has generated substantial interest in business and academic circles. My supervisor, Richard Vines, and I designed the study. I then performed the analysis, produced the study's tables, graphs, and conclusions, and wrote the Methodology and Example sections of the study.

This account of my activities over the past few months supplements the description, which you already have, of my duties at Halperin-Smythe (see original application). If you want further elaboration of any item, please write or call. Thank you for your interest.

Note how specific this candidate's update is. He is giving specific *new* evidence to influence the admission decision in his favor. Needless to say, his extra effort was rewarded by admission. If you are wait-listed, think of your application as suspended on evenly balanced scales, equally weighted on the "admit" and "reject" sides. Throw something, anything, onto the admit side.

● ● ●

If, after all of this, you actually do not get in, do not despair. Almost every one of the successful students I interviewed for this book had been rejected from other programs, and many had been rejected by *all* the schools they applied to in an earlier year. The first thing to do is call the admissions representative asking why you were rejected, and what you can do to correct any deficiencies in order to submit a successful application to them, or someone else, in the future. Don't be angry or upset or accusatory over the phone; say something like this: "I know you probably made the right decision, and I'm not calling at all to complain about that decision. I am just very committed to my goals, and I wonder if you would take a moment and tell me how to improve my chances in a future year, either with your school or another. Can you help me see which deficiencies I should concentrate on?" You may have to call a few times, but asking politely in this manner will almost always get a helpful response.

SO HE SAID, "NO WAY CAN YOU EARN A MASTER'S DEGREE IN ONE SEMESTER."

—WHAT TO DO IF YOU DON'T GET IN—

1. Apply to more schools.

2. Apply to more safe schools.

3. Apply earlier.

4. Get an intermediate degree.

5. Take one class at a time as a nonmatriculated student.

6. Go to summer school at one of your targeted schools.

7. Get an internship in the targeted field.

8. Get a "real job" in the targeted field.

9. Visit in person and wow them.

10. Get older and try again.

It is official NAGAP policy not to hide the decision rationale from rejected candidates, and the CGS also endorses this approach. If you have to, quote this: "When a student is denied admission, it is important that the specific reasons are stated in the student's file. A student who requests the information should also be informed of the reasons for the rejection" (*An Essential Guide to Graduate Admissions,* Council of Graduate Schools, p. 34). You do, however, need to know that sometimes the answer really is, "We had so many applicants that we are sometimes forced to accept some and reject others that are overwhelmingly similar in preparation and academic performance to date." *C'est la vie.*

If you are still committed to your educational goals, then pursue them. Perhaps you did not apply early enough or to enough schools, and simply reapplying in a timely manner to a larger number of programs will result in success. Perhaps you need to apply to a lower rung of schools. If you applied only to top schools, you may very well have passed on an opportunity to study at a perfectly good school without such competitive admissions. Taking an interim degree was the source of success for many of the students I interviewed; for example, if they wanted a Ph.D. in clinical psychology and were rejected for doctoral programs on their first round of applications, they would get a master's degree in psychology and apply again. Other students found success by taking a few additional prerequisites and related classes and concentrating on getting outstanding grades. You can sign up for classes as a nonmatriculated student at most universities, on a class-by-class basis, with instructor approval. I actually know of one Ph.D. who, by using this method, never had to take the GRE; she had taken several graduate courses—always earning an A—and just wrote a letter saying she'd like to convert to full-time attendance. It was approved.

Still other students gained workplace experience related to their future career. Workplace experience can prove especially valuable for applicants to law and medical schools. (Many applicants are drawn to these professions without a clue as to the real challenges practitioners face on a daily basis, and admissions committees are more comfortable with applicants who know what they are getting into.) One student I spoke with discovered that one of his letters of recommendation was less than laudatory; when he replaced it, he found success on his next round of applications. Finally, I spoke with a few students who thought they were considered "too young." They did nothing whatsoever to improve their preparedness for graduate studies except to live for a few more years before applying again; nevertheless, they were successful in these later applications.

I know of one student who was rejected by all the schools he applied to on his first round of applications. Then he bought this book. Using the techniques I've shared with you, he was admitted to ten out of fourteen programs and was fully funded to pursue the Ph.D. He could have given up, decided that his academic credentials were not as worthy as he thought, and become a wage slave for the rest of his life, but he did not. *He knew what he wanted and he tried again.* There are too many variables in the graduate admissions process to warrant giving up on your goals if you are not successful in your first round of applications. Try again, start earlier, and apply to more schools.

5

Getting Ready to Write

This chapter is a series of exercises designed to prepare you to write the first draft of your graduate admissions essay. Do not worry if much of the information generated by these exercises seems, at first, tangential to your educational goals or unlike what you had planned to include in your application. The goal is to build a pool of possible topics and points, most of which will not be included in your essay. You can draw both inspiration and details from this pool of data, and it will make your first draft flow more easily when you start writing.

No one student is expected to write detailed answers for every single exercise in this chapter, but you *are* expected to answer *every single question,* at least in your mind. Read and think and write as many notes as you can. You may even find yourself in the library or going through old labs and papers to find inspiration, but keep moving along so that you finish this section and go on to your first draft in a timely manner.

· · ·

One of the complaints most admissions readers make is that "so many of the essays seem almost the same." Take a moment and imagine that admissions reader sitting down with twenty or thirty or a hundred essays from applicants. Can you see her eyes beginning to glaze over after several essays that all seem vaguely similar? Can you imagine her relief when she reads a first line like this:

> I was taking out the garbage one morning on the Serengeti Plain when I realized what had been bothering me . . .

What makes you unique? Different? Unusual? I once interviewed a medical school admissions committee who let a woman into their school because she had been in a plane wreck. Is that a qualification for medical school? Perhaps not, but it is a qualification for getting noticed if you are otherwise qualified for medical school.

Sometimes the thing that makes a person really different is a personal or family matter.

> At the age of forty-eight, I left my two adult children, my husband, and the dishes in the sink, and moved into a college dorm to become a freshman. And because I was a first-generation college student, I had no one to tell me that a college dorm is not the serene, academic refuge I had always imagined!

With this opening she immediately sets apart from the bulk of applicants. Many students turn something unusual about themselves into an interesting way to launch their essays. However, note the tones of such introductions—there should be nothing frivolous about these writers. They are as serious as can be, just different. They will not seem "just the same" as all the other applicants.

Take a moment right now, pull out a fresh notebook or piece of paper, and write down the most unusual things about you as a person—not you as an applicant or you as a student, but you as a unique and unusual person. Consider your whole life, and maybe even your ancestors' lives. Remember to include personal material, even if you know you would never include it in your essay.

Some students attempting this exercise have said that there is nothing unusual about them. One even told me, "I'm as typical as they come. I'm a white girl from the 'burbs. I know about minivans, big dogs, soccer, and going to the mall." "Try really hard," I said, "It doesn't have to be something unique, just something that you've experienced or done or are that will not seem that common to the people who will read your essay." The workshop was in California. She came running up to me later: "I've got my first line! Here it is: 'When the earthquake struck, I was the only one in charge of my dorm. I got all twenty-two of my dormies out alive . . .'"

Why didn't she think of this right away? Because all of her friends had gone through the same earthquake. It wasn't even that big an earthquake. Earthquakes are common in California, but on the East Coast they're pretty exotic. What's common in your town that might be interesting somewhere else? I've read great essays that mentioned peach farming in southern Missouri, going to the rodeo in central Washington, and being meticulously honest in New York City. Try to list a few things that are unusual about you, your family, your upbringing, your travels, your college, and your part of the country. You don't have to use any of this, but wouldn't it be an interesting challenge to list out ten things right now?

•   •   •

As you begin the process of applying to graduate schools, it is a good time to remember who and what your intellectual influences have been. The next set of exercises will assist you in tracing these influences. Answer each of the following questions with at least a full sentence but less than half a page:

- What writers and which particular articles in your field of study have had the greatest influence on the development of your thought?

- Who were your favorite professors in college, and why? How has each influenced you?

- What is the best paper or exam you ever wrote in your major, and what makes it good?

- What do you consider the most important book, play, article, or film you have ever read/ seen, and how has it influenced you?

- What is the single most important concept you have learned in college?

If you can think of other educational milestones or guideposts, write about them in the same fashion—at least a sentence, but no more than half a page.

• • •

What are some of the encouraging words others have said to or about you over the years? Did a particular teacher or professor encourage you to pursue your studies, go beyond your abilities, or pursue a goal or dream? Write the *actual words* of the professor or teacher, and give the time and place you heard them. For example:

"Julie, you're good at math. Why don't you consider tutoring for the department?"
— Dr. Lee, sophomore year, in front of the math building

"Paul, you're really onto something here. Do you realize that if this works, intergalactic travel will be possible on a human time scale?!"
— Prof. Wilson, in the theoretical physics laboratory, last year

• • •

Where were you and what were you doing when you first thought of pursuing this particular direction of graduate study? One student told me that she was talking with her professor in an English class, and she suddenly realized that the whole class had become a dialogue between her and the prof. The other students were just staring at her, open-mouthed, as they scribbled furiously to get down what she was saying. In that moment, she decided to become a college professor.

I once interviewed a student who told a long story that started out like this:

There are a lot of doctors in my family, and I could never decide whether to be a doctor or go into zoology. I got this chance to be a volunteer for an ethology study in equatorial Africa, studying the behavior of a particular monkey. I spent six weeks staring up into the canopy and making marks on this waterproof clipboard with a grease pencil. Then I got a weekend pass, and went to town. I still couldn't decide—medical school, or zoology. I thought about it every day. In town I saw this sign on a concrete building, HOSPITAL. No doors, no windows, tin roof. Typical. The sun is really bright in Africa. I couldn't see inside at all. So I stuck my head in the door. My body was outside in the sunlight, and just my head was in the shadows. I wanted to see, but I didn't want to disturb anybody. There were two rows of metal cots, all empty except the last one. There were no medicines, no supplies of any kind in sight, just a nun and this boy, maybe nine or ten, it's hard to tell, and he was surrounded by his entire family, and they were just kind of moaning and rocking back and forth. That's when I decided I didn't care about monkey behavior. Right then, in that doorway, I decided to become a doctor.

What were you doing when you decided to pursue this particular area of graduate study?

• • •

Now, answer these questions to build a historical overview of the etiology of your career choice:

- How has your interest evolved, and what specific turning points can you identify?
- What work experiences have led you to believe you would like to pursue graduate education?
- What experiences as a volunteer or traveler have influenced your career direction?
- What experiences from your family life have contributed to this choice?

Throughout all this, remember that you are building a pool of information from which to draw the first draft of your essay. Can you think of any other life experiences that you might want to include? Make a few notes on them and go on to the next exercise.

• • •

Not all applicants to graduate school have a specific career direction in mind when they apply. Although it is fine to be open to different possibilities, you might think twice before pursuing two to six years of specialized education without any plan to utilize it at all. (Incidentally, do not try to become a college professor just because you are smart and cannot decide what else to do with your life.)

Your next exercise is to define your career goal, as nearly as you can. Consider why you have chosen the particular path you are now pursuing, and make a list of your real reasons for doing so. What attracts you to this career? What do you hope to gain? Write these items down the left-hand side of a piece of paper. Be honest! Remember, nobody is going to see this list but you.

• • •

When this list of your true motivations is complete, use the right-hand side of your paper to write down other ways you could achieve or obtain each item. This is a way of getting you to consider your other career options, what they are, and exactly why you reject them, and perhaps to reconsider if you reject them. For example, if your goal is to be a college professor of English, you may have written, "opportunity to work with language around articulate and talented people" on the left-hand side of your paper; on the right-hand side, you might write, "advertising agency, publishing company, magazine, newspaper, online content provider or zine" as other options that could satisfy that desire. Is your career choice really the best one for you?

• • •

Next, consider your academic background:

- How have you prepared yourself to succeed in graduate school?

- What body of relevant knowledge will you take with you?

- What study or laboratory skills have you honed to date?

- What personal attributes or physical characteristics make you particularly likely to succeed in your new career?

• • •

What is your biggest accomplishment to date? Take a little time with this one, as it may not be obvious. While you are thinking about it, make a list of "many things I am proud of."

• • •

What research have you completed to date? Make a list of major research projects and your role in them. If the research is published, look up the exact citation. If it is not published, devise a working title based on what it would have been named had you published it. This is good practice for when you start publishing articles regularly. (Be careful not to misrepresent a working title as a published work.) If you think the work is good enough to be published, get a professor to advise you, prepare it in the correct format, and submit it for publication. You have nothing to lose, and the practice will be educational.

Be ready to describe your level of participation in the research. On one project you may wish to point out that you "designed experimental methodologies, scheduled and conducted experiments, analyzed the data, and drafted preliminary conclusions." In another you may have done less, in which case you can still say that you "assisted Dr. R. Simmons on a study of possible medicinal derivatives of the venom of the southern copperhead, *Agkistrodon contortrix contortrix.*" Be ready to describe the hypothesis, methodology, and findings, or you should not be talking about the research in your essay!

It is also a good idea to spell out the ramifications of the research. Too often, students list research without indicating that they have any idea of its purpose. Link your inquiry into the light sensitivity of a certain barnacle to a possible treatment for a class of allergies and the reader will be more impressed.

Finally, list what you really learned from the research. Perhaps you gained specific knowledge of a concept, a technique, how to work with others, or even an emotion. For instance, you could have learned compassion, empathy, or even humility.

• • •

You have already noted the major writers and thinkers in your field and how they have influenced your development. Can you add any professors currently associated with your targeted school? One of the best opening lines is some version of this:

In my frequent correspondence with Drs. Wilson, Lee, and Wu, I have come to discover that your program and my academic interests perfectly align.

An administrator once advised me that the best opening line of all time is this: "My uncle, for whom your library is named . . ." Now, *that's* an opening line!

The following excerpt is from a successful application for a scholarship offered by the Urban Land Institute (ULI). The gentleman named was, at the time, on the ULI board of directors:

> I had the good fortune to hear Jon Q. Reynolds speak in a lecture this semester. At the end of his presentation, a student asked, "Do you see land development as a right or as a privilege?" Mr. Reynolds replied that it is a responsibility. I share this opinion; because of the longevity of land use and development decisions, they must be undertaken with a sense of responsibility to the public and to the future as well as to the investor. These decisions also . . .

An important note about this type of citation: You must be totally sincere or the reader can smell it. If you cannot be honest in your use of another's name, then do not mention it at all. Avoid featuring the most reviled professor in the program or the great leader who left last year; you need to know politics as well as names.

Of course, you will want to mention your major advisers to date, as well. It is standard academic protocol at the graduate level to do so, so show a little savvy and name your key undergraduate advisers. In graduate school, you are never a lone wolf; you are part of an academic department or a laboratory, and you operate under the supervision of an adviser or chief. Furthermore, you usually give her full title in any formal communiqué, including any honorary appointments. For example, you don't work for the Thin Film Laboratory, you work for the Thin Film Laboratory *under the guidance of Dr. Diana Centornella, Laboratory Chief and the Harlan J. Dansworth Materials Science Scholar.*

Another type of "name dropping" involves minority-related organizations. If you are a member of a minority group and you want to mention it in your essay, you need not say anything outright. Somewhere in your essay you can mention your participation in the African American Student Conference or your membership in the Asian Political Caucus. Such affiliation does not explicitly state that you are a member of said minority, but in the unofficial admissions code it amounts to the same thing. (If you are Caucasian and you have the desire to go out and raise funds for The College Fund just so you can mention it in your essay, then go for it; raise at least a thousand dollars, maybe ten thousand.)

Names of major thinkers and theorists are a powerful addition to any essay. In many of the essay samples in this book you will see frequent citations of those writers and thinkers who have most influenced the student.

Make a list of names you might want to work into your essay, but do not make any firm plans yet as to who you want to include. Your list may include the following:

- Influential undergraduate professors

- Specific professors at the targeted institution who interest you

- Major writers and thinkers in the field who have influenced you

- Professors with whom you have visited or corresponded or spoken

- Any other people you may have in common with the targeted institution

—STATEMENT OF PURPOSE PREWRITING EXERCISE—

Build a table of undergraduate research projects

Suggestions:

- List projects in order of interest to your targeted reader.

- Use working titles to describe your research projects.

- Name your professor/adviser/supervisor.

EXAMPLE

Sample Undergraduate Research Projects

- Designed original research into the ultrafiltration of proteins, including developing a theoretical model for design, design and actual prototyping of cross-flow ultrafiltration unit, and experimentation to determine optimal settings for maximal permeate flux. A Biochemical Engineering Laboratory senior project under the direction of Prof. L. Hintzer.

- Designed a stream remediation project involving liquid-liquid extraction to remove *m*-zylene from contaminated water; also used EPA QUAL2E to model the effects of DO, BOD, and Nitrogen cycle, under the guidance of Prof. L. Hintzer.

- Conducted research into mathematical models of potential use for codifying chaotic systems such as watersheds, an independent study under NSF grant supervised by Prof. P. Cenczynksy. Abstract and draft findings available at http://www.HarveyMudd.edu/~czynsky/models2.html.

- Designed and conducted original research into quantitative and qualitative properties of a meteorite sample using atomic absorption spectrophotometry, emission spectrophotometry, induction coupled plasma, and laser spectrophotometry under the direction of Prof. R. Hull-Wallace. Results presented at the Argonne National Laboratory during annual meeting of the International Association of Amateur Astronomers.

This is not just for science students! Here's a liberal arts example:

- Designed and conducted an in-depth analysis of the use of lightness and darkness to convey moral authority in the Elizabethan poetry of Hallbeck, Smythe, and Colbin, resulting in a 28-page paper presented in summary to the Anderson College English Department Colloquium.

• • •

Can you describe an experience that demonstrates remarkable drive or perseverance? Are you involved in sports? What do you do with your leisure time? Do you have any hobbies or pastimes to soften the stress of graduate study? What can you tell someone that would lead them to believe they'd enjoy your company?

• • •

Students routinely "hide" information that members of the admissions committee would certainly consider pertinent. This is almost always a misguided approach. For example, one applicant to law school developed an undistinguished essay that failed to mention the fact that her father was a superior court judge. Her counselors told her to rewrite the essay and include her father. She crafted an incredibly powerful new essay centering on how her father used to drive her to tears in dinner-table debates, and how she grew to challenge her father and win, using his own rules of logic and argument. She wrote, "I feel as though I have ten years of litigation experience already." This new essay won her admission to all the top law schools.

Do not leave out the obvious. One of the authors of your recommendation letters may mention it anyway. Make a list of all those things you hope the admissions committee doesn't find out about you.

• • •

What do you know about the city, geographic region, or state where you will be applying? Have you ever visited? Did you like it? Is the weather there like the weather where you have lived in the past? Do you have close friends or relatives living near there now? Did your family live there in prior generations? How can you establish any kind of geographical connection with the location of the graduate schools you have targeted? Write down your responses to these questions.

• • •

Finally, consider the future as well as the past. Consider your immediate future; that is, the time between when you apply and when graduate classes start:

- What classes are you going to take between now and your arrival at your targeted graduate school? What laboratory or research skills will you learn?

- What research projects will you complete between now and when you begin graduate school? Will you complete a thesis or capstone project?

- Will you present your findings at any type of conference or meeting?

- Will you be going to summer school before graduate school starts? What classes might you take?

- If you are working, what will you try to get accomplished before you depart for graduate school?

Students often fail to communicate important parts of their preparation that fall between application and matriculation at a graduate program. Be sure to cover this.

Also, consider your long-term future:

- What are your specific post-graduate career plans?

- How will this graduate education facilitate those plans?

- What is your five-year goal? Your ten-year goal?

- Will you be pursuing additional education or professional training beyond the program you are applying to now?

Envision as specific a future as you can, then write a few lines about where you see yourself going. If you cannot do this exercise comfortably, there's no need to force it. Many, many top students cannot see a specific career future for themselves.

•   •   •

As you have probably guessed by now, the miscellaneous notes you have been collecting throughout this chapter are, in fact, the basis for your essay. You may have painlessly drafted most of your essay without realizing it, and need only to string your notes together, or you may choose one single note and build your entire essay around it. Or, in a few rare cases, you may end up throwing all of these items away and writing something entirely new. In any case, if you have been thinking as you read this chapter, the self-assessment process *has* prepared you to write the first draft of your essay.

Warning

Again, the prewriting exercises in this chapter are designed to generate lists and a collection of rough draft paragraphs. This is not an invitation to include any of this material in your application essay without intelligent reflection. In the course of interviewing an applicant to top business programs, I discovered he was a belly dancer. In fact, he let me know, he was an *instructor* of belly dancing. I told him to be sure not to mention this in his essay. Another student confided to me that she was an exotic dancer and had paid her way through college with this unusual occupation. I advised her that this was a classic example of something a candidate should *not* share with top law schools. There's more on this in chapter 7, "Subsequent Drafts: From the Page into the Reader's Brain."

Your First Draft:
From Your Heart onto the Page

The topics for graduate admissions essays are usually specified by the school to which you are applying. The wording may vary, but the topic is usually some version of "Where are you coming from? Why are you coming here? Where are you going after this?"

Although most schools ask essentially the same questions, they each ask them in a slightly different way. Because of this, plan to write the essay for your first-choice school first, then modify it as needed for your other targeted schools. As a general rule, do not mail in your first-choice school's application until you have finished three complete applications. Some of the ideas you use in other essays can help you fine-tune the application to your first-choice school.

The first thing to do is **RTGDQ**. One of my teachers in high school had a big rubber stamp, "RTGDQ," which he claimed stood for "**R**ead **T**he **G**osh **D**arn **Q**uestion." No matter how eloquent your exam answer was, if you failed to address the question directly, you could expect the dreaded **RTGDQ** to appear in your blue book. So open the application or catalog to the exact wording of the essay question, and **RTGDQ**. Then answer it. Truthfully.

Your first draft should be totally, brutally honest. Do not try to second-guess your reader at all. Every sentence should come straight from your heart. Write like you talk, using straightforward language. Tape record your first draft, or pretend you are writing a letter to a friend, if it will help you simplify your language. Keep the emphasis on content, not style; avoid pseudo-academese; and don't think too much.

Write when you write, edit when you edit. In this chapter you will write, and in the next chapter you will edit. Do not let anybody tell you what to write, and do not let anybody see your first draft;

read the next chapter and complete a second draft before you show your work to anyone. The first rule of brainstorming is to fill the blackboard with ideas before evaluating any of them; as you draft your essay, do not critique it. Just keep writing and moving forward.

•   •   •

As general rules of style, avoid footnotes and minimize narrative exposition. Narrative exposition is that style of writing you learned in high school: "Should the student feel compelled to build labyrinthine semantic structures, and thereby disguise the relationship between modalities of meaning and the true self . . ."

Be confident in your writing. Assume that you will be admitted.

•   •   •

An interesting first line or paragraph is a gift to your reader. If you are applying to a highly competitive preprofessional program, you will want to pay particular attention to your opening line or paragraph. You have already seen some interesting opening paragraphs in the last chapter. If you are an unusual candidate, or anyone who has had an unusual experience, launching your essay on that note can be a good idea.

One candidate told me her goal was to tell who she was in one sentence. She wrote, "I am the sixth of seven children from a large blue-collar Irish-Catholic family in the Midwest." Another candidate wrote, "As a member of the Pokagon Band of Potawatomi Indians, the seven grandmother teachings play a large role in my life. Honesty, bravery, love, truth, humility, respect, and wisdom take on a new meaning in my everyday life. The most important lesson that I have learned is to strive each day to gain wisdom." This is certainly an arresting opening line:

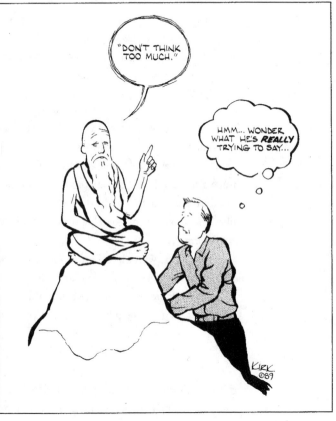

> If this information were to fall into the wrong hands, my father could go to jail. If you cannot honor my need for confidentiality, please do not read further.

Can you imagine coming onto that line while sifting through a stack of barely differentiable applications?

One of the best types of opening paragraph relates an epiphany. This can be the moment you decided to pursue your current goals or the moment you discovered just what might be entailed to pursue those goals. Look again at the "zoology or medicine" story on page 57. It's a classic epiphany tale. Here are two more epiphany openings:

> I made an "A" in labor relations, but I learned more about labor-management issues in one summer working on a union construction crew than I learned in the class . . .

———————

> When the old man urinated on my leg, it ran down my pants and into my shoe. I could not let go of him, as I was holding him up, trying to move him from a wheelchair onto the bed. That's when I first realized that medicine was not going to be just starched white lab coats and golf at four. I looked again at medicine, the actual practice of medicine on real people, and saw that it often involved messy fluids, imprecision, and an element of surprise . . .

Don't be afraid to use vivid detail to make points. Most AMCAS essays start out with some version of "I always wanted to be a doctor because I like science and I want to help people." If you are a medical college admissions reader, you come to hate this sentence. It is unbelievably common, in one version or another. Also, since the student has not *always* existed, he can't *always* have wanted to be a doctor, so he's proposed an ontological impossibility right in the opening phrase. Just for the record, the candidate in the last example above goes on to convey exactly that—that he likes science and wants to help people—but he conveys this message through a series of vignettes employing vivid detail.

Avoid using words like these in your essay: *meaningful, challenging, beautiful, wonderful, invaluable, rewarding.* Say what you mean; either describe the event in question, or report your emotions and thoughts in more basic detail. Replace these vague words with a personal statement, something from your own unique point of view. If you have difficulty with this, start sentences with: "I" "I felt . . ." "I realized . . ." "I saw that . . ."

• • •

Some candidates take a bold position in their first few lines, implicitly promising their readers that there will be more to follow. Here are two examples:

> "Why in the world do you want to go to law school? Heaven knows we don't need any more lawyers." Having worked for the large, prestigious law firm of Bells & Motley since mid-July, it continues to surprise me how frequently I have been asked that particular question.

———————

> Learning outside in a 9,000-acre forest was more engaging and exciting than sitting in a lab waiting for some bacteria to grow.

You do not need a fancy opening, but if one comes naturally to you, use it. Do not spend all day writing first lines; keep moving along. If composing a first line is a problem, just skip it for now. You can come back to it later.

*   *   *

As your essay progresses, be sure to **RTGDQ** over and over again, and address the questions as asked, in the order asked. Be specific and provide details, details, details. You will discover that this approach to writing favors qualitative analysis over quantitative listings. In other words, it is far better to give a rich description of one incident than to cram your essay full of activities and accomplishments without any hint of what you learned from them and what emotions they evoked in you during the process.

Do not be overly redundant with other parts of your application. For example, your complete work history may be listed somewhere else on the application, so mention a particular job, a particular accomplishment, or a particular supervisor only to give a new perspective or to let the committee know what one of these has meant to you personally. However, you should refer the reader to other parts of your application when they are important. Hint that there is far more to you than you have room to discuss in this short essay. Tie your essay to the rest of your application with notes like these: "See letter of recommendation," "See résumé," "See bibliography for additional articles," "See awards." You will notice this technique in many of the essays selected for this book.

*   *   *

Demonstrate that you have read the catalog carefully, researched the program, and considered your reasons for applying to this particular school. Find a common thread, a point at which your philosophy and theirs meet in happy confluence, as in these examples:

> I was especially impressed by Dean Jaedicke's statement in your brochure that the school "strives to imbue students with a sense of 'incompleteness.'" At Reed we called it "learning how to learn," and finding out how much I don't know was the most valuable lesson I left Reed with.

> I want to enroll in the program at [major university] because of its excellent reputation in real estate and urban land economics; I have not found such strength at other M.B.A. programs. I am also familiar with the admirable work of the Center for Real Estate and Urban Economics, and I particularly look forward to working with Professors Edelstein, Rosen, and Wallace.

> The Government and Foreign Affairs graduate program at Virginia is attractive to me because of the faculty members' areas of specialization and my corresponding academic and research interests. I am particularly excited about the prospect of working with Profs. Ceaser, Milkis, and Sabato. Dr. Ceaser's *Liberal Democracy and Political Science* and *Reconstructing America* have

had an impact on my view of political science as a field. Specifically, I am intrigued with his view that political science should be a defender of liberal democracy and the implications of this. These books are also engaging because Ceaser uses the field of political theory to complement the field of American government, which I would eventually like to do. I am also interested in Dr. Milkis's use of historical examples to show that executive power has weakened the party system in his book, *The President and the Parties.* Finally, I became familiar with Dr. Sabato's work as an undergraduate and would enjoy the opportunity to study the media and elections under him.

I like reductionism: (1) it is efficient, (2) it shows clarity of thought, (3) it is accessible to the reader, and (4) it makes for an easy transition from notes to paragraphs. The previous sentence is an example of reductionism, as is the following paragraph:

> I of course know of the reputation of Tufts, which led me to investigate the school. The primary factors drawing me to apply are: (1) opportunity for clinical contact from the very first year, (2) opportunity for small group learning, (3) the "selectives" (pre-electives, as I understand them) available to first- and second-year students, (4) possibility of taking M.P.H.-related electives or joining the M.D./M.P.H. program, (5) opportunity for overseas assignment from the International Affairs Office.

A whole essay full of such paragraphs would feel disjointed and be tiring to read, so use this technique sparingly.

• • •

After you have addressed the specific questions asked by the admissions committee, you are free to weave in any specific additional points you may wish to impart. Check over all of your notes from the last chapter. Once you have given them what *they* want, you can give them what *you* want. Think of this as phase two of your first draft.

Whether they ask you to or not, substantiating your dedication to your career goal often makes for a strong essay. Saying you have "always wanted to be a _____" is not as convincing as reporting specific actions that demonstrate the truth of that statement. Similarly, it is a good idea to demonstrate that you understand the real challenges and drawbacks to both the course of study and the eventual career you have chosen. Admissions committees are reluctant to admit candidates to rigorous programs leading to demanding careers if the applicant seems not to have a clear idea of what lies ahead. Dropout, burnout, chronic fatigue, divorce, alcoholism, drug abuse, and suicide plague certain professions in staggering proportions, and these problems are exacerbated when people join these professions for the wrong reasons. If you have a real understanding of what your life will be like (1) as a graduate student, (2) as a trainee in this new profession, and (3) as a skilled practitioner, then convey this to the admissions committee.

• • •

Some of the most thoughtful admissions readers told me that they like to learn something while reading applicants' essays. If you know a tremendous amount about something, whether it is a molecule or a minstrel singer, you might want to let the reader in on what's interesting about that topic. Don't make self-important and grandiose statements about the nature of chemistry, or folklore—instead, give the kinds of specifics that can only come from in-depth knowledge of a particular topic—ideally, one closely related to the professor's own area of specialization.

• • •

Although many essay questions do not require you to delineate your future career plans, a student with logical, clearly defined career plans often comes across as mature and directed. Your image of your future career goals and anticipated contributions to your field and to society in general may be of interest to admissions readers, especially when you seem to have a mission. Think of this as the "purpose" part of a "statement of purpose."

If you intend to use skills or talents in unusual combinations, be sure to let your reader know. For example, an applicant to medical school made no secret of his real ambition: to combine his knowledge of physics and electrical engineering with an education in medicine so that he could design a new generation of medical technology.

If you cannot imagine what kind of attorney or physician or educator you will eventually become, do not fake it. Your uncertainty will show through in your language or, even worse, your ignorance of realistic career options in your chosen field may offend an admissions reader. If you have a well-thought-out mission in life and in your career, state it; if you do not, you need not mention it at all.

• • •

Occasionally students will decide not to respond to the essay questions exactly as they are asked. If you deviate from the requested format, address the issue and let the admissions reader know your rationale for doing so:

> Please note that I have combined questions A and B into a single essay, rather than submitting a separate autobiography. I have chosen to focus in detail on my particular experiences during the past two years in Africa —what I learned from them, how they affected me, and why these experiences have led me to pursue an M.B.A. I believe such a detailed description will give you a better picture of who I am than could a general autobiographical essay of the same length.

• • •

A difficult essay technique, which is definitely not recommended for everybody, is to build your essay around a theme. All essays have topics, but few have themes. A topic is *what* you are going

—HOW TO SHAVE A YEAR OFF A PH.D.—

1.   Follow your Program of Study. Your Program of Study is the sequence of classes, milestones, and events that leads to completion. You create your Program of Study with your advisor. In graduate school, the milestones and events are more important than the classes. For example, if you miss a deadline to file a form, it can cost you a whole year. Update your Program of Study often, and post it over your desk. Look at it every day.

2.   Come in the door with at least a vague dissertation idea, *but do not rigidly hang on to it.* Grad school is a transformative process, so your initial idea is a jump start, not a printed road map. Write all your papers for every class, as many as you can, on some aspect related to your dissertation interest.

3.   Choose a mentor with a high completion rate. This is a professional relationship. It is irrelevant whether you are "buddies" with this person. Ask your mentor to suggest other people to serve on your committee. Start shopping, casually, for committee members right from the first day of grad school. Watch out for young professors out to make a name for themselves; they can be hardasses. Watch out for old profs that might not survive your dissertation. Keep an eye out for your external reviewer; they are hard to find and hard to recruit, and be sure to check to see whether they dislike your mentor, school, topic, methodology, epistemology, or politics. In fact, check all members of your committee for reservations like this.

4.   Think up a very narrow question that has an experimental answer. Very narrow. Definitive answer. Most research has these three components: population, problem, theory (or topic, problem, theory). Remember, a dissertation is a training process. This is not the most important work you will ever do. In fact, it should be some of the least important work you will ever do. What's better: A perfect dissertation or a done dissertation? (Duh.)

5.   Write a paper that is a dry run of your dissertation idea in the first two years. Ask a professor for (a) permission to do this, and (b) feedback on your idea, research question, methodology, etc.

6. Students who finish theses have higher completion rates for completing dissertations. If your program offers a thesis as a master's option, take it. It may slow you down a bit at the time, but when you get to the dissertation you'll go faster.

7. Do your own research before you get to the proposal stage. This sounds obvious, but a lot of students don't do this. They work on other people's projects, and don't get their feet wet as the director of a project.

8. Go through the IRB (Institutional Review Board for the Protection of Human Subjects) process before you get to your dissertation project. Same reasons. IRB is like learning a new language, and you want to get through unscathed and with minimum delays. (A smart student *expects* IRB delays, by the way.)

9. Take an independent study and use it to do the entire literature review for your proposal *before* you submit your proposal. (Some proposals require lit review and methodology chapters anyway, but you'll have the whole lit review done rather than a prelim version.) You'll probably have to rewrite your proposal (this is normal), but if you're smart you'll be able to salvage almost all of your lit review even if you have to refine your question or methods.

10. Write your proposal before you take your comps. Most places you cannot submit the proposal before passing comps, but this allows you to drop the proposal the day you receive notice of passing comprehensive exams. This, alone, saves as much as six months.

11. Stay on campus! If you stay on campus through your research and writing stages, you have a much higher chance of finishing in a timely manner, and you'll have access to your committee, campus resources, etc. It may be tempting to go get "a real job" and do your dissertation while you work, but there's a much higher risk factor against completing.

12. Keep your eyes on the prize! Have a life plan that requires the Ph.D. to be behind you. If you lust for that future, you will finish the Ph.D. If grad school is more attractive to you than that vision, or if you don't have that vision, you're at great risk of not finishing.

These tips could shave a year, or more, off your process.

to write. The topic of your essay is you: your intellectual preparation, your future goals, your rationale for picking a particular program. A theme is *why* you are going to write, the message or concept or point that strings all your paragraphs together into a comprehensive whole. Themes can include: the high cost of medical services in a modern technological world, white-collar crime, the role of the teacher, how dance and physics are one discipline, and so on. In chapter 8, essays 15 and 22 deal with the theme of overcoming adversity as a means of strengthing character and motivation. Essay 34 develops the opposite theme, that *not* having to overcome adversity can also be an advantage. Essay 18 has an obvious theme—"Why I want to be a lawyer"—but it is carried out with great cleverness and humor. If this approach makes sense to you, you may wish to try it. However, some people have taken good, clean presentations and ruined them by trying to be more clever than their writing skills allowed.

· · ·

If you have faced a particular challenge in the course of your life or your education, it may be to your benefit to let the admissions committee know about it. A few years ago at the University of California, Berkeley, a student fell asleep during a preprofessional advising meeting. Her adviser, who had met with her before, was quite perturbed. After the group was dismissed, he woke her up and demanded to know why she had even bothered to come to the meeting. She apologized, explaining that she had worked all night.

"Do you work all night very often?" he asked. She told him that she did, eight to ten hours per night, five to six nights a week.

"Why?" he asked, now concerned for her health.

It turned out her father had died, her mother was an invalid, there wasn't any insurance, she was already a senior, and she decided to just tough it out and work to support herself and her mother.

"Why isn't any of this in your personal statement?" he asked.

"Well," she replied, "I didn't think they were really interested in the personal affairs of my life."

"Well, they are," he told her. "By the way, what kind of work do you do?"

"Oh," she said, "I'm a private detective."

Hmm. I wonder if a law school would be interested in that. . . .

Here is how one student introduces very important personal information at the end of his application for dental school:

On the personal side, I have been living on my own since I was thirteen, when my father sent me to England to boarding school to avoid the war in Iraq. I did not see my family again for four years. I made my own decisions, including relocating to the United States to pursue the superior science education available here. I believe this early independence has given me a strong sense of purpose, especially for someone my age. This experience has instilled in me a confidence in my own abilities, a deep appreciation for others, and natural and sincere ability to empathize with them. I believe these qualities to be crucial for the successful practice of dentistry.

· · ·

If you have grades or test scores that do not represent your true potential, you can explain them in your essay. As a general rule, it is better to keep your main statement of purpose as positive as possible. Do not make long, involved excuses; keep it simple and devoid of drama; no whining and no feeling sorry for yourself. Also, sometimes it is helpful to compute your GPA according to a more beneficial formula. Your problem must meet these criteria:

- It has to be in the past.

- It has to be resolved.

- It has to be sympathetic.

- It should be unlikely to recur in graduate school.

First of all, you need to get your transcripts and analyze your grades in the following categories: overall, in your major, in math and science, in math, in science, excepting English and comp, year by year, semester by semester, over the last four semesters, not counting your freshman year, since you declared your current major, in classes that meet after noon, and so on, ad infinitum. Then, look for patterns. The best pattern of all is for your grades to go up each year. Then you can say, "My grades have gone up every year. I feel as though I have not yet hit my stride as a scholar." Identify your worst semester and your worst grade, and ask yourself what was going on in that class or semester. Is this a problem you have permanently resolved? Can you assure the admissions reader that this was an anomalous problem?

Copyright 1991 John Grimes. Used with permission.

One student I interviewed came from an ethnic background that did not allow one to defy one's father. He was the first in his family to go to college, and his father didn't really understand how college worked. The family owned a restaurant, though, and his father certainly understood how restaurants worked: When the help no-shows, you call your son. So his father kept calling him in to work when he had finals, when he had papers due, and so on. To solve this problem, the son transferred to a university at the far end of the state. His grades went up and stayed up. His problem was in the past, it was resolved, and, as long as he applied to graduate schools far from this restaurant, it was not likely to recur.

Another young woman told me she had to work full time when in college. "Gosh," I said, "that must have impacted your ability to study."

"Oh, yes," she said, "I hardly had time to study at all."

"Why did you have to work so much?" I asked.

Warning

Keep all excuses and explanations such as those mentioned in this section to the absolute minimum—a sentence if possible, a paragraph at most. Do not make long, involved excuses; keep it simple and devoid of drama; again, *no whining and no feeling sorry for yourself.* Also, sometimes it is helpful to compute your GPA according to more favorable formulae, as in some of the examples on this page and the next.

"I like to buy a lot of clothes, and I ran my credit cards up. I didn't have any choice!" she cried.

I think you get it: This problem is not resolved, not sympathetic, and likely to recur.

Be careful of shining a light on a small problem and making it look like a big one. Students are always asking me something like this: "I made a C on organic chem. Then I retook it and made a B. Should I talk about that?" These are very common grade patterns, and unless something awful happened to you the first time you took the course, you're probably better off not to address the issue at all.

By the way, if your grades are more than ten years old, most admissions readers won't give them much weight, whether they were outstanding or abysmal. It's a good idea to get a few recent grades before applying to graduate school, so you can say, "My recent GPA is 4.0, including both graduate and undergraduate classes I've been taking in geography. As a mature adult, I'm looking forward to returning to school and focusing on my studies in a way I did not the first time around."

Here's how some other students have addressed problems with their backgrounds:

I withdrew from three classes in the fall of my junior year due to the death of my mother.

———

I went to a very strict military boarding school when I was in high school, and when I came to college I am afraid I let the freedom erode my first year's studies. Please note that my GPA for the last two-and-a-half years is 3.25, 3.68 in my major. I feel that my test scores and my GPA in the last two-and-a-half years are indicative of the performance you can expect of me.

———

Finally, I would like to address the issue of my academic career. As you have my transcripts, you can clearly see that I was not especially serious in my first few years as an undergraduate, and you can also see that I have improved dramatically. I have a 3.9 GPA in graduate school, and I expect to continue to do as well in the doctoral program.

———

I am writing to request that you disregard the first GRE score on my records instead of averaging it in with my second score. On my way to take the first test I was involved in a major accident (see attached police report) and I was very emotionally agitated during the test. I realize now that I should have just skipped the test, but I was in a state of shock from the accident and was not thinking clearly. As you can see, there is a big difference between the two scores. Thank you for your consideration.

———

My father experienced some unexpected business reversals in the spring of my freshman year, and I took a full-time job in order to complete the academic term. By the spring of my sophomore year, I qualified for financial aid, and was able to drop down to a part-time job. If you do not count the year when I was working full time and going to school full time, my GPA would be 3.35 overall and 3.53 in my major.

———

Though my undergraduate grades are less than average for graduate school applicants, I feel that the graduate climate is better suited to my type of academic personality. I have never been a good test taker in engineering courses, and exams always lower my grades for a course. However, my lab marks and other scores are always well above average, and I particularly excel at unconstrained projects, both within courses and in independent research.

———

Although I have always been a premed student, I would like to point out that I did not follow that premed strategy of taking only "safe" classes I knew I could make an A in. I took an overload for three out of eight semesters, mostly so I could take classes like "History of the U.S. before 1865," "Greco-Roman Religion," "Native American Cultures," "Classical Greek Philosophy," and two years of Latin. My GPA in all math and science classes is 3.78, and I think that is representative of my ability to complete the medical school curriculum.

———

To make sense of my transcripts you will need to know that I changed my major four times before I finished my sophomore year, which is also why I extended my undergraduate career to a fifth year. I always made straight A's in math and science, but I just didn't connect that to engineering until . . .

Again, be careful not to lose more than you gain by bringing up negatives, especially if your rationale is not as compelling as those presented here. Unless you have a really good reason for mentioned weak grades or irregularities in your background, do not mention them at all.

Although you should never be slave to a formula, you can draw from a set of key ingredients that many successful essays share. They have great opening lines or paragraphs. They convey at least a glimpse of the applicant's personality, substantiate specific academic preparation and knowledge of subject matter, and demonstrate an understanding of the challenges as well as the rewards of a chosen career. They often give a sense of the candidate's maturity, compassion, stamina, teamwork skills, leadership potential, and general likability, usually *without addressing these issues directly.* They name specific professors at the targeted program with whom the candidate is interested in working, and specific directions they expect to take with their studies. Then they go on to show how the applicant plans to use the graduate education in her planned career, and establish that the student has an understanding of her place in the "big picture."

The essay is an opportunity to tie all the disparate pieces of your application together into a comprehensive, coherent whole. Some admissions directors have told me that they are not always looking for new information in the essay; rather, they are interested in having the essay "make sense" of the rest of the application.

It is often better to describe one or two events in detail than to reproduce your entire resume in your essay.

Remember, there is no one right way to craft these essays. Students continually devise new ways to wow and amaze admissions counselors. Some of the most interesting essays will not follow the above formula or any other. However, the best essays will have one thing in common: They will be honest and forthcoming.

In your first draft, answer each question with complete and total sincerity. There is something about the reverberating ring of truth that cannot be faked and never seems overwrought. You will worry about the wisdom of your responses in the next chapter. For now, **RTGDQ**, let your heart do the talking, and just write down what it says.

Here are some random sample paragraphs to get your juices flowing:

I know now that I want to be a big-city, big-time, international lawyer. This is my goal, and I am not embarrassed by it. Washington is an amazing place to live, and the developing international environment is to me the most dynamic game in town.I love long hours and high stress. Give me an impossible job, a laptop, two Advil and a soft drink, and I am where I do my best work. This is who I am.

———

From the aforementioned programs, I have gained experience with such biological techniques as electrophoresis, Southern blots, transformations, recombinant DNA techniques, PCR, chromatography, and sequence analysis.

———

A machine gun to my father's head very quickly shattered the crystal bubble of complacency in which I lived. A dusty road stop in Honduras, a Volvo station wagon sitting idly on sun-roasted gravel, and a perspiring family witnessing a silhouetted gun muzzle protruding through the driver's window; these are images which rocked my stable world. Yet, these images also provide me with an unshakable concern for international affairs.

———

Grasping Jeff's wrist, I could see his anguished gaze. His feet dangled from a 200-foot French citadel wall. If my grip failed, he would plunge into the evaporated remains of a rocky moat.

There was no singular way I could pull Jeff from the edge. Just as my strength was fading, the third member of our trio, Kevin, grabbed my other arm and dug in his heels. The three of us managed to retrieve Jeff from the moss-covered ledge. The importance of this life experience was that individually each of us would have failed to pull Jeff from the edge. However, working together we were able to help Jeff help himself, and we achieved our group goal.

————

The historical periods in which I am considering working are from ca. 1160–1400 (emphasizing Machaut), ca. 1575–1650 (concentrating on the Florentine Camerata), and the 19th and 20th centuries (especially Schumann, Berlioz, Berg, Varèse, Bartók, Messiaen, and Birtwistle). Within these periods I am particularly interested in studying program music, opera, and sacred music—all genres with extramusical meaning. While the range of my interests is currently rather broad, I expect it to narrow with further study.

————

"In my class, ladies and gentlemen," she announced, eyes narrowing, "you will learn to think critically. You do not need to take this class. Right down the hall is another section, which is much easier. I will pause for you to make a decision." This was Ms. Mary Fulweiler's signature introduction to American history. Ms. Fulweiler was a high-school teacher who looked disturbingly like the subject she taught: old and hard. She wore a George Washington-style hairdo, and she wielded a merciless red pen to slash through weekly three- to five-page papers. My first one was returned to me wrapped in a web of red arrows and circles and question marks. She gave me a C+. I had never received a C+ in my life. "You don't even define any of the questions your paper raises," she wrote on the bottom of the title page. "You must learn to think and write critically." A C+. The hair on the back of my eleventh-grade neck bristled. This critical thinking business was the first real academic challenge that I would have to work to meet.

I learned that questions, not answers, burn at the core of the critical thinker. "Any textbook can list who, what, where, and when," Ms. Fulweiler criticized. "Ask yourself the questions that cannot be answered on a multiple-choice test." I can trace the questions I'm currently asking back to Ms. Fulweiler's challenge.

————

Finally, you should know that my uncle lives within a short bicycle ride from campus, and I have arranged to live rent-free for the first year of my graduate education. I grew up spending summers in Ithaca and already know every inch of town and campus.

————

I have a rather unusual connection to your school: I am named after it.

————

I finally got hands-on experience in biochemical engineering research when I was selected as a sophomore to serve as a laboratory assistant to Prof. Douglas C. Cameron. I found actual research to be different from my prior education. I had expected neat experiments with instant results, almost like a 50-minute television program with all the problems solved until next week. Instead, it took a great deal of time to do one experiment, often with an unsatisfactory result in the end. There were many false starts, many failures, wrong hypotheses, and some very long hours as experiments took an unforeseen turn. There is no greater satisfaction, however, than completing an experiment with good results. It is better than the feeling when you get the highest score on an exam.

Dr. Cameron is very demanding, an absolute zealot for precision in methodology and data capture. I am very proud to say that he has retained me each year, and this year named me as his laboratory manager. I am the first undergraduate in the history of the department to be so named. (See letter of recommendation.)

———

You should note that between now and my arrival at graduate school I will complete courses in statistics and research methodologies, and conduct an independent research project culminating in a capstone paper. My topic proposal is currently under faculty review, but I've been told it will be accepted as submitted. My intent is to investigate . . .

———

For these reasons, I particularly look forward to the opportunity to study with Profs. Ronald Walters and JoAnne Brown for their work in 20th-century topics of political and popular cultural history, respectively, and with Prof. Toby Ditz, who discussed with me her work in women's and family history and cultural history.

———

It is my goal to become the superintendent of education for the state of California, or to become an educational theorist with similar potential to impact the lives of our future citizens.

———

Seven years old, needle in shaky hand, sweat dripping down my forehead, I stood in front of a gaping tear on the chest of a two-thousand-pound animal. One of our horses had been chased through a fence by wild dogs and had ripped most of the skin off of its chest. My father was away on business and money was too tight for a vet. I had to decide whether to try and suture up this beast with a small sewing kit meant to replace buttons on my Sunday shirt—or to pull out my pistol and use the 45-cent solution. After 37 stitches and a lot of adrenalin, I knew what my new life goal was

Subsequent Drafts:
From the Page into the Reader's Brain

In creating the first draft of your essay, the emphasis of the writing was all on you. This was to ensure the authenticity of your work—that it originate in you. Now it is time to introduce some admissions readers and hear what they have to say. The following points are all culled from interviews with admissions readers at the top programs in the nation. You should pay close attention to these comments, but never forget that *every admissions reader is different.*

The Essay Hall of Shame

- "Errors and sloppiness, misspellings, even an occasional handwritten essay. You have to wonder how they made the grades on their transcripts."

- "Spelling errors, poor English."

- "Anything that starts out, 'I've always wanted to be a _____.'"

- "Sometimes they don't really answer the question. We ask each question for a reason."

- "When they just seem to be saying what they think we want to hear. We can pick up on that right away."

- "Our application is a little different. We want original work. I hate it when I can tell that they're recycling material they wrote for other schools."

- "The essay sounds like they want to be the next Mother Teresa, but there's nothing in the rest of the application to back up any claims of altruism."

- "We ask for dates on activities. It's a red flag if all the activities are brand new."

- "A whole essay on deep personal problems or excuses for past performance. It's amazing how common that is. The essay should be upbeat, convincing, persuasive."

- "Too long. It shows no discipline."

- "Every year there is always at least one essay from someone who tells us how proud he would be to be admitted to _____, but this isn't that school."

- "Students are so afraid to take a risk that they don't really tell us anything. That throws us right back on the numbers."

- "Don't tell me what _____ is. I know what my own discipline is! What can they be thinking? Tell me what _____ means to you."

- "Some students think they can use the essay to manufacture a person who doesn't exist. It doesn't work."

Review your essay in light of these comments. Would it earn a place in the Essay Hall of Shame? How would you like to read a whole lot of this:

> I have been fondly looking forward to a bright entry at your faculty. In making this assertion, I hope I am not just facile enough to make a claim, for, the facts about my academic antecedents vouch for my superior academic credentials—if I should borrow a phrase out of the vernacular parlance. In this regard, let me crave your indulgence in what I furnish below, concerning my prospective career related to Graduate Studies.

This is from an actual application, and it went on like this for pages.

Admissions readers are actually quite forgiving—every year they admit people in spite of serious errors. I reviewed one law school essay that had two grammatical errors in the first sentence, yet the student was admitted to Harvard, Michigan, Chicago, NYU, Columbia, University of California Boalt Hall, and Stanford law schools. This is because those two errors in the first sentence were followed by an inspiring essay revealing who the candidate *really* was. (On the other hand, I sat in with a law school admissions committee while they sorted the maybe pile one last time. They didn't read beyond the first mistake. The first error in spelling, punctuation, syntax, semantics, word usage, or consistency of style, and they tossed the whole folio on the reject pile. If the error was in the first line, they didn't read the second line. Late in the season the decision-making process can get brutal.)

If "I" is the first word of your essay, restructure the sentence. For example, turn "I have always been fascinated by highly successful people" into "Highly successful people have always fascinated me." Also, get the target school right. Every year I talk to students who apply to John Hopkins and Colombia. Somehow, they never get in.

If your first draft was truly written from your heart, the material will represent the real you. Now, however, it is time to make sure there is not *too much* of the real you in your essay.

Write your second draft as though you were sitting in the reader's brain. In other words, really *read* each section of your essay and ask yourself, "How will the reader respond to this?" The problem with this editing approach is that students tend to overanalyze and overanticipate their reader. In your first-pass edit, just look for the obvious. For example, one student applying to business schools drafted an essay about how her greatest accomplishment was moving away from her family. She had a very close family, and this was her honest response to the essay question, "What is your greatest accomplishment?" In editing her draft, she decided to replace that first response with another one citing her proposal of contract terms that saved her company a considerable amount of money. This was not what she considered her greatest accomplishment, but to a business-oriented admissions reader it was certainly more encouraging.

Warning

Read your essay as though you were sitting in the reader's brain, and correct only the obvious answers. Do not overanalyze!

Incidentally, one of the best "greatest accomplishment" essays I ever read was not about success, but about dealing with failure. This is a risky approach, but in this particular case, it worked. As you retreat from the gut honesty of your first draft, do not revert to entirely safe and boring responses.

For example, you may wish to think twice about responses that criticize past professors, denigrate other programs, espouse intolerant religious beliefs, or feature trendy political concerns that have nothing to do with the rest of your application. It is usually not a good idea to reveal that you are singularly motivated by money (although if you are eloquent enough about it, it might work). Writing about your triumph over past personal problems can result in a powerful essay, but do avoid writing about ongoing mental anguish. Finally, you might bear in mind what one admissions reader told me: "I am simply not moved by the claim that someone's status as a Christian is a qualification for medical school."

Watch for displays of arrogance and omniscience, as exemplified in such statements as "X *must* Y." Choose less inflammatory language, such as "X *would greatly benefit from* Y." Sometimes just a few word changes can fix an overly certain tone. It is fine to disagree with the entire profession you are about to join, but do not insult your reader with high-handed narrative exposition. "Buildings will never make sense until architects learn to . . ." should be rewritten into a first-person personal statement such as "as an architect, my passionate interest will be to improve the. . . ." There are many revolutions going on right now in medicine, anthropology, business, and other fields, and you can be part of those revolutions, but not by alienating the first admissions reader you come across. Give her a chance to be on your side.

Avoid writing anything like, "My longtime friend died and after I saw how he was treated in the hospital, I wanted to become a doctor so I would never let that happen again." Such sentiments reveal a lack of sophistication, a certain solipsism, a lack of understanding of the harsh realities and tough decisions that go with a career in medicine. Read your essay from an admissions counselor's point of view, and see if you want to change or remove any unintentional self-revelations.

Be especially wary of revealing character weaknesses such as sloth, dishonesty, or egocentricity. Unfortunately, some secondary essays actually ask questions like, "What are your weaknesses?" Try to describe weaknesses that are actually strengths turned inside out, such as "I study too much and forget to have fun," or "I try to do too much," or "Sometimes I spend a lot of time in the library just looking up interesting articles and forget to apply myself to the task at hand." Unfortunately, admissions directors report that they have "heard it all" on this front and are a little tired of this approach. However, anybody who says, "I drink too much," or "I am not as motivated as I could be," or "I get depressed a lot," is simply begging for a rejection.

Finally, it is very important that you audit your essay for sexist language or points of view. Do not use male pronouns unless you are referring only to the male gender. Unfortunately, it is probably not a good idea to replace a sexist male singular pronoun (he, him) with the neuter plural (they, them), an awkward solution that some have proposed in response to our lack of neuter singular pronouns; your readers may assume that you have made an unwitting grammatical error. Instead, be laborious with your "he or she," "his or her," and "him or her" constructions, as you do not have room in an essay to establish a pattern of gender interchangeability that seems so much more graceful a solution. Never address letters to "Dear Sirs"; use "Dear Admissions Committee" or just "Ladies and Gentlemen." The ultimate sin would be to discuss your future contributions to "the brotherhood of man." If you do not understand how to approach language in a gender-neutral manner, now would be a good time to start learning. This is taught in high school, so there's no excuse for getting it wrong.

•   •   •

If sitting in the brain of your reader causes you to throw out the majority of your first draft, you are probably being too critical. This is only an editing exercise and should not cause you to start over. You will lose the integrity and authenticity of your essay if you write only what you think the reader wants. This is specifically what admissions directors do *not* want.

Once you have taken a pass at the draft using the above methodology, the bulk of the material before you is probably going to make it into your final draft. It will become better written as you go through more drafts, but the points presented will probably remain the same. Only now might you show your draft to another human being, but my recommendation is to wait until you think you have a final draft.

•   •   •

The next editing exercises are more fun than sitting around in someone else's brain pretending to be an admissions reader. First, read your draft for lines that you can "spice up." Try to infuse your essay with another dose of life. For example, "I worked as a teacher's aide at a daycare school" sounds rather mundane and onerous. Using both detail and accomplishment, here is another way to represent the same fact:

> Last spring and summer I was a teacher's aide at a daycare school espousing the principles of Rheikofkian development theory, using only positive interaction. I was commended by the head teacher for devising new games that exemplified Rheikofkian theory in practice and for reaching a particular student who had been diagnosed as borderline emotionally disturbed. After one semester under my tutelage, this student was able to be mainstreamed when she entered the public school system. (See letter of recommendation.)

Less is more in a statement of purpose. If a point is worth mentioning at all, it is worth illustrating for your reader. If your essay is too long, resist the temptation to keep all the points, saying less about each. It is better to throw out some points and topics, and perhaps even enrich your presentation of those that are left, than to turn your essay into a brutish list of activities. Trust your reader to look over the rest of your application and see supporting material, especially if you refer to it with citations like "See résumé for additional volunteer experience."

Avoid self-promotions such as "I am an intelligent, compassionate, and caring individual" in favor of describing scenes and events where you act in an intelligent, compassionate, and caring manner. If you feel compelled to self-describe, soften the statements with qualifying clauses such as "I think of myself as . . ." or "people have often said that I am . . ." or "I have often been told by others that I am. . . ."

If you still have the phrase "I have always wanted to be a _____" in your essay, remove it. You have not always *anything*. If you want to take this approach, try telling a story about the moment at which you first became interested in your future career. Do you remember that moment?

Watch out for possible negative connotations that can sneak in with the words you select! We are becoming a society seemingly blind to connotations, as I see advertisement after advertisement with as much negative emotive impact as positive. You should not fall for this sloppy way of communicating. Words are rich signifiers, bringing a whole baggage of extra meaning with them wherever they go. If your essay is full of words like "work," "study," "laborious," and "exhaustive," your reader may be tired and exhausted by the end of the essay. If you write, "I practice piano for three hours every day no matter what," you are certainly getting a message across, but a better message might be "I enjoy music a great deal, and I play the piano for three hours or more every day. My favorite composers are . . ." So read your essay again, and see if there are word selections and phrases with negative connotations that you could turn into more positive constructions.

• • •

Edit to make sure that you get your message across. Do not worry overmuch about the finer points of style. Rough transitions and a few belabored sentence structures are fine as long as you convey the message you want. Do not let your language draw attention to itself; it should be a medium for your message, not a message in itself.

Your spelling and grammar should be perfect, however. Absolutely perfect. You should have a final draft of your essay proofread by somebody you consider to be an expert in grammar and spelling, but do not seek such expertise until you have a final draft.

Be careful not to edit the life out of your essay. A grammarian and a stylist would have a tumultuous marriage. It is hard for some grammarians to accept, but the English language is like a snake, and it is always getting away from them. The erosion of the distinction between "that" and "which," the acceptance of "like" for "such as," dangling participles sneaking in, and, horror of horrors, the begrudging acknowledgment that splitting an infinitive is sometimes the way to best wring the exact meaning out of a sentence—all of these cause dilettante grammarians to have sphincter-tightening paroxysms. If you are applying to a graduate program in English, you may wish to be hyperconservative, but otherwise, write like you talk and take the advice of an overly picky

WARREN EDITED HIS
PERSONAL STATEMENT
A BIT TOO FAR.

I am
who I am.

Copyright 1991 Kirk Anderson. Used with permission.

grammarian with a grain of salt. A primer on this subject is *Miss Thistlebottom's Hobgoblins* by Theodore M. Bernstein. Other good books on style and editing are *Edit Yourself* by Bruce Ross-Larson, *Nitty-Gritty Grammar* by Edith Fine and Judith Josephson, *Write Right!* by Jan Venolia, *On Writing Well* by William Zinsser, and of course the classic *The Elements of Style* by Strunk and White. The ultimate usage reference is Fowler's *The New Fowler's Modern English Usage,* but it's pretty dense. Your most important desk reference, in any case, is a good dictionary. If you do not own one, buy one before tomorrow noon. If you accidentally get into grad school, you're going to need it. The one that came with your computer is inadequate; trust me on this.

Although this book does not pretend to be a stylebook, I would like to warn against two very common errors I ran into in reading thousands of graduate admissions essays. First, unless a noun is a proper noun, you do not need to capitalize it. Fields of study, such as chemistry, history, mathematics, are not proper nouns even though they are commonly capitalized in academic settings. Second, the quotation mark always goes on the outside of the comma or period, so this is "the right way," and this is always "the wrong way", unless you are in the United Kingdom, where they always do it "the wrong way". If you have doubts about punctuation, capitalization, and similar technical matters, learn to use such writers' desktop references as *The Chicago Manual of Style* and *The Associated Press Stylebook.* Finally, all citations need to be in the style that is standard for your field. Chemistry has one set of citation conventions, psychology another. See your adviser for a style sheet. For the humanities as a whole, use the Modern Language Association's *MLA Handbook for Writers of Research Papers.*

Write your essay first, as it is far more important that your creative and intellectual energy be expended on content than on worrying about stylistic details. Once you have your essay, though, be sure that you do attend to those stylistic details—every last one of them. In my research for this book, basic errors in spelling and usage were cited by admissions readers more often than any other specific complaint about applications essays. However, if you find an error after the application is submitted, it is probably better just to live with it than to send in a "corrected" version; doing so only adds insult to injury.

• • •

There is no correct or ideal number of drafts, but fewer than three is probably too few. Once you have what you consider to be a final draft, you can begin to road test it on a few people you respect. Do not be alarmed if you show your essay to six people and get ten strong opinions. Listen to your readers, but do not let them make decisions for you. In the end, this is your essay. If you delete or soften every presentation in your essay in response to criticism from readers, you will end up with a tasteless, textureless mush. Too many cooks spoil the broth, and too many engineers make an ugly bridge. When you think your essay is perfect, submit it.

Put at least your full name and Social Security number at the top of each page. Here is one example of a page heading:

Christopher Xavier Hylands   Page 2
SS# 915-78-4967
(applicant for the doctoral program in educational administration, University of
Massachusetts, Amherst, fall 2009 incoming class)

Identifying information such as this should be on *all* submitted documents. Try to use your complete name on everything; avoid initials and shortened forms such as Chris or Jon or Nan.

If you submit anything on paper, never print on both sides of the paper unless you really do not care if nobody reads the back side. If your essay is longer than the specified length, you should know that some admissions readers will not read beyond that length (most will, but a few will not). If your essay is very good, however, do not worry too much about its length. That said, watch out for word or character counters that may lop off a too long essay. Some students sign their essays, which I find to be a nice touch; it vouches for the sincerity and truth of the essay's content. It's easy to scan in a signature.

More and more graduate schools are accepting standardized applications, where you apply to a "clearinghouse," and that service forwards your collected materials to the individual schools. These include Project 1000, American Medical College Application Service (AMCAS), Law School Data Assembly Service (LSDAS), American Association of Colleges of Osteopathic Medicine Application Service (AACOMAS), American Association of Colleges of Podiatric Medicine Application Service (AACPMAS), and the American Association of Dental Schools Application Service (AADSAS). Each works a little differently from the others. Every few years some organization threatens to launch one of these in the humanities or the general sciences, as well.

These standardized methods will save you time, but further homogenize your application just as you are working your dead level best to individualize your materials! Think about it. Be sure you don't let ease of application keep you from making your best application. I recommend that you apply directly to the schools whenever you can, answering their unique questions, and submitting supporting documentation and work samples and materials to suit yourself.

—A DISCLAIMER EVERY APPLICANT SHOULD READ!—

Before we launch into the chapter of samples, you need to know of four major cautions. First, **this book is not designed to take the place of faculty advice and counsel.** It is designed to complement faculty advice and to make you savvy on the mechanics of the graduate application process so that you can get the most out of your contacts with faculty. The sooner in the process you can involve faculty, the better. Seek out faculty guidance, and do not disregard it. If your adviser disagrees with advice in this book, he or she is probably right. This book is designed to address the essay-writing needs of a very wide range of applicants, and your faculty adviser knows more about *your particular case.*

Second, it remains for you, the reader, to adjust the suggestions and information contained herein to your particular goal. At one end of the spectrum are doctoral and postdoctoral candidates in highly technical areas. Candidates for such programs need more focus on substantiating their intellectual preparation and specifying their research goals, and less on the personal details of their lives. For some of these applicants, an appropriate application may be virtually devoid of personal information.

At the other end of the spectrum are candidates for fine arts programs, candidates for non-subject-specific scholarships, and occasionally a candidate for a preprofessional program such as law or medical school. For some of these candidates, a fully appropriate essay may contain *only* personal information, or it may consist of just a scene or vignette, providing virtually no information about the applicant's academic preparation and career plans. You should be sensitive both to the range of possibilities and to what would be considered an appropriate mix of information for your own particular type of application. One correspondent wrote: "My sense is that graduate programs in some areas are not concerned much about an individual's life story. Rather, they need to know that the applicant is mature and devoted to his or her field of study; the applicant needs every opportunity to prove his or her writing to be in the academic style. The difference might be that some need to write *statements of purpose,* while others need to write *personal statements.*" The samples that follow run the gamut from autobiographical sketches (personal) to summaries of research (as impersonal as you can get).

A third caution: although this book is in places irreverent, nothing presented here should be construed as an invitation to be flippant, flighty, glib, or "cute." Such a tone would be a huge mistake in a statement of purpose. Although I have tried to reveal a greater range of approaches to these essays than students normally consider, I most certainly do not encourage you to write anything that does not reveal a proper respect for the admissions process. Although the other books in this genre often say something like "and a little humor never hurts," in the essays I read I find that humor falls flat rather often. One admissions director called humor a "high-wire act," and said that he appreciated it when applicants could pull it off, but that they did not seem to be able to predict when it would work. You should take risks in your writing, but take them in the areas of revealing personality, revealing whatever about you is unusual or unique, or taking a well-presented controversial stand. If you choose to make a joke, make it a subtle one, indeed. Humor should be a garnish, never an entrée. Humor that fails is often interpreted as immaturity, and immaturity is almost universally believed to be detrimental to success in graduate school. Be different, take a risk, but in general be serious and purposeful.

Finally, do not measure yourself against the samples and examples in this book. Statistically it would be *much* easier to be admitted to one of the most competitive programs in the nation than to be selected for a book such as this. I have selected these particular essays according to two criteria: either I found them to be almost perfect stylistically or I found the candidate to have a particularly strong application, or both.

Many of the candidates selected for this book are a little different. One of the priorities of most graduate admissions professionals is to create and/or preserve diversity in each year's incoming class. This means racial and socioeconomic diversity, certainly, but it also means recruiting people who have had different life experiences and people who have unusual career plans. However, you do not have to go to Africa or join the carnival to have a successful graduate application. If the most unusual thing about you is how utterly normal you are, then maybe you should build your essay around that. No matter who you are, you can follow the principles outlined in this book, take a risk, and make your best application.

As soon as you are done with your essay, feel free to send it to me for consideration for the next edition of this book:

> Donald Asher
> *Graduate Admissions Essays*
> c/o Ten Speed Press
> P.O. Box 7123
> Berkeley, CA 94707

Or just email me at don@donaldasher.com. Be sure to include both an email address and a permanent address and telephone number. All such correspondence shall be considered submitted for publication and subject to editing and revision. Recompense is limited to a copy of the new edition. I look forward to hearing from you, and *best of luck!*

8

Samples, Samples, Samples

Read several essays to discover what style may be best for the unique combination of your objective and your background. All 50 essays are listed by a number and a "nickname." In the Sample Essay Index beginning on page 235, you will find both specific details and general issues to help you locate a specific essay. You should also check the general index beginning on page 239 for mention of specific academic subjects that may appear elsewhere in the book.

Having said this, I urge you to begin by browsing the entire collection of samples without regard to a specific subject matter, stopping to read essays that interest you. Do not just flip to the ones in your field, or in fields most like yours, to see what others have done. Take time to explore a number of essays. Some of the stories represented there are so fascinating that another whole book could be written on them.

Whatever you do, remember this: **Do not even think about modeling your essay closely on one of the examples in this book;** *essays in this book are provided so that you may learn how to write the best statement for your own unique background. Admissions people have also seen this book, and if you copy material, they will notice it right away.*

Having trouble finding an essay? Check the Sample Essay Index on page 235.

Essay #1 "From Working Poor to Elite Scholar"

Statement of Purpose, Dept. of History

One of the proudest accomplishments of my life was earning my college degree, despite the fact that my early adulthood pointed in the opposite direction, beginning with my marriage at the age of 19. Throughout the 1990s I lived as one of the "working poor," someone who slipped through the cracks of supposedly historic prosperity. By the age of 25 I was divorced and frustrated with menial, low-paying jobs: clerk, receptionist, housecleaner. There is nothing like scrubbing someone else's toilet to inspire one with determination toward obtaining an education. Because of my absolute commitment toward earning my degree, I got a flexible shift at a retail warehouse which enabled me to acquire my degree while supporting myself financially.

Enrolled at the local community college, I experienced a different world opening up to me; excited by a new encouraging environment, I excelled academically. I learned that if I tried hard, I could succeed; if I wanted something badly enough, I possessed the ability to take advantage of these opportunities. I worked a minimum 35-hour workweek for five years to put myself through school without succumbing to the temptation of a student loan. I paid tuition up front with the money I earned. It was the example of my mother, a Puerto Rican immigrant working diligently to provide for her family, who instilled a work ethic into me that has stood me in good stead.

With a lifelong passion for history, I have developed an interest in the cultural history of early modern and modern Europeans, especially women's history. The experiences of ordinary women fascinate me: how they constitute their world through popular folk tales and literature; how the seemingly irrational paradoxes of the past to modern eyes are completely rational when taken within the historical context; and finally, how these historical changes and transformations in culture constitute the present. I enjoy studying the early modern period of English history, especially the Tudor-Stuart period, because of the tensions that existed between medieval philosophies and the rising Enlightenment intellectualism. My influences have been diverse. I read the popular historian Barbara Tuchman, not for her technical accuracy, but for her beautiful prose. Natalie Zemon Davis's research inspires me in the way that she cleverly picks out fresh life from tired sources. And finally, Michel Foucault's philosophies have profoundly influenced the way I write, for now I have a philosophical grounding that makes me highly sensitive to my own biases. In fact, Foucault's post-structuralist matrix has been instrumental in shaping my current project focusing on the 17th-century midwife Elizabeth Cellier. In this project, I am reexamining the current histories of English midwifery using Cellier as a case study, detecting a decided bias embedded within them. The underlying assumption of these histories is that pre-industrial professional women—and Cellier in particular—struggled against patriarchy and oppression from the male medical community, when in fact Cellier's literature shows that she utilized the accepted discourses of patriarchy available to her in her writing and turned them into useful tools of political and religious power.

This essay uses an outstanding combination of personal information and academic exposition. The personal information makes the reader interested in this young woman as a person, and the academic information proves that such interest is warranted. Notice that the woman is matter-of-fact about some rather large challenges she has faced in her life; she doesn't ask for special consideration, rather she explains certain decision-making processes and turning points in her development as a person and a scholar. This is an outstanding essay overall.

#1   "From Working Poor to Elite Scholar"   *(continued)*

As a student, I feel that my success lies in the fact that I approached my studies as if I were a professional (historian, not student, that is). I always enrolled in the most challenging courses and worked with professors I felt were the most qualified in my areas of interest. Never did I settle for an A– or B+. If I got one, I would ask what I could do to improve—and ultimately, I utilized the advice to strengthen my work. My personal academic milestone occurred while I was completing a research seminar on historical methods. This required course was taught by an Americanist—Dr. Julie Worth, director of the [school withheld] history department—so our research topics were limited to American sources. I was able to work within my main interest, which is marginalized women, while using the primary sources of *The New York Times*. The resulting paper, "Biologically Unsound: Women, Murder, and the Insanity Plea in the Progressive Era" examined the preponderant use of the insanity plea for women who went outside their "innate nature" and murdered, regardless of the circumstances which drove them to kill. Although the topic was outside my focus, which is European history, this paper was selected for publication in the Phi Alpha Theta journal, *The Historian*.

My focus as an undergraduate has always been with an eye toward graduate school and a career as a professional historian. Aware of the rigors of graduate study, I have not only completed an undergraduate language requirement in Spanish, but I am also currently enrolled in an accelerated French course. In addition, I have become active in the historical honor society, Phi Alpha Theta, including serving as chapter president. During my tenure our chapter hosted the Phi Alpha Theta Regional Conference, the largest regional conference in the nation. With the help of faculty adviser Dr. Judith Gaillard, I created the conference sessions, chose appropriate student commentators for those sessions, and gave a keynote speech. The experience taught me that I have a flair for organization as well as mediation. Under my leadership, our chapter also published its first journal, and hosted a variety of campus activities. This year I am working with the Computer Society in order to establish a Web site for students who need help succeeding in history courses; we are going to call it the Clio home page. My position as an authority figure both in classroom work and within these various organizations has awakened a desire to embrace teaching, for I enjoy sharing the excitement of education with my peers, as well as helping them achieve their own academic success.

I feel that my life experiences as well as my commitment to education would be an asset to Cornell's doctoral program in history. Cornell has a exciting interdisciplinary program that is exceptionally impressive. In particular, Dr. Rayna Wilhelm's specialty in Tudor-Stuart social and cultural history complements my own interest in studying the experiences of English pre-industrial women. This combination will provide the strong background I desire in order to shape my future research interests. I feel that Cornell is a premier institution for an aspiring Ph.D. candidate and as such, a very competitive program. But I know I have the tools and the determination to excel in such a stimulating and challenging environment.

Here is a nice exposition of a specific academic project, leading to publication. Do you have a paper that you could submit for publication before you apply to graduate school? Your professors can guide you in this process.

Always name your advisers and mentors.

When you have identified specific professors at the targeted graduate program who could be mentors to you, mention them by name.

ESSAY #2: "The Sound of Kittywakes"

While my coworkers stared at the amazing sight of thousands of black-legged kittywakes exploding off the cliff face, I closed my eyes and listened. I had been working in Prince William Sound, Alaska, for a number of months and had noticed that when a colony of these sea birds was flushed by a predator, they made a particular descending warble vocalization. In fact, in the hectic life of a kittywake colony with up to 16,000 birds coming and going, this distinct call seemed to be the trigger for the only coordinated activity in which I ever saw them participate. Later that afternoon, I practiced making the "flush call" until the researchers with me were sick of it, then climbed onto the colony and did my best imitation. The thunder of the entire colony lifting off, as other birds picked up the call, cemented my long-held intention: I want to work with sound. My purpose for undertaking doctoral work in acoustics and animal behavior is twofold. First, my professional goal is to contribute to the existing research on biological systems which use sound. Second, my personal goal is to convey in-depth understanding and love of these systems to the students I teach.

With regard to advancing current research, the concept of coevolution has always held special fascination for me. Its importance to the theory of evolution, so central to the study of biology, is made more relevant by vivid examples in the area of echolocation. Certain bats and moths have evolved for so long in their predator-prey relationship that the moths have actually developed acoustic countermeasures to help them evade the bat's echolocation.

The highly specialized nature of these countermeasures, which include Doppler shifts, and both broad and narrow band interference, reveal how strong an evolutionary pressure the predation of the bats must be. Though my reading of articles has turned up extensive research with regard to bats, I have not found any work dealing with any similar predator-prey relationships among marine organisms. I plan to explore whether cetacean predation over thousands of years has caused prey species such as squid or fish (which are heavily preyed upon by sperm whales and dolphins respectively) to evolve acoustic evasive techniques similar to those utilized by moths on land. This work may show us not only how coevolution has influenced marine echolocation, but how convergent evolution may have led both marine and terrestrial prey to similar defense mechanisms.

I have strong preparation to help me realize both my personal and professional goals. Since completing my undergraduate degree, I have participated in Exxon Valdez–funded research in Alaska and National Parks research on endangered species in Hawaii. I have successfully brought this active participation in research to the students I have taught. Classes I have designed and taught have varied from public education programs to high-school-level courses in biology, evolution, chemistry, and physics. These teaching experiences have confirmed that I have the desire and aptitude to convey my knowledge of the sciences to others. Though my position running the science department for a private high school provided significant teaching satisfaction and latitude, I want to teach upper-division college courses to advanced students. My willingness to sacrifice this rewarding position should be seen as a reflection of my desire to pursue a career in higher education.

Science essays can be somewhat personal, such as this one, or highly impersonal, such as the next one. One style is not "right" and the other "wrong"; you need to pick the style that matches your background, your interests, the assigned topic, and the institution to which you are applying. This student has done considerable work to identify alignment between his academic preparation and interests, and the focus of this particular graduate program. Even if you apply to fifteen programs, try to make each application as focused and specific as this one.

Graduate school is an excellent place to combine two disciplines that might not be so easily combined as an undergraduate.

#2 "The Sound of Kittywakes" *(continued)*

Teaching, tutoring, and proctoring experiences are important for winning assistantships and are in general highly regarded by graduate programs. Be sure to mention them. This candidate not only has teaching experience, but he also has a teaching philosophy, as mentioned here.

The departmental philosophy at UCSC parallels my own. I was pleased to read of the biological sciences department's requirement that all graduate students teach for a number of quarters. This stems from my firmly held belief that you may possess information, but that it has not yet become knowledge, and thus truly yours, unless you can teach it to others. Doctoral study at UCSC would be an opportunity for me to work directly with Drs. Costa, Oritz, and Williams in developing my research interests, and the teaching requirement will provide a perfect opportunity for me to hone my instructional skills. It is this kind of departmental commitment to developing multidimensional graduate students that I am looking for.

In conclusion, the combination of my two goals—to contribute to the existing research on biological systems which use sound, and to convey in-depth understanding and love of these systems to the students I teach—have led me to pursue an advanced degree in biology. In return for UCSC's commitment to provide an environment conducive to higher learning, I would like to offer a young man confident in his ability to take advantage of all you have to offer. I would like to offer you an experienced teacher and researcher who would like to contribute to the body of work you are producing.

I would like to offer myself.

ESSAY #3: "Nitrogen"

Summary of Current Research

My current work with Dr. Raganasik is on the activation of nitrogen regulated promoters. Earlier work in this laboratory has shown that transcription of the *glnALG* operon of *E. coli*, coding for glutamine synthetase and two nitrogen regulatory proteins, is initiated at *glnAp2* by σ^{54}-RNA polymerase. Under nitrogen-limiting conditions the regulatory protein NR_I is phosphorylated by NR_{II}. NR_I-phosphate (NR_I-P) binds to two sites, located 100 and 130 bp upstream from the transcription start site, and catalyzes the isomerization of the closed σ^{54}-RNA polymerase-*glnAp2* complex to the open complex. We have now shown that NR_I-P cannot activate a σ^{70} promoter, like the *lac* promoter, containing NIR_I-binding sites but can activate other σ^{54} promoters like *nifHp*. These results suggested that the activation by NR_I-P is not solely dependent on the presence of the NR_I-binding sites but also on the nucleotide sequence of the downstream promoter region. In collaboration with Dr. Vona White, we studied the effect of phosphorylation of NR_I on its DNA binding properties. Our results showed that phosphorylation greatly increases cooperative binding of the activator to two adjacent binding sites, and that the interaction between two NR_I-P dimers is required for activation.

Furthermore, I am studying the activation of *glnHp2*, also a nitrogen-regulated promoter, of the glutamine permease operon of *E. coli*. I have shown that open complex formation at *glnHp2* is activated by NR_I-P, and that the activation is stimulated by integration host factor (IHF), a DNA-bending protein. IHF binds to a site between the NR_I-binding sites and the promoter. A single nucleotide mutation in *glnHp2* (T to G at position -14) increases the affinity of σ^{54}-RNA polymerase for the promoter. Using an *in vitro* transcription assay, I showed that the stimulation by IHF takes place only in promoters that form weak closed complexes with RNA polymerase. Activation of the mutant promoter is not stimulated by IHF. On the other hand, when the binding sites for NR_I or IHF were placed on the opposite side of the DNA helix, IHF inhibited the open complex formation. We conclude from these results that the stiffening produced by the IHF-induced bend can facilitate or prevent interactions between the upstream bound NR_I-P and the closed RNA polymerase-promoter complex, depending on the relative location of the binding sites for these proteins. In this manner a regulatory protein, IHF, can stimulate or block transcription without itself contacting either the RNA polymerase or the activator.

Recently, we have found that σ^{54} binds specifically to the *glnHp2* promoter in the absence of the core RNA polymerase subunits. In collaboration with Weslia Carson and Malcolm Blick (AFRC Nitrogen Fixation Laboratory, University of Sussex, England), we have demonstrated a new role for core RNA polymerase in transcription: that it assists the binding of σ^{54} to promoter DNA. An altered form of σ^{54} with a deletion within the N terminus showed increased DNA binding properties. Our results suggest σ^{54} has a latent DNA binding activity which is revealed by core RNA polymerase.

Graduate applications may require a statement of purpose, an autobiography, an essay or two or six on assigned topics, a summary of research, or all of the above. All these writing assignments are slightly different, and you should be sensitive to the instructions. Remember, **RTGDQ.** This two-part essay is in response to the assignment: "Describe your research experience to date."

Research summaries are a common part of laboratory science applications. The focus should be on the science, not the scientist. Presenting your research in a clean, impersonal format—as this candidate did—is the best approach.

#3 "Nitrogen"	*(continued)*

Summary of Previous Research

Be sure to name your advisers, as it is bad form to imply that you did high-level work all by yourself, without any advice or counsel from a senior scientist.

As a postdoctoral associate in the laboratory of Dr. Kirschner, I was involved in two research projects. One project was to characterize the *ams* gene, which is involved in decay of *Escherichia coli* mRNA. I cloned the *ams* gene by complementation, mapped the transcription start site, and determined the size and the N terminus sequence of the *ams* protein. We used a T7 RNA polymerase-promoter system to overexpress the *ams* locus. We determined the nucleotide sequence of the *ams* gene, and these data showed that the C terminus of the protein has homology to a mitochondrial ribosomal protein of *Neurospora crassa*. More recently, it has been shown that *ams* encodes RNase E, an endoribonuclease that plays a general role in the chemical decay of *E. coli* mRNA. The other project was the characterization and secretion of protease III (*ptr*) of *E. coli*. I mapped and sequenced the *ptr* promoter and determined the N terminus sequence of protease III. This N terminus contains a signal sequence which is needed for secretion of protease III to the periplasm. Using the cloned *ptr* gene and protease III-alkaline phosphatase fusions, we found evidence that protease III is also secreted to the growth medium.

In my Ph.D. work, I studied the chemistry and ultrastructure of the spore wall of *Aspergillus nidulans* conidia, and the effect of cell wall components in the uptake of chemicals. I used electron microscopy to study the ultrastructure of the conidial wall and found that it is composed of several layers. The outer layer is covered by regularly arranged fibers (rodlets) which can be removed by sonication. Chemical analysis of purified conidial walls from a wild-type strain showed the presence of neutral sugars (glucose, galactose and mannose), protein, chitin, melanin and small amounts of lipid. Chemical fractionation experiments showed the presence of alpha-1,3-glucan in the electron-dense outer layer. Conidial walls of a white mutant strain lacked melanin and alpha-1,3-glucan. I also purified the rodlets, which contain protein and melanin in equal amounts and some carbohydrate. Histidine, aspartic acid, glutamic acid, glycine, and alanine are the most prominent amino acids of the rodlet protein. The presence of melanin and possible cross-linkages between it and amino acids like aspartic acid, glutamic acid and glycine makes the rodlets resistant to proteases. I also studied the effect of conidial wall components on the uptake of sugar analogs and amino acids by conidia. Conidia were first treated with sonication to remove the rodlet layer, and then with proteases or glucanases. The removal of glucan and protein from the outer layer of the conidial wall allowed an increased uptake of 2-deoxy-D-glucose, 3-O-methyl-glucose and L-alanine. These results indicate that certain components of the conidial wall act as a barrier to penetration of chemicals.

ESSAY #4: "Law School Essay of B. T. Powers"

Law School Personal Statement

B. T. Powers, Applicant Code 325917

"So this is police work," I thought, sitting at a shaky table in a downtown pancake house one freezing afternoon three years ago. Beside me sat a Deputy DA with little experience in the courtroom. Across from both of us sat our case's star witness, Scottie Wasserman, a transient in tattered and worn clothing. The bulk of the restaurant patrons had migrated to the other half of the establishment upon our entrance. Whether this was due to Scottie's appearance or my police uniform, I didn't know.

Weeks earlier, Scottie had been the only person around to witness a homeless woman being thrown against a fence and strangled. As the DA saw Scottie walking into the courthouse that day, I could see the horrifying visions in her head of an intoxicated transient taking the stand, slurring his speech, and repelling the jurors out of a guilty verdict.

As the initiator of this lunch, I sat wondering how it would feel to be the DA in charge of such a case, being responsible for a witness like Scottie, and helping in the defense of an indigent woman. Your tax dollars at work, some might think in a cynical tone, but I could still recite those words without cynicism.

All of my college peers were still working through their senior year, while I had decided to race to earn my degree in three years in order to join the police academy sooner. My high GPA should be viewed in light of my class load at the time. In a way it was a sacrifice, but by joining the police department early, I was able to see the difference I could make—differences like that day in the pancake house with Mr. Wasserman.

The table continued to tremble under Scottie's arms and legs as he tried to balance his fork and ignore his condition. Seeing him and his compatriots on a daily basis on my beat had given me an insight into alcoholism and the dependence on addiction that the homeless are often burdened with. I thought about how the elements of my education and my life experience could help the situation. As a community patrol officer, I was supposed to be quick on my feet, a problem solver, as well as a humanitarian. Being raised in a police family meant knowing the limitations and realities of social services. Having gained the outlines of the criminal law and justice system in college, I thought I had forged a bit of a unique vision of the crucible. I thought I understood where theory met practice.

I had already tried out my most idealistic side. I tutored freshmen undergraduates in college; I helped build a criminal justice forum to aid those who wanted to help. And I volunteered at a police assistance program on weekends.

None of those things seemed to matter, though, to Mr. Wasserman. He flattened the hair on his head, trying for presentable with whatever will he could muster. Scottie's blood alcohol content was always more than three times the legal limit for drivers. The DA tried to smile. I could tell she was calling on all her law school training, all her knowledge. This was to be her first case. From her recent studies, she knew the law she would be trying, she knew how to handle a jury. But she didn't know how to present someone like Scottie.

Vivid depiction of a scenario or event can be a powerful essay for professional schools.

The underlying theme to this essay is "where theory meets practice."

#4: "Law School Essay of B. T. Powers" *(continued)*

Sitting there, I envied her challenge and considered what I could bring to the table in such a situation. I thought about the transition from enforcing laws to studying law to *using the law*. I watched as the DA grew more and more nervous. "Why do you shake like that, Scottie?" she asked, faking a calm demeanor.

She didn't appear to know why we were sitting in a pancake house, feeding Scottie a heavy dose of sugars before he testified. Scottie knew. "It's withdrawal, ma'am. Officer Powers knew I wouldn't be any good at the trial if I was drinking. I don't think it's right, hitting a woman, and I want to be sober for this. I haven't had a drink since last night, and I wouldn't have been able to hold it past lunch if given the chance. Officer Powers has been with me all day now so I don't drink."

I knew that my upbringing and my experience on the department had provided me with a knowledge base that few lawyers would have the luxury to attain—the ability to understand the people who go through our legal system, the ability to reason as they would reason in times of crisis. Whether civil or criminal, almost every U.S. citizen who is involved in our legal system is experiencing what for them is a crisis. I wanted to be able to understand what they were going through.

Scottie stayed sober and gave the testimony that earned the DA her win, a unanimous guilty, and the two of them together took a dangerous criminal off the streets. I drove Scottie to the west side that evening and let him out, and watched him walk into the corner store to buy what he needed to stop his shaking. I don't have a bleeding heart. But I understand a bit about nuance and complexity, about what it means to be a human.

It's not enough to simply believe in people, or hope for the best, or throw around platitudes that are at their root condescending. I think driving a black and white all day has given me a perspective of the gray area that most people don't get to see.

I am hoping that my police career gives me a greater understanding of the laws that I will some day enforce and the statutes that have been fought for in our judicial system. I'm eager to take what I've learned so far, and add it to a rigorous education in the law. I know this combination can be used for a greater good. It is my goal to be of service.

ESSAY #5: "Library Floors and Literature"

Personal Statement

It happened two years ago as I lay sprawled out on the floor of the library lounge at the Université de Grenoble in Grenoble, France. I was working on an *explication du texte* of Guillaume Apollinaire's poem "La Loreley" for my *Poèmes et Proses du XXe Siècle* class when I suddenly put it together: this was *my* approach to literature. Close reading, formalism. Staying close, very close, to the text. I was certain.

Certainty, however, proved rather unstable. I knew it was important not to close myself off from other approaches to literature, so when I returned to Swarthmore from Grenoble, I took two courses which I knew would be highly theoretical—*Women Writers 1790–1830* and *Feminist Literary Criticism.* These courses brought me around to a kind of hybrid approach to literature which I find rich, effective, and enjoyable. In this approach I maintain a close connection to the text at the same time that I apply theoretical work.

I am using this approach to literature in two major projects this year.

First, I received a $2,400 National Endowment for the Humanities Younger Scholars Summer Research Grant. I proposed to expand on a prior research project, looking at the use of silence in the novels of Elie Wiesel, and at the ways Wiesel both demonstrates and gets around the fact that conventional language simply breaks down when it is used to talk about the Holocaust. I plan to expand on the same project for my senior English thesis. For this thesis I am studying the ways Wiesel uses silence in the literal content of his novels and in his writing technique, and am working toward explanations as to how he gives these silences meaning. My fluency in French from my semester of study in Grenoble has been invaluable since most of Wiesel's works were written originally in French. My thesis involves close, formalist readings of Wiesel's novels, and is enriched by theoretical work. (This thesis appears as "Senior Essay" on my transcript; that designation will change next semester to "Thesis.")

My second major project this year is a self-designed research project which has just replaced comprehensive exams in the Swarthmore English Department. I am working with British poetry just following World War I, looking at how these poets write about a kind of war that truly had no precedent since it was the first war in which death could be so effectively and impersonally mass-produced. I am focusing on my observation that a surprising number of these poems rely heavily on biblical or mythical images, as though more contemporary images simply were not applicable any more.

I have known for several years that I want my graduate work to be in the field of English, but my approach to literature has been enriched by my double major in English and sociology-anthropology. Twice my interest in anthropology has led me to study literature of non-European cultures, both times with great personal satisfaction. My papers for *The Black African Writer* combine theoretical research with a good deal of formalist textual analysis and close reading. I had several long conversations about these papers with Prof. Wallace Mann, the R. Talbot Sondheim Professor of African Studies at Swarthmore.

This is a great experiential opening. The reader can "see" the student "sprawled out," and the essay offers an exotic setting. This candidate displays amazing breadth while leading the reader through distinct phases in her intellectual development. The masterful way the candidate weaves in theorists, theories, authors, and names of works lightens what could otherwise be heavy exposition. The essay as a whole amounts to an intellectual argument, the point of which is this: This candidate's background points to the inevitable conclusion that this student is ready to excel at the targeted graduate program.

#5: "Library Floors and Literature" *(continued)*

My second excursion into less-traveled territory was a paper I wrote for *Introduction to Hebrew Scriptures*. I chose to do an exegesis of Isaiah 65:17–25. I worked from the original Hebrew text since I had taken a course in biblical Hebrew (Religion 93) and have a moderate level of reading comprehension of the language. I had a marvelous time digging so deeply into each word, and sometimes even individual letters, as is required in an exegesis of a Hebrew passage.

My two major projects this year—my thesis and my senior project—are related by the theme of war literature, and my work on one project gives me new ideas for the other. I feel fortunate that this has worked out, and at the University of Colorado-Boulder I want to continue studying twentieth-century literature. However, I am also ready to start widening my base, casting out in some new directions. I have found over and over that if I have a long-standing gut-level enjoyment of some kind of literature I almost invariably have a wonderful time and do a particularly good job taking an academic approach to that literature. Old English literature is in this category for me.

I have never done academic work in Old English literature, but for years I have treasured a cassette tape on which are recorded in Old English the stories of *Sir Gawain and the Green Knight, Caedmon,* and *The Wedding of Sir Gawain and Dame Ragnell.* And when I am feeling particularly harried, I often go to the Swarthmore library and treat myself to an old, scratchy recording of a reading of Beowulf, following along in the Old English text and in a modern English translation. By imitating the voice I hear and following in translation, I have taught myself a tiny amount of this language. I want to follow up on this interest.

My interest in studying at the University of Colorado-Boulder has grown out of conversations I have had with numerous people, including Prof. Laurie Langbauer who had a lot of specific information since she taught there one summer. When I spoke about my interests with Abbe Blum, another professor of English at Swarthmore, she recommended that I call Prof. Margaret Ferguson. I did so, and had a wonderful conversation which helped me to confirm that I would feel very much at home in the department. I am especially excited about the department's strength in twentieth-century, Renaissance, and Old English literature.

I am also genuinely pleased about the distribution requirements, since they will help me to explore areas that I did not or could not at Swarthmore. Only by doing that will I continue to learn new things about myself as a student of literature. I do not want my experience in the Université de Grenoble library to be a unique blip in my development. I want to continue changing, refining, playing around with the ways in which I approach literature. This ever-changing, ever-learning approach will help me to be a lifelong scholar and lover of literature.

These paragraphs show the depth of specific interest this student has in this specific graduate program. Be sure to customize your essays to this level of detail. Also note the use of professors' names, both at the undergraduate alma mater and the targeted graduate program.

ESSAY #6: "64,000 Miles to Law School"

I have known since junior high school that I would be a lawyer. But I did not take the traditional road to law school.

I finished my undergraduate coursework at U.C. Davis and was awarded a B.A. with a major in political science/public service and a minor in Spanish. I did not consider applying to law school immediately, for I felt that I had lived a sheltered life in a white, middle-class suburb of Sacramento, and that I knew little of the real world. So I packed my bags, and with two thousand dollars in traveler's checks in my pocket, I took the train to Guadalajara, Mexico, determined to make a new life and face whatever rigors it had to offer. I knew no one in Mexico and had no connections, but I got a hotel room and began to look for work the next day.

I was to remain in Mexico for three years. One of my first jobs was as an English teacher at the Tourism School of the state-run University of Guadalajara. Ostensibly set up to give free educational opportunities in a career in tourism to disadvantaged Mexicans, the school was as much "real world" as I could have asked for. The directors would delay our payroll checks and then offer personal loans, at high interest rates, so that the teachers could cover expenses until the checks "arrived." Student union strongmen packed pistols on campus and hijacked city buses when they grew tired of waiting at bus stops. Leaders of the student union passed my classes regardless of their failing grades or lack of attendance. My outrage, frustration, and helplessness left a deep impression on me; for the first time in my life, I was a foreigner with no civil rights.

Despite a low salary (U.S. $250 dollars per month) and poor working conditions, I stayed on in Mexico, resolved to perfect my Spanish, for I felt certain that it would be important in a legal-related career in California upon my return. I eventually found work at the Instituto Anglo-Mexicano de Cultura, a private English institute under the auspices of the British Council. I studied there in a one-year program and received a teaching certificate. My work consisted of writing the curriculum for and teaching six English classes per day to groups of thirty teenagers and adults. In my free time, I studied Spanish, Portuguese, French, and Latin in a program I developed for myself. On holidays, I travelled around the country by bus to familiarize myself with different dialects and to see the wonders of Mexico.

When I returned to California, I immediately began studies for the California Court Interpreters examination in Spanish. I did not yet feel ready for law school, and decided that court interpreting would be the best way to be in contact with the law and at the same time use my Spanish to work with the Mexican people, for whom I had developed a deep appreciation.

I passed the exam on my first sitting, the first candidate to pass in Sacramento in two years, and began working freelance in the Sacramento municipal and superior courts. From the first day, I was thrust into interviews between attorney and client and onto the witness stand in cases ranging from family law disputes to forcible rape to drunk driving to first-degree murder. In the interpreter's position, literally between the lawyer and his Spanish-speaking

This student involves the reader in a fascinating life story—in this case, an adventure that the student voluntarily pursued. Note that he conveys his rationale for pursuing each stage of the adventure, and doesn't just drag the reader along for a travelogue. This essay exemplifies the writing edict, "don't tell, show"; for example, rather than telling us that he has compassion, intellectual curiosity, uncommon drive, and that his journey resulted in the maturity he was seeking, he shows us all these points without ever mentioning them directly. This is an impressive presentation for an uncommon candidate.

Note how this student took a circuitous route to his goal, but without ever once losing sight of the object of his intentions.

Provide context for
accomplishments,
as this student did
above by citing the
pass rates for this
exam. Isn't this more
impressive than
simply writing that
he passed? The
context lets us know
this is an impressive
accomplishment.

#6:   "64,000 Miles to Law School"   (continued)

client, I saw the criminal lawyer's job as it really is: the frustrations, the heartache, the human element, the tactical considerations, the negotiations with opposing counsel, the grinding work and long, long hours, the hard-won victories and the saddening defeats.

In my first year as a court interpreter, I worked in conjunction with the U.C. Davis Extension college to develop a training course for court interpreter candidates in Spanish. I wrote the curriculum and the California Court Interpreters Association provided some of the materials. I gave the course solo for the first spring and fall semesters, and then team-taught the course with federal interpreters and colleagues Yolanda Portal and Carol Meredith. I am proud to say that six of the students from those courses went on to pass the state interpreter exam; they now make up an important segment of the court interpreter pool in the northern Sacramento Valley.

I then passed the Spanish interpreter examination for the U.S. federal courts. This exam has an overall pass rate of 3.9%; of the 11, 457 candidates who have taken the exam since its first offering, 442 have passed. (Official statistics provided by Ramon Castaneda, Staff Interpreter, U.S. District Court, Sacramento.) I began working as a freelancer in the Sacramento federal court. The work was high-pressure and fast-paced, and I learned much about the changing state of sentencing under the recently approved federal guidelines. I stood beside young men accused of trafficking hundreds of kilos of cocaine and interpreted their tear-choked pleas for mercy as judges handed down sentences of twenty and twenty-five years in the federal penitentiary.

For three years I divided my work between the Sacramento federal courts and the California state courts in a ten-city area stretching from Stockton to Shasta Lake and the Nevada border at Lake Tahoe. In my extensive travels, I saw how the law was applied differently around the state, and I became especially aware of the tremendous shortage of bilingual, bicultural attorneys to serve the needs of California's growing Hispanic population.

In legal interviews, despite my best efforts to convey the meaning of the words, I sensed a lack of understanding at a deeper level. I wanted to break in and explain to the attorney the realities of Mexico's legal system; I wanted to explain to the defendant how our judicial system was different from his or hers. But I could not. I saw more than a few Spanish-speaking defendants walk through the system as if in a daze. I grew frustrated and more convinced than ever that if I wanted to make a real difference, it would have to be as an advocate.

But there was one more step to be taken on the long road to law school before I would feel ready. After three years of saving and extensive planning, I set off in a 1971 Volkswagen bus with the goal of driving overland to the tip of South America and back up to the Arctic Sea in Alaska. Twenty countries, thirty months, forty border crossings, and sixty-four thousand miles later, I achieved that goal.

Along the way, I gave interviews on Brazilian television in Belo Horizonte, Goiania, and Santa Rosa. I made presentations to school groups of twenty to two hundred students

---

#6: "64,000 Miles to Law School"   *(continued)*

---

in Brazil and Canada. I interpreted at a judicial conference between Justice Edward Panelli of the California Supreme Court and members of the Supreme Court of Bolivia in Sucre, Bolivia. Throughout Latin America, I negotiated prices with mechanics, immigration officers, customs officials, policemen, soldiers, and on one occasion, with armed men wearing masks. I had to make my way through red tape and bureaucracy in Spanish, Portuguese, and French. I managed a twenty-five-thousand-dollar budget through countless ups and downs and returned the Volkswagen safely to California last September. In sum, I gathered the real-world experience I felt was necessary to be an effective lawyer. At present I am writing a book about my experiences, *A Passage to Patagonia: 64,000 Miles of Driving the Americas.*

> Note how the candidate makes this more than an adventure, by pointing out how this adventure relates to law.

I look forward to working as a lawyer in areas where I can employ my language skills and my court experience together with my law school education. I am particularly interested in the Jerome N. Frank Legal Services Organization's immigration project and the immigration level services course at Yale. My interest has a personal facet as well, for my wife is an immigrant from Uruguay. I am also very interested in your course "U.S.-Mexico relations after NAFTA." This will be an important field of law in the years ahead as U.S.-Mexico ties expand, and the boundaries of the law in many specialties will be stretched and redefined. I intend to be a part of that dynamic process.

I think others would say that I am a hard worker, a good organizer, an enthusiastic speaker, and an avid student. I believe I can make a positive contribution to the student body of the Yale Law School, and with a Yale Law School degree, I can make a positive contribution to the legal profession and to the welfare of immigrants in the years of change which lie ahead.

> Predict success for yourself as a graduate student, and later as a professional practicing in your chosen field. This is a highly effective close to a statement of purpose.

ESSAY #7: "Physics"

This type of personal
opening creates
reader interest, *but*
it is only effective
when wedded to a
no-nonsense exposi-
tion of academic
preparation. You can-
not "charm" your way
into an elite graduate
school. But you cer-
tainly can charm your
way into getting full
consideration—rather
than a perfunctory
review. This applicant
has it just about right.

Twenty-two years ago I entered this world riding shotgun in an Oldsmobile station wagon traveling 60 miles per hour down interstate 280 nearing Mountain View, California. Though my parents' accident, in all ways unexpected, I have always received the credit for this feat of being born in motion. My fast-paced style, passion for life, and love of adventure show in my relationships with family and friends, in the way I approach sports and hobbies, but even more tellingly in my studies. This spring, I will hold a bachelor of science in physics with a math minor, as well as a bachelor of arts in Spanish. To reach this point, I studied abroad in Spain, Japan, and Chile and completed four internships—one in mechanical engineering, one in material science, one in particle physics, and one in astrophysics. The following fall, I will begin another adventure; instead of climbing a mountain, running a marathon, or completing a bike tour, I will enter graduate school to earn a doctorate in physics. My eagerness, excitement, and determination for success, together with a supportive network of mentors and colleagues, provide a strong basis for achievement in graduate study—making a substantial contribution to my future and eventually to that of my preferred graduate institution, Stanford University. As my mother says: "That child was born driven."

My first significant encounter with experimental physics took place three years ago half a mile underground in Sudan Mine in northern Minnesota. Staring at the huge neutrino detector, I realized that my future lay in experimental physics. Since that experience, my goal in seeking an advanced degree has been to build foundations in the experimental, modeling and computational skills needed to understand, exploit and enhance knowledge of the universe. While I hope to make initial contributions to the field of physics through research at the graduate level, I plan on continuing my research as a professor. Earning my doctorate at Stanford University will provide me the experience necessary to be successful in my goals.

This past summer I worked under Dr. Michael Kelsey at the Stanford Linear Accelerator Center (SLAC) on building a computer simulation of the BaBar drift chamber. I compared the simulated time-to-distance calibration to that of the actual BaBar drift chamber to check for discrepancies. I also used the model to vary parameters to learn what effects variance might have on the system, and to look for possible improvements. This internship included the opportunity to attend graduate summer school talks, as well as take part in departmental meetings. The former provided me interesting information about dark matter, quantum computing, and current projects at CERN. The latter placed me in the situation of an expert describing BaBar drift chamber simulation to researchers at Stanford, CERN, and others members of the BaBar Collaboration around the world. This last internship at SLAC confirmed my desire to pursue graduate school at Stanford University. I had a very positive experience working under Michael Kelsey, and aspire to continue my education at Stanford in accelerator physics research.

Physics, math, and chemistry courses, complemented by undergraduate research experi-ences, have built my confidence in physics concepts, experimental design, as well as data

---

#7: "Physics" (continued)

---

analysis methods. Two years ago, I worked with University of Wisconsin - Eau Claire physics professor, Kim Pierson, researching both Large Aspect Ratio Trench Fill and Thin-Film Deposition Technique for Photovoltaic Cells. These projects required that I operate a bell jar vacuum system, a DC-Triode sputtering system, and a scanning electron microscope. The summer before, I collaborated with Dr. Paul Strykowski of the mechanical engineering department of the University of Minnesota where we researched Thrust Vector Control of a High Speed Jet, as well as Flow through a Micro Orifice. I assembled a wind tunnel, designed an experiment to increase the efficiency of an industrial operation, and engineered an apparatus to enclose a micro orifice plate. My diverse undergraduate research experiences, along with Stanford's rotation research assistantship, will help in relating one research area to the other, as well as solidify my choice of a research interest.

The act of being born did not end the interesting part of my upbringing. As the fifth of thirteen children, I made my distinction known. Clare might be a teacher, Amethyst a writer, and Gideon a fireman, but I would be the physicist. Home-schooled through eighth grade, I often did every problem in my math texts without being told. My father fostered my independent researcher bent, often encouraging me to, "Look it up." Immersed in our set of World Book Encyclopedias, I would frequently find myself waylaid in such interesting byways as Nobel Prize winner Georges Charpak's multiwire particle detector chamber en route to the exploration of blue whale migratory paths. Teaching too started at home, where I assumed responsibility for my younger siblings' lessons while my parents worked. In college I have tutored in math and physics, assisted a fourth grader in increasing his comprehension and reading ability in the Reading Partners Program, and currently teach accelerated math to talented elementary and secondary students through the Math for Young Achievers program. My leadership training took a significant leap ahead during my two years in NJROTC in high school, where I achieved the rank of Cadet Lieutenant and the position of Platoon Commander. In college I captained UW-Eau Claire's varsity women's cross-country team for two years, leading my team to nationals for the first time in seven years. My experiences as an independent researcher, leader, and team player have prepared me to be a valuable and conscientious member of a research team.

Clieve Davis once said, "This is work, but it is awakening to what was to become a life's passion." This statement rings true to me, for while I know I will have to work hard to stay ahead, the physics field is one that inspires me, and one I truly have a passion for. My memberships in the American Physics Society and the Sigma Pi Sigma Honor Society reflect my certainty and deepening interest in physics. As I continue on this path, I aim to advance and enrich the spectrum of scientific tools and physical models for predicting and understanding our universe, and I hope it is a path that Stanford can help me on.

ESSAY #8: "The Real History"

Raina L. Croff   Personal Statement

This experiential opening grabs the reader, and leaves them thinking "What's going to happen next?"

This essay is extremely powerful, using personal and emotional information combined with an intellectual argument about the owner-ship of history and historical perspective. Showing this level of passion in an applica-tion essay is—quite frankly—risky. But this candidate pulls it off expertly. The candi-date takes a strong and critical stand, without making the reader feel criticized. Of course, without the academic prepara-tion recounted in this essay, it would not be nearly as effective.

It was February again and I could feel that familiar uneasiness returning to me. My fourth grade classmates' stares seemed to chain me to my seat with unbearable weight. I slumped in my chair, head lowered, eyes downcast staring at my open textbook. My nine-year-old body looked the physical portrayal of the effects of racism—degradation, self-consciousness, and embarrassment. My teacher's voice still rang in my mind, "Raina, would you like to read to the class the chapter on slavery?"

At the time, all I knew about my cultural background as an African American was what the textbooks had made sure I understood—my history in this country began as a slave. This was among the only roles in the history books in which I was shown a reflection of myself—an image painted by someone else, an outsider looking in. I too felt as an outsider when my fourth grade teacher picked me out because of my color, asking me to read for my race to the rest of the class. It was not what the textbooks told me about my African American heritage that had the greatest impact on me as a young person developing a worldview and a self-perspective. Rather, it was what the writers had strategically left out that stunted my knowledge, pride, and self-worth as a human being contributing to the achievements of the world.

African history before its transplanting, or "before its beginning again" in the New World, has been repeatedly and systematically written out of human history. This is one of the greatest oppressions affecting the African Diaspora. This failure to acknowledge and appreciate African contributions to human civilization creates a void in the self-development and self-perspective of the New World African individual. In turn, its ramifications ripple outward to contort how the rest of the world perceives us. As a developing African American thinker, I was unable to connect myself to a cultural context greater than what my education had spoon-fed me: redundant images of slave auctions and sardine-packed cargo trains of which the textbooks seemed to never tire. Since that fourth grade experience my parents have taught me that in order to learn anything about myself I must take my own initiatives. It is imperative that I choose my own sources and find accounts of my people's experiences written from their own minds. This is my passion—actively investigating sources of knowledge from which I can draw my own conclusions. The systematic suppression of African history in conventional education has only added fuel to my curiosity to learn about a history in which a reflection of myself emanates from the center. I want to share my passion and my research findings with others, especially reaching children at an early age so that they may have firm foundations on which to build knowledgeable minds and healthy self-esteems.

As a double major at Beloit College in anthropology and classical civilizations I have a strong background from which I can develop a successful future *doing* my passion— researching and teaching. I want to concentrate on the sociocultural traditions of West Africa, as well as studying her great achievements and contributions of antiquity. I want to research how traditional social patterns have been transplanted among the Diaspora in

#8: "The Real History"	*(continued)*

the New World, especially among African Americans. I want to investigate this through a historical-archaeological approach as well as from a modern perspective through cultural anthropology. In order to achieve this goal I must interact between a web of disciplines: African and African American studies; archaeology; and cultural anthropology. Ultimately my goal is to actively engage the public. I plan to do this through volunteer and professional training programs that focus primarily but not only on African Americans, targeting our youth and immersing them in the rediscovery of African history and contribution through education in archaeology.

My vision works from my mindset that African history is world history. It belongs to all of us as a part of our collective human history. I also believe in the educating of the peoples from the inside out—instilling a solid foundation of African knowledge in the black community and reaching out from there. My vision begins in the teaching of primarily African Americans with emphasis on the educating and hands-on involvement of our youth, but ultimately it is to equip them with the tools to be the educators of a wider, cross-cultural audience. A major part of my vision is in leading excavations, both in the New World and in Africa, where African Americans will have the opportunity to dig, learn, and hopefully develop a deeply seeded respect and passion for their long-neglected histories. In addition, I want to set up an internship program where African American students can be African archaeological research assistants, training them in excavation techniques and mentoring them in scholarly research methodology.

I want my brothers and sisters to experience the same excitement and inspiration that I feel through the empowerment of research and re-discovery of themselves and their history. I want them to share the feeling I had during a visit to Howard University when I laid my eyes on the bones of first-generation New World Africans whose remains had been salvaged from a black burial ground in New York. I was fascinated and moved to learn how they had kept their West African tradition alive even in their death through the details of their burial ritual. Archaeology is an eye-opening and mind-enriching avenue for the education of our youth. It is a field of ever-advancing scientific technology while simultaneously a science of human imagination through the employment of individual interpretation. After all, archaeology is the material evidence of human ritual. It is the byproduct of behavior, which is itself a manifestation of an ideology. This is what I want to re-discover and teach—African *ideas* that have been forgotten, mis-credited, or stealthily lost from the pages of history. It is time they were recognized and repatriated to and by their own people.

I have already made some progress toward my goal of becoming an Afrocentric archaeologist. As both a McNair Scholar and an Associated Colleges of the Midwest Minority Scholar, I designed an archaeological research project. This past summer I was the research assistant to archaeologist Dr. Robert Salzer. I spent 13 weeks at the internationally recognized southwest Wisconsin Gottschall rockshelter site doing intense excavations and conducting original research. As the assistant ceramics analyst at the site, my project was to research

---

#8: "The Real History" *(continued)*

Here is a very clean exposition of an outside research project. Notice the candidate mentions a lecture and publication that are going to happen in the future.

and record the style category and vertical distribution of each of the 2,000 pottery sherds unearthed over the past 14 years of excavations at this site. In addition to this, I had to format a computer program into which this data could be stored and re-opened as new sherds are uncovered over the following years. Ultimately, in addition to an in-depth research paper, I will speak about my project results at a professional archaeological conference in the spring. Also, my findings will culminate in a joint publication by me and my mentor in a professional journal—an article which will challenge the pre-established ceramics chronology for that region. This research and analyst assistantship and publication has equipped me with the archaeological training and exposure that I will need in order to be successful in my further studies in Old and New World African Archaeology—a rare opportunity for an undergraduate.

Here, again, the candidate provides an excellent example of recounting activities that will take place between this application and the date of matriculation.

In addition to this experience, by the time this essay is received, I will be in Senegal, West Africa, studying anthropology at the Universite de Cheikh Anta Diop—the father of and greatest mind of his time in Afrocentric anthropology. Finally, I will be doing what I am passionate about—experiencing firsthand West African culture. This trip will be the physical reconnection for which I have been mentally preparing myself. I see this experience as the launch pad toward a successful future as a student in the Ph.D. program in African studies at Temple University.

I am the first person on both sides of my family to attend college, let alone to continue my education into the graduate level. I have made it this far, but if I am to make my goals into achievements, I must find my future at Temple University. I see myself as a dedicated, serious, and passionate student and leader, and I am confident that I possess the drive and self-discipline to successfully complete my doctoral study at Temple University. I strongly feel I have found my *nia*, or purpose, and now I must take the next step toward making my vision a reality. I have researched African studies and anthropology programs at Temple University and am excited to find that they align perfectly with what I want to study and teach others. I am enthusiastic about my field of study and anticipate the day when I will be teaching. In my study of Professor Molefi Kete Asante's book *Afrocentricity,* in speaking of his writing and the transformation of one's worldview through Afrocentricity he states, "Formless becomes form; black spaces are filled with truth . . . a new perspective, a new approach, a new consciousness invades our behavior" (pg. 6). I think of my own vision taking form, becoming reality. I will know the reward of the pursuit of my goal when I will see a

Outstanding finish!

young person sitting tall, head raised, and voice loud and confident as I ask her to read to the rest of the class about her ancestors and the mighty West African kingdom of Cayor.

ESSAY #9: "Chemistry into Law"

Personal Statement for Law School

I waited patiently by the bench in what all Harvey Mudd chemistry majors call the "Super Lab," staring for what seemed to be hours at a small flask bubbling with something that looked like a cross between Pepto-Bismol and whipped cream. I was waiting for the color to turn just the right shade of blue before I could go home for a late dinner, but it was obvious that this solution was as far from blue as baseball is from rugby. I realized then that Super Lab was not so Super, and neither was a career as a chemist.

Every summer since high school, I worked at Lawrence Livermore Laboratory as a research assistant. One of my major projects involved working on a team to develop probes for the detection of radioactive substances. When I turned in my final report, a computer program that would give the same results in five minutes as four people would in a week, my pride turned into disappointment when my supervisor took credit for all of my hard work. Unbeknownst to me, somewhere in tiny print in the contract I signed as an employee, it said something to the effect that as an employee I would relinquish all rights to everything that I developed at Lawrence Livermore National Laboratory. I felt that it was unfair for a company to claim such rights to its employees' innovations and wished to learn more about the issues that surround intellectual property.

I was introduced to the field of intellectual property law in industrial chemistry, taught by Professor Gerald Van Hecke. For my final report, I researched the development of the Gore-Tex fiber by procuring its patent from an online patent service. At that time, I was considering a career in the management sector of the chemical industry because I wanted to be able to use my knowledge of applied chemistry while at the same time work with people. However, once I was introduced to industrial chemistry law, I realized that a career in law would not only incorporate all of my skills but would give me more breadth than management in a chemical company. Whereas management would limit me to a particular industry, IP law would expose me to a number of industries. IP law would also not confine me to a particular strategy in dealing with problems but force me to develop different strategies based on the industry and the problem that I am dealing with. Law school suddenly became a very attractive career path to me, especially because it would allow me to use my education creatively to help protect the product of peoples' ideas.

Although I am an applied chemistry major, what I have learned as a undergraduate can be applied in many ways to law. Because I have a strong technical background, I have been trained extensively in solving problems both alone and in teams. Although the problems themselves have been technical, the analytical skills that I have acquired in solving such problems can be applied to the world of law. Harvey Mudd's unique engineering clinic program allowed me to work on a team of five students to develop a project plan for General Electric Nuclear Energy to bring the concentration of toxic organic compounds in their waste system down to environmentally safe levels. I have also worked on student teams to solve problems for Habitat for Humanity, and during my summer internships to solve

---

This is an outstanding and humorous opening paragraph, bringing the reader right into the story. An opening like this makes a promise: "I promise not to be boring, no matter how many essays you've read today and how tired you may be of brilliant, accomplished candidates."

The second paragraph traces the origin of the candidate's interest in law. This is always a good topic to cover in an essay.

Always name your advisers.

This student provides a rationale for her transition from studying chemistry as an undergraduate to studying law as a graduate student. She follows two tracks to explain the transition: first, explicating her personal transformation from being interested in chemistry to being interested

➔

#9:   "Chemistry into Law"   *(continued)*

in law, and second, exploring how her chemistry education could be useful in a legal career. Finally, note how she reveals herself as an interesting and independently willed person by recounting her experiences in debate and foreign study. To really grasp this essay, it helps to know that Harvey Mudd is one of the most elite and difficult engineering colleges in the United States. This student can afford to poke a little fun at herself because she has succeeded in a program renowned for its intellectual rigor.

Once you prove you can do the work, *then* you can address the issue of whether you are a nice or interesting person.

problems for the government. Because I am an applicant from a nontraditional background, I can provide a different perspective to problems encountered in law, and can even introduce vastly different but equally effective approaches to solving these problems.

My technical background is not the only factor that sets me apart from the traditional law school applicant. Because Harvey Mudd balances its technical program with an equally strong emphasis in the humanities, I am not only leaving Mudd with a great education in chemistry but I am leaving Mudd as a technically educated student who is skilled in writing and communication. In addition to possessing a liberal arts background that is unequaled by most technical applicants to law school, I also possess a background that is unique even for a Harvey Mudder. The typical Harvey Mudd student studies at Mudd for four years, then pursues graduate school in a science or engineering field, and then works in either industry or academia. Unlike the typical Mudd student, I have managed not only to perform well academically, but to take advantage of nonacademic opportunities in order to better balance my life. My experience as the resident assistant of my dorm has given me tools that are necessary to a lawyer such as time management, interpersonal and conflict resolution skills, as well as the ability to effectively deal with crisis situations. Having to juggle my responsibilities as a resident assistant, a student, and an athlete have increased my organizational skills by orders of magnitude. As freshman and sophomore class president, and team leader of an engineering project, I learned how to be more assertive and gained valuable leadership skills in the process. In addition, my membership in the National Forensics League and participation in Lincoln-Douglas debates have provided me with the skills of impromptu speech, oral communication, and the art of persuasion using sound facts as the basis for arguments.

I finally managed to completely break the mold of the typical Harvey Mudd student by attempting to study abroad for one semester. This was the greatest challenge of my undergraduate career because not many science and engineering majors, let alone Harvey Mudd students, leave to study at foreign institutions. Many attribute this to the specificity of the science curriculum and the resulting difficulty in finding compatible curricula at foreign institutions. After making use of all the resources possible, I realized that although it is indeed an arduous task to find a university abroad that matches our curriculum to a tee, it is not impossible to do so. After one year of persuading some reluctant administrators to make it easier for a Harvey Mudd student to leave for one semester, I found myself at the University of New South Wales in Australia where I had some of the most valuable experiences in my life. I returned much more independent, and especially aware of the world around me. Upon my return, and due in part to my own example, I discovered that the school had proposed many changes to allow more flexibility in the students' education so that studying abroad would be possible for others who follow me.

I once had the misperception that those who are educated in disciplines such as political science, public policy, or pre-law are more likely to be prepared for a graduate education in

---

#9: "Chemistry into Law"   *(continued)*

law than most other students. Now I believe that a student coming from a more nontraditional background can contribute in many ways to society as a lawyer. In a world where technology is the dominant means of progress and is advancing at such a breakneck pace, it can be a great advantage to society to have knowledgeable people working with laws concerning technology. I not only believe that I am qualified to perform this service to society as a lawyer, but I am convinced that [school withheld] possesses the quality of education and diversity in student body that can best help me fulfill these goals.

This is a nice summation of her entire argument.

ESSAY #10:   "Goodbye, CFO"

Personal Statement

As the firm's attorneys escorted the former chief financial officer from the building, his files confiscated and his office sealed and locked by a locksmith, I realized more than ever that teamwork and cooperation are essential management skills. The CFO had a vision and an action plan for the future of the company, but his methodologies led to his own downfall, damage to the shareholders, and disruption in every aspect of the organization. As he walked out the door, I resolved to go to graduate school at the University of Texas-Austin (U.T.) and pursue the M.B.A.

My twenty-one months at Cascade Capital Companies (CCC) have been a true education in real world business issues. Due to my abilities and my desire to excel on behalf of my employer, I was promoted three times in nineteen months *at the same time as the company was downsizing rapidly.*

I was originally hired as an analyst for a subsidiary broker/ dealer, conducting due diligence reviews on investment products ranging from REITs to capital leasing, real estate, and mortgage-related limited partnerships. I also managed the firm's database operations, prepared budgeting and variance reports, and monitored the securities and insurance licenses for 23 representatives in three branches.

Then, as part of a reorganization, 24 people were laid off and I was promoted into management of the parent company. I was told they gave me the position because I could "talk the lingo, crunch the numbers, and work the hours." I certainly did work long hours, but it was mostly because I really liked my job and the work needed to be done. In my new position, I was in charge of three professionals, all of whom were older and more experienced than I, but I had developed a closer understanding of the mission of the department and the priorities of senior management. I managed relations with approximately 400 broker/dealers and a total of approximately 5000 sales representatives available to sell our products.

I tracked sales and commissions and managed marketing projects through a computer database I reorganized and managed myself. I created sales incentives for the representatives, designed and desktop published promotional materials, and prepared the quarterly reports on the seven REITs we were offering. I created a useful subset of the total universe of reps by calling all 400 broker/ dealers and getting them to identify their top players. This allowed us to build closer relations with the most active and promising reps.

My performance in this position gained the attention of senior management, and the SVP tapped me to assist him and the product manager in developing two new products. As the rest of the company was suffering another layoff and plummeting asset values and gross revenues, we designed a corporate sale-leaseback fund that generated $13 million from retail investors by taking advantage of the LBO climate. Then we decided to develop the company's first product targeting institutional investors, a secondary offering of Cascade Capital's Trust 6, in the process of which I prepared all the analysis upon which we structured the offering and participated in the proxy solicitation process. Then, I called up pension fund consultants

---

Can't you just see the CFO being led off in handcuffs? This opening is a grabber!

Business schools like to see solid quantitative skills, a series of rapid promotions, and a high income for your age. This business school candidate does an outstanding job of introducing you to his "ten-year career compressed into less than two years." This essay strongly suggests that the author is an unusually competent manager, able to generate a high performance for himself and able to engender that performance in others. He explains the intent behind his actions and is good at telling a business story. Any business school would be happy to recruit this *wunderkind.*

These paragraphs show both smart work and hard work.

#10: "Goodbye, CFO"   (continued)

and sold them on the product, creating relationships with 150 reps and consultants. (This was a particularly strong accomplishment in light of the performance of real estate–backed investments at this time.) I also wrote all the presentations for the pension plans. With this new product we raised $12 million in commitments in six weeks of intense activity.

Then, in a reorganization of the marketing department and a re-focus of the company's strategic direction, I avoided another layoff and was promoted to the position of associate of a CCC subsidiary, Cascade Capital Institutional Advisers (CCIA), working directly with Donald Kugel, president of both CCIA and CCC. I monitor our total portfolio, prepare in-depth analysis of our products, design quarterly updates, prepare proposals, and correspond with real estate consultants and with institutional investors directly.

As I was climbing this corporate ladder, a ten-year career compressed into less than two years (I am by far the youngest person in my company), at every step of the way I was promoted because I identified with management's objectives and because I kept delivery and performance well in excess of their desires. This has been at times difficult, as the company is run by five highly talented individuals (four now) who do not often agree on much. Teamwork and cooperation were words used only in the marketing literature.

In fact, there was a time when senior management seemed to be in a logjam, and every partner seemed determined to advance a separate agenda. We in middle management were actually being choked off from vital information to do our jobs. To help facilitate communication between departments, I founded a twice-monthly, informal gathering of departmental representatives to discuss issues and problems. This quickly became known as the "Breakfast Club," and it has been instrumental in creating a friendly and cooperative working environment in which information can be shared openly and constructively. I can now pick up my phone and call any middle manager in the company directly to learn what I need to know. Middle management in the company is actually much more effective as a business than the top brass.

> You have to show initiative. It's not enough just to be good at your job.

In spite of his personal brilliance, the CFO went out the door for failing to see any common purpose with the rest of management. When I saw Dean Witt's message in the U.T. catalog, "We strive to create an academic community of student and faculty working toward the achievement of a common goal—the attainment of excellence," I knew I was headed in the right direction. The combination of advanced technical instruction and a real teamwork philosophy has become a central criterion in my evaluation of M.B.A. programs.

I am drawn to U.T. for several reasons: (1) I am a Texan, and the opportunity to pursue my graduate education in Texas is preferred, (2) I intend to start a real estate–related company in Texas, and the personal connections available to me as a U.T. graduate would be invaluable, (3) my "bottom line" nature is drawn to the combination of low cost and high value available at the University of Texas at Austin's Graduate School of Business, and the faculty is one of the most respected in the nation (I've done my homework), (4) my weakness is one of

> This is an example of reductionism. Remember, (1) it's efficient, (2) it's easy to read, and (3) it makes for an easy transition from outline to essay.

#10:   "Goodbye, CFO" *(continued)*

---

your greatest strengths: accounting, and (5) I believe the economy of Texas is headed for the stratosphere, and I want to be there for it.

Ever since I was 13 years old and working on a construction site for my father's commercial/residential development company, I have wanted to launch a real estate–related company. My first job was "debris remover." The next summer, the foreman gave me my first promotion: he gave me his old tool belt complete with a hammer and a measuring tape! Ever since that time I have pursued excellence in real estate–related areas (see resume). My experience in mortgage brokerage, real estate brokerage, real estate law, development and syndication has provided me with a broad background. I am eager for the University of Texas at Austin's Graduate School of Business to round out my business education so that I can continue to pursue my goals. I hope to be the kind of graduate who will be a credit to U.T. throughout his career.

Thank you for your attention, and I look forward to meeting you personally.

ESSAY #11: "Sports, Presidents, and Public Relations"

The Question: "What are the reasons you wish to pursue the graduate program and how does it relate to your career goals?"

Roger Belton, SS# 148-16-3129
Applicant—Master of Arts in Strategic Public Relations
University of Southern California

The Catalyst   A burst blood vessel in the brain of my former university president provided the tragic high and low point in my young public relations career.

It began with a jarring call at six A.M. on a Sunday morning. The president of George Fox University—where I serve as assistant director of public information—had suffered a life-threatening stroke caused by a brain tumor. I was called in to deal with the news media. I served as the university spokesperson, doing all media interviews, writing press releases, and recording a daily voicemail line with health updates. The situation was made even more hectic by the fact that two of my university relations colleagues were out of the office.

I found myself hurting for our president and his family but caught up in the action. Even when the director of public information returned, I remained as the media spokesperson. A year later, cancer claimed the life of our president, and I was asked to summarize the personality of this remarkable man in our alumni newspaper. (See writing sample.)

That was one experience which has led me to apply to University of Southern California for further training in public relations.

Beyond Age 30   Although I am assistant director of public information, much of my time is consumed by my work as sports information director for George Fox's athletic program.

Not long ago, a co-worker asked me, "Are you going to be a sports information director when you're 65?"

My instinctive reply surprised even myself: "I don't plan to be one when I'm 30."

Since I'm 28 today, I've got two years to engineer a career change.

I feel I've gone about as far as I can in small-college sports information. Since graduation—when I moved from a 20-hour-a-week student position to full-time employee—I've elevated the coverage of nonrevenue sports by improving their publications and press releases.

When I began, media guides were produced only for men's basketball. Now all 13 varsity sports have a media guide. Many guides have received national honors. My women's basketball guide is perhaps my favorite. Created from scratch, it has been honored as the second best in the nation among colleges at our level of athletic competition. (I've enclosed the most recent copy.)

Here's another arresting opening line, grabbing the reader right from the opening clause.

This essay is a little chatty, but it does an outstanding job of conveying the enthusiasm and decency of this remarkable man. One gets the impression that if life served him a pile of lemons, he wouldn't start a lemonade stand, he'd start a franchise operation. Also, he has done a good job of adopting the writing tips espoused by this book, such as referring to supporting documentation (as in "See writing sample"). His essay traces the history of his decision to pursue graduate education and details his preparations to succeed. This is a natural theme on which to organize any essay.

#11: "Sports, Presidents, and Public Relations"   *(continued)*

Feel free to spice up
your essay with direct
quotes that sup-
port your points or
advance your narra-
tive, as demonstrated
in the last paragraphs
of the prior page.

With the assistance of student assistants, I produce weekly news releases for each sport. They often are used verbatim by local newspapers. While speaking about athletic media relations at a recent conference, a sports reporter from a Portland radio station declared George Fox the "King of News Releases."

At George Fox we strive to stand above the crowd. While most schools at our level photocopy their basketball programs, my office puts together a 12-page program that generates about $7,000 in advertising revenue.

This year, I supervise a staff of up to seven students who assist me in stat keeping, ticket selling, ad selling, news release writing and office work. I also recruit and manage about a dozen volunteers to staff games during basketball season.

I enjoy my job. I like working with my student assistants and seeing them mature as writers and persons. It's fun to be part of the "team" with coaches and student-athletes. I still find my palms sweaty in the ninth inning of a tight baseball game, but the amount of coverage available to small colleges is frustratingly small. So much work for so little return.

Stepping Outside the Sports Arena

Although I often find myself consumed with the promotion of my athletic department, I don't want to be pigeonholed as a sports fanatic.

After earning a number of state awards as a high school trumpet player, I received a music scholarship at George Fox. I continue to play occasionally at weddings and church services and teach lessons.

The death of a college roommate from leukemia led me to volunteer at a camp for kids with cancer run by the American Cancer Society. For the past six summers, I've been known as the bugle-blowing counselor "Mr. Toad."

My Destination

I still tell people I don't know what I want to be when I grow up, but I'd like it to be in the public relations field.

I believe I have the talent for it.

I was recently honored with the "Rising Star" award in the field of communications by the Council for Advancement and Support of Education (CASE) District VIII. It's an award given to professionals in their first five years in the field. The district is made up of development, alumni and public relations professionals at educational institutions in five states and six Canadian provinces. George Fox University — with 2,300 students — is one of the smallest colleges in CASE.

I take an active role in George Fox's weekly university relations meetings where we discuss potential news stories and a wide variety of PR issues. Topics have ranged from: "How can we improve internal communication on our campus intranet system?" to "What do we put in our alumni newspaper when one of our newly admitted freshmen has been arrested for a double homicide?"

#11: "Sports, Presidents, and Public Relations" *(continued)*

I get a thrill out of trying to capture the interest of the news media with a story tip and have achieved local and national success. *U.S. News & World Report* magazine used one of my submissions about a unique George Fox campus tradition in its annual college ranking guide.

Although I don't believe I want to be a full-time writer, I consider writing one of my strengths. My story about a record-setting female pole vaulter this summer was used by the National Association of Intercollegiate Athletics (NAIA) in the inaugural edition of its Internet magazine *NAIA News*. (See writing sample.) Another feature about a women's basketball senior citizen fan club received a national award from the College Sports Information Directors Association.

An Itch to Explore   After 11 years as a student and administrator at George Fox, I feel very comfortable here, but I want to broaden my horizons. It's an itch. Perhaps I picked it up from my father, who packed my family up when I was 12 and took us to live in Brazil for a year. Twenty countries later, I'm still hungry to explore. In the last three summers, I've had coffee at the home of a Bosnian war widow; seen Belfast, Northern Ireland, during Protestant marching season; and crossed from Hong Kong to China with a relief worker to see her work on an island inhabited by lepers. Travel has opened my eyes to a world larger than a basketball game.

> After you've established intellectual capacity, it's okay to throw in a human-interest section.

I enjoy the academic environment. Going back to school excites me. Education always has been a part of my life. My parents are both teachers. Since I have an interest in possibly following in their footsteps later in life, I would appreciate being considered for a teaching assistantship. (See separate application packet.) I believe I would be an excellent candidate since I have spent the last seven years editing sports and general news releases written by college students.

Why USC?   I believe USC would provide me with excellent training in my profession. After finding its high ranking in the *Gourman Report,* I visited the school's Web site for more information. The idea of receiving hands-on training from L.A.'s PR professionals is extremely attractive. I contacted Alan MacDonald, who earned his master's degree in PR from USC, and current journalism graduate student Jennifer Prosser, to ask about their experiences. Both gave the school and the professors high marks.

> The more persuasive your answer to "Why here?" the more likely you'll be admitted. Students who do not customize their essays waste an opportunity to impress admissions decision makers.

Although I could see myself returning to a public relations position at George Fox, I'm intrigued by the variety of options that would be available to me after graduation. Alan MacDonald told me that USC stood for University of Social Connections. In addition to my current experience, a degree from USC would give me additional credibility. During my January visit to USC, I met with Tim Burgess and was impressed that the Annenberg School of Communications had its own career advising office.

#11:   "Sports, Presidents, and Public Relations"   *(continued)*

I have done quite a bit of research on master's degrees in communications, but USC's public relations program was the first and only one to excite me. I am applying to no other program.

I do not go into this application process halfheartedly. This has been my passionate intention for over a year. In preparation for the cost of full-time graduate school, I became ·frugal. I decided to continue driving my 12-year-old car, and I moved out of a house where I rented alone to save costs in a shared duplex with four roommates.

I feel that I am ready to perform in your program—mentally, financially, academically—and that I have honed the skills necessary to excel. I would like the opportunity to fulfill my capacity at USC.

Thank you for considering my application.

Preparing yourself fiscally for graduate school is just as important as preparing yourself intellectually. When you've made prudent financial preparations, let readers know.

ESSAY #12: "Personally Related to God"

Statement of Purpose for Architectural School

Leon Battista Alberti is my great, great, great . . . great uncle on my mother's side. His name is neatly inscribed in a genealogy contained in one of our family Bibles. It was only after I became interested in architecture that I discovered who my relative was, although it is common knowledge that everyone on this side of my family can draw or paint, as if by genetic decree.

I grew up in a lower-middle-class neighborhood in Detroit, one of three girls. My father was a blue-collar worker who instilled in me a strong work ethic and a respect for all creations of manual labor. He taught me how to take things apart, fix them, and put them back together again. He taught me to be proud of any job well done, no matter how trivial or how complex. He taught me to be honest.

My sister is developmentally delayed. This fact sensitized me at an early age about learning to live with disabilities. My mother went back to school in her thirties to become a deaf-education teacher. So I grew up with an unusually strong feeling of social responsibility, of obligation to help others. Instead of being angry about my sister, we responded by "going to work."

I took my interest in drawing, painting, and sculpting and decided to pursue a career in occupational therapy. Occupational therapy helps teach basic living skills to the mentally ill, developmentally disabled, and those who have suffered a stroke, trauma, or other serious central nervous system debilitation. My specialty was occupational therapy using art as a treatment modality. I especially preferred three-dimensional media, such as ceramics, woodworking, handicrafts and horticulture. I was also taught to use skilled observation techniques in order to develop an activity analysis, or a breakdown of the minute, specific steps needed to successfully complete a basic task.

As an occupational therapist, I also designed and fabricated adaptive equipment for use by patients. I learned how to manipulate and structure a patient's immediate environment in order to promote his or her highest level of independence and functioning. I designed treatment aids, detachable wheelchair fixtures, and for one client I designed kitchen modifications to allow her to return to her role as a homemaker in spite of her disability from muscular dystrophy (I obtained funding for the work, as well). I have often been the staff member called upon to repair the furniture, fix the ping-pong table, fine-tune the equipment, wire the new stereo. . . .

All of this experience, I feel, will be directly applied in my future career as an architect with a specialty in universal design.

In my experiences as an occupational therapist, I was often struck at how poorly designed clinic and treatment areas were for the patients they were supposed to serve. In Michigan I was a consultant to Easter Seals on a group project to evaluate buildings for barrier-free design. For the same organization, I contributed to a project to map all the wheelchair-accessible buildings in Kalamazoo, Michigan.

This opening paragraph is powerful and auspicious, since Leon Battista Alberti is the Leonardo da Vinci of architecture.

This essay is wonderfully honest and forthcoming, and for several reasons it is a nearly perfect application essay. The applicant puts a "spin" on her essay, featuring her intent to pursue a specialized career and demonstrating how her rather unusual background is uniquely suited to achieving excellence in that career. Finally, her essay ties together the rest of her application in a compelling manner. The candidate has clearly thought about her goals and plotted a serious path.

#12:   "Personally Related to God"   *(continued)*

At one program where I served, the physical surroundings were so austere that I launched a project to paint children's hospital corridors, wards, and gymnasium in colorful wall graphics. At another program, a psychiatric facility, a "decorator" with good intentions had painted the ward in electric orange complete with vinyl floors to match. The colors proved overly stimulating and disorienting for the sicker patients, and the nurses and I succeeded in lobbying the director for a more appropriate and calming color scheme. I have seen nurses scramble to fill dozens of medication trays with 100 percent accuracy, while spinning and turning and reaching around in a dispensing room that is only 4' by 6' in dimension. I have seen shower rooms too small to accommodate the patient and the nurse. I have seen grab bars installed at useless angles and levels, door knobs that an arthritic hand cannot turn, chairs for patients that tip over easily or are hard to get out of, counters and corridors that are invisible to the visually impaired (they lack a simple border line; how easy it would have been to do it correctly). So I have observed the pleasures that simple, inexpensive design can bring to patient populations and staff, and the heavy-handed errors that are all too commonly committed by designers who have no real awareness of the hospital environment.

I have come to believe that humanity will be better served if healthcare facilities are renovated or built by individuals who have some sensitivity to the people actually working in them and some knowledge of patients' specialized needs. I am very interested in universal design of medical and treatment facilities, design of hospice environments, and residential design for the differently abled and for the rapidly increasing geriatric population. I view these as exciting areas for change and growth in modern architecture. The design training that I would receive at Berkeley, combined with my knowledge of the needs of these population groups, would allow me to bring a unique perspective to my career as a practicing architect.

To facilitate a smooth entry to your program, I have been taking the prerequisite math classes (which will be completed by July). I have a straight "A" average in these classes, and I find myself very eager to return to full-time studies. I have selected Berkeley as my program of choice because of its reputation for commitment to handicapped access, universal design, and related areas of modern architecture and design. I am applying to no other program.

This applicant, like the last one, is applying to only one school. Although this is always risky, any time your reasoning for doing so is due to a complete confluence of your interests and the offerings of that particular program, mentioning that fact can only strengthen your candidacy.

ESSAY #13: "Arabism and Islam"

Statement of Purpose

In 1933 the Syrian-Egyptian scholar Muhammad Rashid Rida, emphasizing the importance of Muslim Arabs' loyalty to the greater Islamic community, wrote that "each man must be a member of a body greater than his own nation." Sixty years later, in a very different context, these words are relevant to my own life. They capture the essence of my principal academic interest, the hierarchy of allegiance to nation and religion in twentieth-century Egypt. In addition, Rashid Rida's words convey the basis of my attraction to a career centering upon the Middle East: my desire to reach beyond my own society to help build closer ties between the United States and the Arab world.

I am applying to UCLA's Islamic studies program to prepare for a career in U.S.–Mideast relations, focusing on Egypt. UCLA's interdisciplinary training, with its emphasis on foreign language, is ideal preparation for such a career. Although I intend to seek a Ph.D. in modern Middle Eastern history, I first would like to complete a master's in Islamic studies. I view the MA program as an opportunity to fill in gaps in my knowledge of Middle Eastern history (economic history, for example), to strengthen my Arabic and French skills, and to focus my research interest before pursuing a Ph.D. Because of my special interest in early twentieth-century Egypt, the opportunity to work with Professor Marsot is a primary factor drawing me to UCLA.

Living in rural Turkey as an AFS student during high school first exposed me to the Middle East and Islam. I entered college planning to concentrate in Middle East history, but, as my transcript suggests, Yale offered few courses in this area. Thus in courses that on the surface seemed to have little to do with the region, I found every possible Middle East angle. For example, for a seminar on British history, I contrasted the British colonial administrations in Egypt and the Sudan; for a course on medieval Europe, I wrote about the characterizations of Arabs in twelfth-century German literature. Reading in my spare time also helped me develop a solid background. Once, to my friends' bewilderment, I took Yvonne Haddad's *Contemporary Islam and the Challenge of History* on a vacation in Florida. A summer internship in the Middle East Studies Division of the Brookings Institution strengthened my knowledge of contemporary Middle East politics. At Brookings, I researched the role of nonviolent resistance in the early months of the *intifada* and prepared a bibliography on the history of the Sudanese civil war. Finally, my undergraduate training included three years of Modern Standard Arabic at Yale and a summer at the Arabic Language Unit of the American University in Cairo.

My interest in the early twentieth-century Islamic reform movement in Egypt began with my senior thesis on Muhammad Rashid Rida. Living in Turkey and Egypt interested me in relations between Arabs and Turks, and the larger issue of the role of nationalism in Islam. For my thesis, I translated Rashid Rida's articles on Arabs and Turks from 1898 to 1916 to examine his views on the connection between Arab political strength and Islamic reform before the collapse of the Ottoman Empire. In contrast to most historical interpretations of

---

This post-Fulbright essay is from an accomplished scholar well into her specialty. Notice how the impact is at once both personal, in the sense of being straightforwardly egocentric, and abstract, in the sense of focusing on the realm of ideas. The writer passes what business school students call "The Airport Test," as in "Is this someone I'd want to spend eight hours stuck in an airport with?" If you are interested in Arabism and Islam, you'd find her company most interesting indeed.

Note how the candidate points out her early focus on Middle Eastern history even though her college didn't have many courses in this topic.

#13: "Arabism and Islam" *(continued)*

Always mention your language skills when they are pertinent to your graduate subject. Don't overstate them; rate them on the scale of native speaker, fluent, proficient, or basic; or use the U.S. State Department scale (I, II, III, IV, V).

Rashid Rida, which categorize him either as a pan-Islamist or the first Arab nationalist, I found that Rashid Rida advocated both Muslim unity and Arab supremacy among Muslims as keys to reforming Islam. He emphasized one or the other according to external political factors. I concluded that Rashid Rida's significance lay in his attempt to resolve what many of his contemporaries, as well as subsequent Egyptian intellectuals, held to be a theoretical conflict between Arabism and Islam.

My experience as a Fulbright scholar in Cairo last academic year was a turning point in my study of the Middle East. First, I improved my Arabic skills dramatically in an intensive program. I am now quite comfortable conducting research in Arabic and am proficient in the Egyptian dialect.

Furthermore, I continued my research on Rashid Rida at the Women's College of al-Azhar University. My project entailed translating a series of Rashid Rida's articles on Arabs and Turks written just before and during World War I to determine how the imminent dissolution of the Ottoman Empire influenced his view of the political role of Arabs in the *umma* and led to his calls for an Arab caliph.

As I witnessed the growing influence of the Muslim Brotherhood in Egypt, however, I shifted the focus on my project to investigate how Rashid Rida's ideas about Islamic reform have influenced the contemporary Egyptian Brotherhood's ideology. My affiliation with al-Azhar was essential to this research. As the only Western woman at the university, I had an unusual opportunity to become well acquainted with a group of female students who belonged to the Brotherhood and the "Islamic Group." In discussions about my research, these young women echoed many of Rashid Rida's articles when they spoke of trying to resolve the "conflict" between their Muslim and Egyptian identities. They brought to mind Rashid Rida's calls for the Caliphate when they emphasized the Muslim world's need for a Muslim Arab leader to foster greater political and spiritual unity. These conversations, along with research on Hassan al-Banna and the Brotherhood in Egypt today, demonstrated to me that Rashid Rida's ideas are not, as some have charged, obsolete. Rather, I believe that the early twentieth-century Islamic reform movement offers an excellent basis from which to analyze Egypt's current Islamic movement. Researching the connections between Muhammad Rashid Rida and this movement will be the core of my graduate study.

Finally, the Fulbright helped to focus my professional goals. Living in Egypt convinced me that a more accurate American interpretation of the Islamic revival movement is central to the long-term success of American-Egyptian relations and spurred my interest in a career in diplomacy or development work focusing on Egypt. Though some Western analysts argue that the rise of "militant" Islam in the region, and the anti-Western sentiment that sometimes accompanies it, diminishes the possibility of good relations with the countries of the Middle East, I believe that the geopolitical importance of the region (especially Egypt) precludes severing any ties. Rather, Americans must explore ways to strengthen our relations with the Arabs, especially if Islamic governments come to power. Whether I pursue a career in

---

#13: "Arabism and Islam"   *(continued)*

---

development or diplomacy, I hope that Arabic will be an integral component of my day-to-day work. (See FLAS fellowship essay, enclosed.)

I recognize the challenges of a career in U.S.–Mideast relations. Discussions with my former professors and other experts, as well as my own experiences, have elucidated the potential limitations for women in this field. I have also weighed the personal implications of devoting my professional life to another part of the world, while there are compelling problems in this country. However, my belief in the need for better mutual understanding between the United States. and the countries of the Middle East assures me that I've made a worthwhile choice.

I look forward to graduate study at UCLA as an exciting, and essential, stage in my scholarly career. I'm eager to apply my academic preparation and enthusiasm in UCLA's program, and I'm certain that Rashid Rida's words about the importance of reaching beyond my own society will continue to guide me.

ESSAY #14: "Iterated Mappings"

Statement of Purpose—Ph.D., Mathematics

Like many essays that focus on science and laboratory research summaries, this essay is about mathematics and nothing else. It could be written by a wealthy urban socialite or a tattooed urchin with a mohawk. It either succeeds or fails based on the math within it.

Over the past few years, I have become interested in the dynamics of iterated mappings. As an independent research project, I have been investigating the dynamics of the quadratic map, $Z_{n+1} = Z_n^2 + C$, when it is applied to algebraic structures other than the complex field, which is used to generate the classic Mandelbrot and Julia sets. I began by exploring the three-dimensional sets that are generated when real-valued 2×2 symmetric matrices are used for Z and C. Later, I extended my investigation to include the four-dimensional sets produced by general real-valued 2×2 matrices, using a basis that is compatible with the matrix representation of complex numbers. To gain intuition into the dynamics of the quadratic map on these structures, I wrote several computer programs to generate slices of these sets and to calculate orbits for given values of Z and C. My original "Mandelbrot set" program starts Z_0 at 0 and lets C range over 2×2 matrix space, which is the same type of algorithm that is commonly used to generate the classic Mandelbrot set. The first programs defined an iterate to have escaped when its Euclidean distance from the origin was greater than or equal to an escape value (usually 2). This is the same escape condition that is used with classic Mandelbrot and Julia sets.

My research has already yielded several interesting results. It is well known that the complex plane is isometric to a two-dimensional slice of 2×2 matrix space. I found that lines in this slice that pass through the origin serve as lines of rotational symmetry in the matrix Mandelbrot set, and the matrix Julia sets are all symmetric about the origin. The images that I have generated have shown an incredible variety of structure depending on the slice viewed, and, in the case of the matrix Julia sets, the value of C. The boundary of the matrix Mandelbrot set is chaotic in some places and perfectly smooth in others. I have been able to calculate the precise shape of the boundary for some of the slices with smooth boundaries. Some of the slices of the matrix Mandelbrot set are perfect squares, circles, or sections of hyperbolic solids. Others are narrow bands that stretch as far as the edges of the circle defined by the escape value will allow. The presence of "arbitrarily bounded" slices such as the hyperbolic solids and the narrow bands reflects the fact that the matrix Mandelbrot set has fixed points whose Euclidean distance from the origin exceeds any escape value. Many of the matrix Julia sets also have arbitrarily bounded components.

The presence of arbitrarily bounded slices raises the question of how to determine whether a particular escape criterion is reasonable for a Mandelbrot or Julia set. The purpose of the escape criterion is to classify orbits as either bounded or unbounded. In the case of the classic sets, all escape conditions that contain the disk of radius 2 centered at the origin will classify all orbits in the same way. This is true because all cycles of the quadratic map on the complex field are contained inside this disk, and all orbits that leave this region tend toward infinity in such a way that each iterate has a greater Euclidean modulus than its predecessor. But for the quadratic mapping on matrix space, any escape condition which relies on a Euclidean metric will exclude some cycles. Based

#14: "Iterated Mappings"	*(continued)*

on the images I have seen and an analysis of the quadratic mapping on 2 × 2 matrices, I conjecture that an escape criterion based on a metric that is half hyperbolic and half Euclidean will provide a better test of boundedness for the matrix Julia and Mandelbrot sets. Although computer images seem to indicate that my candidate for an escape criterion will be effective, a proof of this demands that I have a better understanding of the dynamics of matrix Julia set orbits. I will also need to consider the mathematical implications of using an escape criterion based on a non-Euclidean metric.

For an analytic mapping on the complex field, all attracting cycles must attract a critical point of the map. Since the quadratic map has only one critical point, 0+0i, a quadratic map with a fixed value for C (corresponding to a specific Julia set) can have at most one attracting cycle, and if one exists it must attract 0. If there is no attracting cycle, then the orbit of 0 escapes to infinity. The Mandelbrot set therefore shows which values of C induce an attracting cycle and which ones do not. Classic Julia sets can be defined equivalently as the closure of the set of repelling periodic points.

I would like to establish whether each of these features of the complex quadratic map can be generalized to the matrix quadratic map. If there is at most one attracting orbit in a matrix Julia set, and if the orbit of 0 is necessarily in its basin of attraction, then an escape condition that respects the dynamics of the Julia sets will also respect the dynamics of the Mandelbrot set. In order to prove that the orbit of 0 behaves in this way, a means of identifying critical points and determining whether a cycle is attracting, repelling, or neutral is needed.

Following the approach used for the complex quadratic map, I have been able to prove the appropriate attracting and repelling cycle theorems using the modulus of the Fréchet derivative. Based on the orbit calculations that I have done, it seems that attracting cycles so defined do attract the orbit of 0. It also seems to be true that there is at most one attracting cycle. For functions of the real numbers, a proof that a critical point of the map must be in the basin of attraction of each attracting cycle can be obtained by using various characteristics of Schwarzian derivatives. This proof cannot be adapted to functions of complex numbers because of the presence of imaginary numbers. The proof in the complex case is a "deep result" that depends on Montel's theorem and the analyticity of the map. One way that I might be able to prove this result for the quadratic mapping on matrix space is to examine matrices that have an imaginary component separately, and use a Schwarzian derivative approach with the symmetric matrices. Another possible approach would involve using the specific dynamics of the quadratic mapping on matrix space to show that there is at most one attracting cycle and that it attracts 0. It is also possible that this conjecture may need to be modified before it is true.

It is possible to recast the quadratic map on 2 × 2 matrices as a Clifford algebra. Thinking about the dynamics of the map in relation to the algebraic structure of the system will allow me to generalize my results to higher-dimensional spaces which result from larger matrices

---

#14: "Iterated Mappings" (continued)

---

or from matrices with complex entries. I am also interested in exploring the connection between the dynamics of the matrix quadratic map and the quadratic map acting on the quaternions, which form the more famous four-dimensional Clifford algebra. One of the principal differences between these two algebras is the presence of zero divisors in the matrix case. I am interested in investigating the implications of this aspect of the algebra on the dynamics of maps on matrix space.

One of the best aspects of doing research is being able to share what I have learned with others. I also enjoy hearing about other people's research at seminars and research conferences. It is especially gratifying to read or hear about work that gives me new insight into my own projects, or to be able to share my results with others who are interested in the implications for their research. I plan to obtain a Ph.D. in mathematics and become a professor. My best professors use what they have learned through their research to make their classes more exciting and to communicate the relevance of important concepts to their students. They also use their knowledge of current research in their field to give students a sense of mathematical history and a sampling of interesting open problems. I look forward to learning more about a wide range of mathematical ideas in graduate school. I am pleased that I have been able to incorporate concepts from many different mathematical fields into my current research project, and I plan to use a similar approach in the future.

Only once the technical material is well established does this candidate turn to more personal topics.

ESSAY #15: "High Water"

When you grow up in a place where isolation is a way of life, just getting to town can be a challenge. Throughout my school years, my family lived on a gravel road with only three outlets to "civilization." One way was across a dry creek bed, another was over a small brook, and the last was a low-water bridge on the Meramec River. When we had a hard rain, each one flooded and we had no way to get to town at all. As a result, I missed many days of school over the years. In a rural area like ours, twenty miles from the nearest grocery store, blocked by three swollen waterways and nearly impassable roads, traveling to another country seems like an impossibility. Yet despite the odds facing a first-generation student with working-class parents, I have been able to surpass my small town boundaries in my struggle to build my own bridge to a better future, plank by plank.

In researching the works of Annie Ernaux, a French working-class woman who forged her own bridge to academia, I came across a phrase that sums up my experiences in education. She said that at the beginning of her academic career, she had believed that education was a land of equality, fraternity and liberty, but she soon found out that some girls were freer than others. Those of us who start out on the bottom just have to work a little harder to find that one way out. As a freshman in high school, I took the one foreign language offered by my high school, which just happened to be the language my mother had learned in high school and the one I most wanted to learn. I made the most of what I was offered, taking all four years of French and reading French novels lent to me by my teacher on the side. At the same time, I chose the most challenging courses offered in all subjects and became as involved as possible in the few activities available at our school. I earned a full scholarship to Truman State University as a result. That was my ticket out and I have never regretted my difficult departure.

Not only did my scholarship offer a bridge to Truman State, but it provided the means to cross the Atlantic, in the form of a stipend for study abroad. I had no difficulty deciding where to go. France had always been a magical place in my imagination. Throughout my studies in high school, I pictured myself in the lavender fields of Provence, on the beaches of the "Méditerranée," and under the Arc de Triomphe in Paris, without ever believing I would one day visit these places. Now I had the chance to make my fantasy a reality. The five weeks I spent in Provence and my week in Paris were real eye-openers for me. The culture was so different from anything I had experienced in Missouri that at times I wanted to catch the next plane back to the States. But when I translated for a group of fellow American students and our new French friends complimented me on my language skills, I felt like a vital link between people of two different cultures. I realized I could adapt to a foreign environment because this connection with people who were not as foreign to my experience as I had assumed eradicated my perception of "us" versus "them."

Back at Truman, I was able to connect the assorted planks that are my intellectual interests (linguistics, literature, international studies, and women's studies) in a cohesive pattern in the study of French and francophone culture. I consider myself lucky to have

This is the type of candidate that admissions professionals are looking for: someone who can transcend her environment and reach for a goal; someone who is primarily, if not overwhelmingly, motivated from within; and someone who will appreciate and capitalize on opportunity. This candidate is vastly preferable to one who may appear statistically similar (vis-à-vis grades and scores) but has been coached and prodded and supported and tutored her whole life.

By quoting historical figures, you can say things you might not dare to say directly yourself.

#15: "High Water" *(continued)*

Name your key
advisers.

studied under Dr. Betty McLane-Iles in courses such as Francophone Women Writers and Francophone Literature of Quebec. Besides encouraging my interest in francophonie and feminism, Dr. McLane-Iles has always challenged me to draw everything I can from each literary work I read or each experience I have with the language. Her assistance has been invaluable in broadening my perspective so greatly that I decided to strive for the Ph.D. in French literature with a focus on francophone women instead of my original goal of a teaching certificate for high school French. With the Ph.D., I will be able to integrate my diverse educational background in research as well as teaching. An entire school year of direct interaction with francophone culture will give me the firsthand knowledge that I will need as a professor to help students traverse the cultural chasm between the United States and the rest of the world.

ESSAY #16: "Nurse Bound for Medical School"

AMCAS Essay for Medical School

When I was an undergraduate at the University of California, Davis, I wanted to be a physician. Although I always excelled in the life sciences, I had to work 20 to 32 hours per week throughout my first years of college, and I graduated without honors status (B.S., human biology, a premedicine major I designed in collaboration with the faculty).

I was very dissatisfied with this performance, as I was sure I could have excelled had I had more time for my studies. I re-affirmed my commitment to healthcare as a career, and I studied nursing at the University of California, Los Angeles. There I applied myself and graduated *magna cum laude* (B.S., nursing).

I then pursued a nursing career with zeal, selecting a path that would allow me to stress medicine, autonomy, and decision making in my work. After serving a year on a medical-surgical floor, I accepted a position with the Kidney Transplant Unit (KTU) at the University of California, San Francisco, Medical Center (UCSF Medical Center). This position allowed me to gain in-depth knowledge of a specific patient population and gave me opportunities to advance my assessment skills. My nursing skill was acknowledged in formal and informal ways, including my nomination for the Sophie Robinson Award for excellence in nursing, and I served on many in-service and quality assurance committees.

Next I was selected for the position of physician extender for the Renal Transplant Service at UCSF Medical Center, where I was hired by the department of surgery to assist house staff in meeting patient needs. I attended twice daily rounds, followed up on radiographic, laboratory and consult reports, performed routine house staff procedures, and occasionally assisted in OR. This was a custom-designed nursing position, and I was allowed to define the role to the extent that I oriented and worked side-by-side with interns. I was also invited to serve as research assistant, collecting data on drug side-effects under direction of Juliet Melzer, M.D., UCSF Medical Center, on a project with the working title of "Investigational drug study on MALG (Minnesota Anti-Lymphocyte Globulin)."

After 18 months of this experience, which I enjoyed thoroughly, I decided to obtain critical care experience and began to apply for competitive positions in this area. I obtained an appointment to the Cornell University Medical Center at New York Hospital as a post-anesthesia care nurse. In this position I provided post-op care for cardiac, neurologic, pediatric, trauma, burn, and vascular patients. This was exciting work, with a diverse patient population. This is also when I decided once again to become a physician. Because of the following event, I realized that the intellectual challenges of nursing were no longer enough for me, and I made my decision to go on to medical school and become a physician.

I received a 42-year-old female with a newly placed peritoneal shunt. (She had had an 11-year history of ovarian cancer, and a chronic ascites problem requiring frequent paracentesis.) She awoke combative, and was quickly extubated by the anesthesiologist. Her recovery deteriorated, as she developed pulmonary edema, a temperature of 40 degrees centigrade, and a right-sided heart failure. I provided the critical direct nursing care to this patient for

This is an AMCAS essay for medical school. It is important to note that with an initial application to AMCAS schools, no letters of recommendation or supporting materials of any kind are allowed. This makes the admission essay extremely important. If schools are interested in the candidate, they will request additional materials, known as secondaries. Notice the straightforward coverage of the candidate's grades in her first undergraduate career.

If you are not admitted to medical school on your first attempt, you should note that many students are admitted after strengthening their backgrounds as this candidate did. Note the proper use in this essay of working titles to describe research in progress.

#16:   "Nurse Bound for Medical School"   *(continued)*

---

hours while the interns consulted on approaches to her treatment. I was acutely aware that my abilities and knowledge were limited to nursing, and I very much wanted to be able to contribute meaningfully to the intellectual debate I was witnessing among the interns.

The attending physician was summoned to survey the problem. He clamped the shunt and put her on antibiotics, recognizing that the patient's heart was not strong enough to handle the large fluid load. The patient went to ICU, and I decided to go to medical school.

I returned to the Kidney Transplant Unit of UCSF Medical Center and began to study for the MCATs. Also, I took a course in hematology from San Francisco State University and served as a research assistant on two additional projects: (1) I conducted GFR studies as an assistant to Nephrology Research Fellow Carlos Stempl, M.D., UCSF Medical Center, on a project with a working title, "Does Verapamil improve GFR in transplant recipients?" and (2) I am currently research assistant under the direction of William Amend, M.D., UCSF Medical Center, performing the retrospective arm of a two-armed study, "Incidence of Cytomegalovirus in transplant patients and the efficacy of Acyclovir prophylaxis."

My ultimate career direction is to practice infectious disease medicine. Witnessing the devastation these organisms can cause on immuno-compromised patients has given me a great appreciation for the role of the physician, to intercede in and reverse the course of infectious disease. I would find this work immensely interesting and rewarding, and I look forward to the opportunity to pursue it.

With more than enough energy and stamina to succeed, I am intellectually, emotionally, and financially prepared for medical school. I will admit no more impediments to my goal. I am eager to begin the process.

This ending shows confidence, determination, and poise. Remember, you are someone who is going to succeed whether you're admitted to their particular graduate program or not.

ESSAY #17:   "Tobacco Mosaic Virus and the Eiffel Tower"

"What is the most important difference between tobacco mosaic virus and the Eiffel Tower?" my professor asked on the last day of my introductory biochemistry class, as he put two slides of the structures up on the screen. "Both are made of precise building blocks which elegantly come together to form the whole unit," he explained, "but only the virus knows how to put itself together." At this point, I had a *Eureka!* response. I truly recognized the beauty and complexity of life at the molecular level. That's when I first knew that I wanted to undertake biomedical research.

Since then, my decision to pursue graduate study has been confirmed by both my undergraduate course work and my research experience. While studying immunology in my sophomore year, I learned for the first time not only the facts about the workings of the immune system, but also the ideas and experiments that led to their discovery. As I became exposed to the experimental side of the information found in the textbook, I began to appreciate the sophisticated thought processes and energy required by scientific research.

The most influential experience in persuading me to attend graduate school, however, has been my current independent research project, which will culminate in an honors thesis. I am examining the antigenicity of a protein in a novel drug delivery system. (Please see the accompanying research summary.) I am eager to bring the concepts I have learned in my project to the level of a graduate program of study. First, I discovered how the power of perseverance can overcome obstacles. When my experimental system, the ELISA, suddenly stopped working, careful troubleshooting led to the discovery of a minor technical problem. Through this experience, I learned how to critically dissect an experiment to find the root of error. In addition, the graduate student with whom I have been working for almost two years has taught me the ability to take an idea and follow it while at the same time demonstrating to me the balancing act involved in allocating time, money, and energy to a project when the direction your results will take you is unknown. My research sponsor, with her contagious energy, has also influenced me with her enthusiastic approach to attacking new research areas, and has motivated me to work harder to reach my goals and the goals of the lab.

The pathobiology graduate program at the College of Physicians and Surgeons of Columbia University is of interest to me for several reasons. First, the affiliation of the University with Presbyterian Hospital, Milstein Hospital, the Institute for Cancer Research and the Institute for Human Nutrition provides students with the opportunity to combine basic scientific studies with clinical applications. The resources available at the hospitals and centers aid students in immediately applying what they learn in the classroom and laboratory to situations where disease demands immediate attention. In addition, the location of the college in Manhattan is attractive because of its proximity to other research institutions and medical schools. Such a dynamic group of scientists provides many opportunities for the exchange of fresh ideas and collaborative efforts. Finally, the range of research conducted by the faculty is appealing. The studies of Nicole Sucio-Foca are of particular interest to me

---

Here is a superb example of using an experiential opening for a science-oriented essay.

There are many career paths and research opportunities related to medicine, pharmaceuticals, and biotechnology that do not involve an M.D. degree. This Ph.D. candidate in medical pathobiology will have many exciting opportunities to contribute to medical science, without suffering through a few years of 80- and 100-hour sleepless clinical internships.

Trace the history of your interest in the topic.

This is a model answer to the question "Why here?" Every program wants an answer to this question, whether they explicitly ask it or not.

#17:   "Tobacco Mosaic Virus and the Eiffel Tower" *(continued)*

because they involve the creation of peptide vaccines, an area of immunological research which has much potential for the treatment or prevention of many diseases.

Once in graduate school, I hope to pursue studies related to the development of vaccines. My interest in this topic stems not only from my course work specific to immunology but also from an additional academic experience in the course, "The Burden of Disease in Developing Nations." In this class I learned that although vaccines are currently available to treat a myriad of diseases, some of these vaccines are useless to people in the developing world because they degrade under the conditions of high temperature or humidity which are often found in these countries. Multiple lines of research can thus address both the development of new vaccines and the improvement of currently existing vaccines so that they may be useful to the greatest number of people.

In trying to create new vaccines for diseases for which they are currently not available, several approaches from immunology, biochemistry, molecular genetics, and organic chemistry can be considered. For example, an understanding of whether a humoral or cell-mediated immune response is best suited to fight a particular disease is needed. Immunologic techniques involving animal models and cell culture studies can be used to determine how B and T cells interact to fight disease. Furthermore, specific pathogenic macromolecules can be used as the antigen in a vaccine rather than an entire protein. This method requires the isolation and purification of protein subunits using biochemical assays such as gel electrophoresis, column chromatography, and protein sequencing. In addition, the gene encoding an antigen can also be used to develop a vaccine. Recombinant DNA techniques such as screening of genomic cDNA libraries, gene sequencing, and the polymerase chain reaction can be use to isolate, characterize, and amplify a specific gene. Finally, specific protein antigens can be chemically synthesized. This method requires not only a rigorous use of synthesis design from organic chemistry, but also principles from biochemistry to determine protein sequence and folding, as the conformation of a protein domain and not just its amino acid sequence is often recognized by antigen presenting cells. Thus, x-ray crystallography and FTIR must be employed. All of these lines of research can lead to the development of new vaccines.

After graduate school, I will consider a career in the pharmaceutical industry. The ability to see an idea about a molecular process evolve into a product which will help make people's lives healthier is my motivation for this choice. However, I am also considering a career in academia because I am interested in the possibility of combining research with teaching and interacting with undergraduates. I am currently tutoring genetics students and have previously tutored organic chemistry students, and the one-on-one interaction has enabled me to teach and learn at the same time. Through my involvement in Women in Science and Engineering as a biochemistry affinity group leader, I have been able to advise students about the selection of courses, summer jobs, and potential professors with whom to do an independent study. The teaching experience which has proven to be the most challenging is serving as a ninth-grade religious education instructor for the past three years. I have

---

#17: "Tobacco Mosaic Virus and the Eiffel Tower" *(continued)*

---

prepared my own lessons and led discussions with a group of twenty, sometimes less than enthusiastic, fourteen-year-olds. Trying to capture their attention has forced me to be creative in my style and presentation of material. Thus, my involvement with students may persuade me to enter the academic research world.

My past experiences have well prepared me to pursue graduate education at the College of Physicians and Surgeons. My undergraduate education in the competitive atmosphere at Brown has enabled me to not merely reiterate ideas stated by my professors but to apply the concepts I have learned to unfamiliar situations. During my four years here both my study skills and my ability to process information have sharpened, as evidenced by an improvement in my grades within my major from a 3.0 grade point average freshman year to a 3.6 junior year. The lack of self-confidence which plagued me during my first two years here was induced by both insufficient study skills and an unusually rigorous course load, wherein I completed my inorganic and organic chemistry courses in three semesters rather than four and took physical chemistry, a course usually reserved for upperclassmen, my sophomore year. In addition, my interactions with people within the Brown community outside the classroom have prepared me for the intellectual atmosphere at Columbia. The need to write and speak effectively on issues of importance, whether it involves a change in the housing policy or creating a new concentration, are requisite to enact positive change. One initiative which I undertook was the creation of a Web site for Women in Science and Engineering, to help create better communication among women scientists both at Brown and at other universities. Therefore, by combining my diverse undergraduate experiences, I will be able to grow as a researcher in your pathobiology graduate program while contributing my ideas about both the research interests of my colleagues and issues facing the Columbia community.

When your grades have markedly improved, always point that out. Readers may look at your GPA without noting your GPA *trend*. Help them see what you want them to see.

Service to your academic community, and the other "communities" to which you belong, is almost always regarded as a positive sign of character and maturity.

ESSAY #18: "Not Like TV Law"

Personal Statement for Law School

The theme of this next essay is rather straightforward: "Why I want to become a lawyer." The exposition of that theme, the interplay between the humorous and the mortally serious, is not so straightforward. This essay is a paradigm of the "less is more" principle. Note how much material is covered so briefly. Instead of dragging the reader through every aspect of the campaign trail and her time in Washington, she trusts that they will infer much of the experience.

Even though everyone warns me that it's not going to be like those lawyer shows on television, I want to go to law school. Despite the thirty-pound textbooks and the long hours, despite the strange vocabulary of torts, procedures, and *Black's Legal Dictionary,* despite the lines at the photocopy machine, I want to go to law school. I ignore the bumper-stickers that read "The last thing our country needs is another lawyer" and that quote from *Henry VI.*

I want to become a lawyer, even though a record number of people are trying: innumerable heads bent over countless test sheets, with candy, extra pencils, clocks resting nearby on empty seats. Those standardized questions wormed their way into the fabric of my thinking, so that I imagined daily disagreements in a "Facts and Issues" format or saw the difficulty of untangling our apartment's phone bill as a logic problem. (If each roommate called Boston, but only Gretchen called Kansas City, who called Detroit?) And graduates confide that these changes intensify, your thinking becomes fundamentally altered, synapses fire in new and permanent directions, and you become habituated to logic and argument. I met a young law-school couple at the beach. They stood waist-deep in the ocean, holding hands, pushed gently by the water as they discussed rights of privacy. But none of these projects dissuades me.

During my year away from school, I worked in Kit Bond's senate campaign and Washington office. For that entire year, my attention was focused on aspects of law; those who make the laws, the laws themselves, and the effects they have on the public. During the campaign, my position as deputy director of issues and policy development showed me the unexpected results laws can have, and how even the most well-intentioned decision can hurt a sector of constituents. Later as a legislative correspondent, I prepared texts which clarified issues to constituents and justified our office's position. Often, however, complaints about Senate actions were well founded. Missourians were hurt by a benignant law which had an unavoidable negative consequence, or by the scrupulous attention to the exact language of a law which worked to subvert, rather than promote, its intent.

But alongside the unfortunate results, I watched the struggle to create a reasonable and articulate code. I saw drafts of legislation change shape as Congress hammered out the final form of a new law; I studied elegant and cogent Supreme Court decisions which exemplify the beauty of a tightly worked argument, carefully expressed, from which the law derives its power.

So I still want to become a lawyer, despite those terrible, ubiquitous jokes, despite all the clichés. Have you read Oliver Wendell Holmes? "But remotely what the lawyer does is to establish, develop, or illuminate rules which are to govern the conduct of men for centuries; to set in motion principles and influences which shape the thought and action of generations which know not by whose command they move."

That's why I want to become a lawyer.

ESSAY #19: "Iditarod Dogs and Molecular Biology"

Statement of Purpose

They call it the last frontier. Last summer I set out for Alaska, to see the true wildness left in this world. This spirit of adventure took me to Homer on the Kenai peninsula, where I became the "dog handler" for Iditarod musher Jack Berry and his sixty huskies. Although I came to Alaska to live among the wild, I found myself spending all my free time teaching English pronunciation to a Brazilian doctor and arguing plant physiology with the old women of the Homer Garden Club, when I wasn't hitchhiking the fifteen miles to the Homer Public Library. For better or for worse I'm obsessed with learning, and I want to take my pursuit of knowledge to a far greater scale.

Theoretical physicists are in pursuit of the grand unifying theory, the set of equations that will make compatible all of this world's macro- and microcosms. As I see it, there is a similar grand objective in the world of biology. I feel a drive to elucidate the mechanisms of life through molecular studies. There are ways, paths, lines of thinking that converge the realm of the biological with the domain of chemical logic. I know that a solid understanding of the physical function of proteins can be that unifying link.

Now it is the rainy winter of my fourth and final year at Reed College. I have been an enthusiastic biochemistry and molecular biology major enrolled in what is possibly the best program of its kind. This past spring I worked independently on a project to determine the preferred conformation of dehydrated isosorbide. While this was interesting in its own right, I think that the knowledge obtained through studies of organic chemistry is most relevant when applied toward macromolecules. Aside from being fascinating structures, they have a significance reaching far beyond the laboratory. I've chosen the topic of my undergraduate thesis with these greater interests in mind. For this thesis I am pipetting toward a crystal structure of xylose isomerase that contains a single active site mutation. I find it absolutely amazing that proteins can catalyze reactions and am obsessed with the relationship between their function and structure. Enzymes catalyze reactions, but an amino acid polymer is also capable of much more. Motor proteins, G-proteins, the amalgamations in the SNARE hypothesis—cells have created proteins for an intense diversity of uses. I am lucky to be a structural biologist at a time when the techniques necessary to decipher the form of these proteins are uncovered. I am intrigued by the functional structure of proteins, and value any laboratory method that can provide molecular insight. I chose to apply to Scripps because I have been uncommonly impressed by the structural research I've seen published by Scripps researchers. Orton Gilula's and Nigel Unwin's investigations of the structure and functional mechanisms of gap-junction and ion channels are especially intriguing. I find ion channels to be wondrous edifices. Ion channels are contraptions straight out of a Dr. Seuss story book: one massive protein that chooses to allow specific ions through it, if and only if it is satisfied with the chemical and electrical environment surrounding it. This, truly, is a level of chemistry where biological decisions are made.

Notice how this graduate-school candidate uses personal stories and a genuine enthusiasm to package his approach to science. This applicant also told me that he wore a Hawaiian shirt to his interviews, to stand out from the crowd in the minds of interviewers who may meet with a dozen candidates in a day. These techniques worked for him, but only because they matched his effusive personality.

Notice the answer to "Why here?" and the mention of specific researchers of interest to this candidate. Customize your essays, or lose out to the candidates like this one, who do.

#19: "Iditarod Dogs and Molecular Biology"   *(continued)*

I could drone on for pages about the research that I find fascinating, as Scripps has a collection of amazing resources. I would love the opportunity to work in a laboratory with this talent. I am enrolling in graduate school to learn more and to understand greater biological systems so that I will be able to apply my molecular knowledge to my own research. I'm fascinated by the biology of the cell; with a thorough understanding of the techniques available to the protein scientist, I will finally possess the ability to address the basic hows and whys of cell function.

Two years ago I spent a semester abroad with the School for Field Studies in the Pacific island nation of Palau. With every mangrove and coral reef transect we took, I wanted to know: "Why do these angel fish live here? How can these trees grow out of the salt sea?" The only answers my professors could give: "Because the fish do best in this biotic environment . . . because they've evolved and adapted for longer than you can imagine." The answers available are just not satisfactory, but I know that with more training I could find those answers for myself. I want answers with a mechanism: answers that resemble not statistical spreadsheets, rather blueprints of ingenious design; answers that might detail how membrane proteins balance harsh extra-cellular conditions with a cytoplasm that is conducive to life. These are answers I need to find, and I'm too stubborn to quit now. I need to go to graduate school, for I've only just learned the principles of protein structure and function. I want to be an expert. The MCSC Program holds the resources that can enable me to continue my quest.

ESSAY #20: "NSF Post-Doc in Chemistry"

Personal Statement for National Science Foundation Postdoctoral Research Fellowship in Chemistry

The training conducted under this grant would be geared toward establishing a new academic laboratory in which biological, chemical, and physical techniques are focused on elucidating the fundamental forces and principles of bioorganic and bioinorganic catalytic mechanisms. The strategy of this laboratory would be to elucidate chemical structure/reactivity properties of enzymes and enzyme-bound intermediates leading to the design of experiments which test the nature of transition state stabilization for a given reaction. As chemical systems, some proteins provide excellent, surprisingly tolerant, structurally definable scaffolds for holding probes of the ground states and transition states of catalyzed reactions. Mutant proteins are truly chemical analogues of the wild type structure, and genetics provides an excellent way to generate and test a large number of these analogues (10/8 structures, which would result from randomizing seven amino acid positions, could reasonably be tested genetically). X-ray crystallography and NMR spectroscopy provide powerful, essential, yet incomplete characterization of enzyme chemistry. Fruitful interpretation of good structures can be limited by a paucity of functional information. Therefore, the proposed laboratory would be primarily responsible for generating functional information through the preparation of enzymes, random and site-directed mutant enzymes, inhibitors, and chemically and isotopically modified substrates and cofactors, and through the characterization of the chemical reactions of these reagents. Characterization of the reactions would routinely include genetic function, reaction product analysis, kinetics, and at a minimum, the preparation of suitable samples for x-ray crystallography, NMR spectroscopy, and any other informative techniques. How far the work of the lab extends into the physically oriented techniques will be determined by the extent of the training I am able to accomplish as well as by personnel in the lab; however, collaborations with specialists in crystallographic or spectroscopic techniques will always be preferable to provide as many perspectives on a given project as possible. To the extent that good, effective mathematical models are available, they will be highly considered during the interpretation of results and tested by the design of experiments; e.g., the computer program Del Phi has proven itself a useful model for electrostatic forces in proteins. The laboratory would study many different enzymes with different chemistries at various stages of development. The study of established enzyme systems would provide the most rigorous testing ground for our knowledge of enzymatic chemistry. The analysis of enzymes with undefined mechanisms would include therapeutic targets where much may be presumed about the chemistry of the enzyme, but where satisfactory, functional inhibitors are still wanted. The social raison d'être for this laboratory would be the development of new therapeutic inhibitors based upon the chemistry derived from pursing an understanding of catalysis. The study of enzymes with unknown mechanisms should provide fertile ground for the discovery of new chemistry.

Notice how different this essay is from the last one, even though both these candidates are applying for laboratory science opportunities. Although the title for this postdoctoral essay, as requested on the application form, is "Personal Statement," there is not a shred of personal information in it. The essay contains a proposal for formulation of a chemistry lab and research project, and mentions several prominent chemists who support the proposal. This type of application entails a whole lobbying campaign and extensive personal contact in support of the project, and this essay needs to be considered in that larger context. The ability to make and utilize personal contacts becomes ever more important as your academic career advances.

#20: "NSF Post-Doc in Chemistry" *(continued)*

The proposed postdoctoral work provides an excellent opportunity to establish a project which has much in common with the future work of the proposed laboratory. The enzyme is a therapeutic target with an unknown mechanism. The project hinges on the synthesis of substrate analogues as inhibitors and involves chemical and kinetic characterization of the inhibition, aspects of enzymology in which I am not well trained. In addition, chemical characterization may involve the preparation and analysis of protein crystals.

The proposed scientific adviser, Prof. Robert Abeles, has established a laboratory where compounds are routinely designed and synthesized with the intent of testing bioorganic and bioinorganic enzymatic mechanisms. As a consequence he provides expertise in an environment where the results of such experiments are routinely analyzed and interpreted. He actively seeks to train his postdoctoral fellows in science while teaching chemistry as it pertains to the analysis of enzyme mechanisms. In short, he operates a laboratory with the focus with which I would like to operate my own. His recommendation would indicate my suitability as the director of such a laboratory.

Brandeis University presents an excellent faculty. In addition to Dr. Abeles, the biochemistry faculty includes Dr. W. P. Jencks, who is also a particularly lucid and careful chemist and enzymologist. As a sign of the continuing support of penetrating enzymology, the university has recently added to the faculty two noted crystallographers, Drs. G. A. Petsko and D. Ringe, whose collaboration with Dr. Abeles is very strong. Their crystallographic program now includes the Laue diffraction technique which allows structural characterization of enzymatic reactions on a millisecond time scale.

Obviously this candidate has been involved in detailed discussions with the researchers named in this essay.

ESSAY #21: "Perception, Reality & Big Pond Communication"

Statement of Purpose—Doctoral Program in Communications

I spent the morning of my eighteenth birthday in an auditorium with two hundred strangers. I said goodbye to my parents at the door of the Cullen Building, the behemoth antique limestone structure which houses all the administrative offices and the majority of the classrooms at tiny Southwestern University, where I had matriculated the day prior. I had forsaken the comfortingly anonymous urban sprawl of Houston for the much-heralded "small pond" of the small private liberal arts university and felt ill-prepared for my first symposium. The course roster consisted of the entire freshman class, which fit easily under one roof with several seats in the front left over. We flipped through Mead notebooks officiously and examined one another suspiciously, shrinking down into our flip-down synthetic woodgrain seats as the day's speaker directed a Vulcan "live long and prosper" salute to the nervously fidgeting audience and calmly inquired of us, "How do you know what you know when you know it?" How, he asked us, do we discover the meaning of our world? Do we actively determine what the world is, or do we merely perceive it passively? In other words, is knowledge mediated? The sound of ballpoints scribbling stopped abruptly; several pens bounced audibly off the industrial carpet. The professor launched into a whirlwind tour of the major epistemological paradigms: the Greek Idealists believed existence originated in a cosmic Ideal; Descartes believed rationality begat phenomenology; Berkeley doubted the reality of all sensations, but Locke believed knowledge was imprinted upon us by experience; Hegel postulated that we could arrive at the truth after participating in a dialectic of reason. I met the eyes of the woman sitting next to me. *Huh?* they seemed to say.

My own confusion gave way to exhilaration shortly after that first symposium lecture. I had exited the realm of generic, standardized learning; it was now possible to think about *thinking*. It was time to consider cognition, the nature of the self, and the relationship between reality, representation, and perception. I developed a keen interest in the ways humans transmit meaning: language, image, and narrative. Within three and a half years, I had picked up a philosophy minor—and a passion for structuralism—while pursuing my undergraduate degree in English. Various advanced courses introduced me to additional interesting paradigms of inquiry, such as New Historicism (who knew simple events in time, such as conversations, were profound enough to be read as literary texts?), psychoanalytic theory, French feminism, discourse theory, and postmodernism. The scope of possibilities for inquiry broadened. When our freshman class reunited for the second and last time—for graduation—I was its valedictorian. More importantly, I had learned that every exchange of negotiated meaning between humans—what we call "communication"—has deeper, fascinating layers of resonance that appear before the lens of concentrated academic scrutiny. At that time, I pledged that by seeking an academic career, I would continue to examine the artifacts of our mediated culture for hidden or even subversive meanings, and that I would strive to teach others to do the same.

This essay for a Ph.D. program in communication reads like a survey course in humanities! The tone is a little lighthearted, but the intellectual mastery is clear. This is another essay organized in a straightforward chronological order. If you have trouble assembling your essay, this is an easy organizational structure. Notice the underplayed way the writer mentions fairly major accomplishments, such as being the valedictorian.

#21: "Perception, Reality & Big Pond Communication" *(cont.)*

I returned to the classroom six months later for a master of science in communication from Boston University (B.U.). At B.U., I applied the feminist/structuralist critical paradigms I had learned to a disparate body of cinematic and literary texts, from the transparent to the prolix. In each, I found a sophisticated and sometimes surprising network of subtexts and metamessages which reinforced my curiosity about the cinema and other forms of mediated mass communication as constructive processes. I investigated the anti-heroic, unromantic character of the Czech New Wave cinema as a response to post–World War II national- ism (see sample) and found evidence of a neo-Victorian obsession with punishing female sexual deviance in the "splatter" films of exploitation kingpin Herschell Gordon Lewis (see sample). I discovered a characteristic ambivalence about the heteropatriarchal world of adult social and sexual relationships in the otherwise conventional studio "teen films" of women directors like Martha Coolidge, Amy Heckerling, and Lisa Gottlieb (see sample). I became intrigued by the interdependence of narrative genre and the sociological characteristics of the viewing imagery, and I examined at length the tendency of marginalized groups to adapt mainstream genre conventions and ideologies to suit their own values (in the case of "women's westerns," the urban rap musicals of the 1980s, and the "blaxploitation" action film cycle, which integrates picaresque Afro-American folk legends like Staggerlee and Br'er Rabbit into the "lone vigilante" narrative template established by the "hard-boiled" Anglo-American detective genre). Finally, I culminated my master's work with the successful defense of my book-length thesis on the symbolic functionalism of the Elvis Presley musical film oeuvre (see sample). I furthermore intend to spend my year-long hiatus from school revising my thesis for possible publication, and I have several articles under consideration at major media journals, including *Wide Angle* and *The Journal of Popular Film and Television*.

Primarily, I have sought—and continue to seek—to work and study in an environment much like the one where my college career began—a environment that is academically chal- lenging, intellectually sophisticated, interdisciplinary in nature, and solidly focused on the exploration of the relationships between human perceivers and the mediated phenomenal world. To this end, I have followed a diverse but rigorous course of interdisciplinary study that I feel has prepared me well for doctoral work at the University of California-San Diego (UCSD) in the communication field. I believe that the program's sweeping emphasis on the cultural, social, and epistemological aspects of the communication process would provide me with a useful holistic framework upon which to base my more specific research interests. I am additionally impressed that the department can offer both a wide range of faculty perspec- tives and a significant number of faculty whose research interests seem to coincide with mine (including Prof. Ellen Seiter, whose emphasis on audience reception theory is encouraging to me, and Prof. Helen Keyssar, whose interest in drama and social functionalism is equally intriguing). Summarily, I am optimistic that UCSD would provide me with precisely the kind of environment I seek, owing to the rare combination of a broad humanistic perspective and a commitment to thorough, demanding research.

Notice the frequent references to writing samples and other materials submitted with the application.

Be sure to mention articles submitted for publication, as well as those accepted and those already published.

Always mention key professors that you would like to work with in the graduate program.

ESSAY #22:   "Seventeen Schools"

Personal Statement

I attended seventeen different schools before high school. I do not come from a family of migrant workers in the traditional sense, but those were nonetheless difficult times for a single woman with three young children, few skills and no education. We moved from town to town and state to state as my mother tried to get better paying, less physically taxing jobs that ranged from tending bar to cleaning salmon to light manufacturing.

This upheaval might have soured some students on school and driven them into a shell. I had the opposite response: I threw myself wholeheartedly into each new school, striving to distinguish myself to new teachers and peers. In some schools this allowed me more opportunity for advanced study, in others—already too overtaxed to adequately educate the forty "average" students in the class—I was seated in the corner with instructions to complete the class lesson and entertain myself non-disruptively for the remaining time. I started reading anything that I could get my hands on, and so began my lifelong pursuit of knowledge.

I knew early on that I would go to college, even when living in small logging towns where such things were almost unknown. My mother was wise enough not to point out that no one else in the family ever had, or that kids from trailer parks get jobs, not degrees. Instead, she did everything within her power to make it possible: When scholarships were available, she put me in private schools; she used addresses of friends or employers in place of our own on school registration forms to keep me in the better public schools; she ensured that I was articulate in "proper" English, in addition to the slang spoken by my friends.

When the time came for me to realize my goal, I made a point of going to a private university, which I funded with scholarships, grants, loans, and part-time jobs. I hid my background and made friends with upper and upper-middle-class students, as though I could become one of them through immersion. While they went to France for the summer, I worked fifty hours a week. I kept up this ruse for three semesters, while taking classes in a number of disciplines. Finally, in the fourth semester, I cracked. I was taking eighteen units, working three jobs, and steadily falling behind on tuition payments. I decided to cut my losses, take a semester of "W" on my transcript, and drop out of school. In retrospect, this may be the smartest thing I've ever done.

I moved home, got a job, and felt like a failure for a while. Out of school for the first time in my life, I had a lot of time to think. I got to know myself as I really am, rather than who I was trying to be for show, possibly for the first time in my life. I discovered that I am who I am because of, rather than in spite of, my experiences. It was my "fortune" to be less fortunate—it made me strong, resourceful and adaptable, among other things.

I returned to Marquette University after a year's leave of absence with renewed vigor and a pronounced sense of responsibility to honor my background instead of denying it. I focused more sharply on issues of gender and social justice. The more globally I studied these issues, the more I saw that the macro scale mirrored the micro scale. I watched *Life on the Global*

As a personal autobiography that segues into an intellectual biography, this is a highly effective essay. Similarly to those in essay #15, the challenges that this applicant has overcome to reach her goals are so significant that one can be sure of her self-motivation and internal drive.

This is a very revealing story of adversity overcome. Remember the rules for addressing adversity in an application essay: It has to be in the past, it has to be resolved, and it has to be sympathetic. This candidate's life is one of triumph over challenges, and this essay represents her well.

#22: "Seventeen Schools" *(continued)*

Assembly Line, a documentary film about women in light industry in the newly industrializing nations, and almost cried. Women used up and discarded by the export electronics industry in Malaysia reminded me of my own mother, whose arms are so plagued with work-related arthritis and tendonitis at age fifty that she can't pick up her grandchildren. But I also saw women's little resistances both in newly industrializing countries and here in the United States, the way they work around the system even under the harshest conditions. These are what call to me—the powerful, small-scale actions that frequently aren't even recognized as political, but that empower these women.

I need to use my gifts for learning, teaching and social analysis to do work relevant to the world I come from—a shadow economy where women barter what they have for what they need: childcare for money, government cheese for meat, a few hours running the community center for used shoes for their children. Because of my own upbringing on the margins of society, I am especially intrigued by community-based women's groups in developing and newly democratizing nations, which constitute the margins of the developed world. Through my research and writing, I want to document the ways in which poor women organize for social democratization in developing nations and what they need to improve their plight; I want to draw parallels between them and poor women in wealthier countries like the U.S., and to examine the extent to which political democracy impacts their efforts to improve their lives.

Much of the information I received in my youth from school, books and television about how American society works did not reflect the activities I witnessed in my own community, where low-income single parents like my mother used informal networks and unusual methods to meet their needs. To supplement their food stamps, some of them gleaned remaining produce from fields that had already been commercially harvested in exchange for 75 percent of what they picked. They would then give a portion of their "earnings" to other women in payment for watching their children while they were in the fields.

At Marquette University, I augmented my politics major with a certificate in women's studies in part to fill in this gap between my experiences and my textbooks. My politics classes gave me a good grounding in institutions, but the subtleties of the informal economy and the oblique ways that some women's groups use to circumvent laws or issues without challenging them directly simply don't fit into the "official" version of political science. Because they focused on the people within the institutions rather than the institutions themselves, sociology and women's studies classes such as "Sociology of Gender," "Women, Men and Violence," "Women, Society and Religion," "Social Movements and Revolutions," "Nonviolence in Theory and Practice," and "Political Sociology" allowed me to explore these interests more fully. In these classes I researched and wrote papers on movements for legal birth control, India's Chipko movement, and women's peace groups like Women Strike for Peace and the Women of Greenham Common. One of these, "The Truth About Women

#22: "Seventeen Schools" (continued)

and Peace," was eventually published in *The Women and War Reader,* a new anthology from NYU Press (see attached article).

Here's a smooth citation of a publication.

Deeper research into issues of gender and social justice revealed that whether one looks at Lagos, Los Angeles or rural Laos, women's groups are organizing for various forms of social democratization, scratching out space for and improving their lives even under the harshest conditions. I propose to research and document the ways in which women in rural Bangladesh attempt to improve their lives and what they need to improve their plight; I want to draw parallels between them and impoverished women in wealthier countries like the U.S., and to examine the extent to which political democracy impacts their efforts to improve their lives. To achieve these goals, I intend to pursue a Ph.D. and become a professor of sociology.

I am not one to go into things rashly. You could say that my last seven years have been a dry run for graduate school. I assisted Marquette politics department chair Raymond Evans with research for his forthcoming books *The Victims' Rights Movement* and *The Post-Cold War Socialism Reader,* and English department chair Catherine Bryan with research on women in medieval and Renaissance drama. I delivered two papers at the annual meeting of the Peace Studies Association, along with helping to organize the conference; I also delivered one paper at the annual Peace Studies Association meeting and attended the American Political Science Association meeting and the American Sociological Association meeting—all within the last year. These conferences allowed me a better understanding of the depth and breadth of current research and the opportunity to present my work to colleagues in several disciplines. I have reviewed the papers of my peers while working as the copy editor of *Discourse Interdisciplinary Philosophy Journal,* a student-run publication, and those of scholars from around the globe as managing editor of *Peace Review.* I recently prepared a scholarly manuscript for associate dean Janine Tryon and religious studies professor Lea Lafayette. Currently, I am experiencing the administrative side of Marquette as assistant to the associate dean for arts, humanities and social sciences. I'm entering graduate school well prepared to meet the challenge.

Whenever you have held positions in educational administration, be sure to mention them in your essay.

There are a number of reasons why the University of California-Berkeley (UCB) is the best setting for my pursuit of these goals. I am extremely impressed by the scholarship of Raka Ray, whose work on women's political groups in India is in many ways similar to the work I wish to pursue. I have read several of her articles and believe that she would be an excellent mentor. Additionally, Latin America and the former Eastern Bloc, regions that I am particularly interested in exploring academically, are strongly represented in the specialties of faculty members Laura Enriquez, Manuel Castells, Victoria Bonnell and Gil Eyal.

UCB's reputation as an innovative, qualitative, and highly regarded program seems to provide the ideal combination of rigor and freedom. A perusal of recent dissertation topics indicated that students are allowed the autonomy to take on projects which don't necessarily

Here's a compelling answer to the concern, "Why here?" Remember, it's generally a good idea to identify more than one professor in whom you are interested, as this candidate does.

#22: "Seventeen Schools"	(continued)

follow the work of their advisers and that are quite ambitious in scope. A meeting with graduate assistant Elaine Talmadge confirmed this impression. As someone with a history of taking on challenging and intensive research projects, I believe that I would thrive in such an environment. I am confident that the knowledge, skills and experience that a Ph.D. from UCB provides will be the base of a long and productive academic career in sociology.

ESSAY #23: "Systems Simulation"

Statement of Purpose, Ph.D. in Systems Engineering

A large chart is slowly unfurled in front of the class as the professor offers excitedly: "This will give us some perspective on what you've been learning these last three semesters!" The chart displays a descending continuum of linearity to nonlinearity on the y-axis. On the x-axis is the number of variables in a system. I sit up attentively, anticipating my professor's introduction to what would become my favorite class, Systems Simulation. The professor directs the laser pointer to the top left corner, highlighting the first- and second-order topics such as radioactive decay and RLC circuits: "We've spent all this time learning the basics of these linear systems." His laser pointer drifts to the lower right and enthusiastically narrates, "Now this is the where it gets interesting. Limit cycles. The immune system. Economics." As his pointer travels to the lower right-most item, he says eagerly, "And finally: *Life.*" It occurs to me then that although I have taken four courses in my intended specialty, I have only begun to learn systems engineering. I am eager cross the frontier to begin learning about life. This revelation motivated me then, and it motivates me still, to pursue a Ph.D. in systems engineering with a specialization in nonlinear control and simulation of interdisciplinary systems for my graduate studies.

I have sought out many opportunities to work on multidisciplinary engineering projects in my undergraduate career. In my most recent summer research position, I had the opportunity to work in a team of three undergraduates under Professor J. Rossmann in designing and constructing Harvey Mudd College's first large-scale subsonic wind tunnel to allow for visualization and quantification of external flows.[1] I had a range of responsibilities within the team that involved a full range of research, design and construction. These included calculating the necessary specifications of the settling chamber, exit diffuser, and axial fan. Furthermore, I worked with a limited budget to design a cost-effective structural support system, negotiated with vendors, and helped assemble and build the test section and flow-straightening screens. This experience gave me a real-world taste of how elegant systems engineering could be—I had the tools to beautifully integrate mechanical, structural, electrical, economical, and project management aspects in order to design a successful wind tunnel. The greatest challenge during the project was completing the design and construction of the wind tunnel over a ten-week period; our team learned the value of efficient time-management, maintaining focus, and good project planning. I look forward to coordinating the documentation of our design and construction process of the wind tunnel in a forthcoming publication by the end of the spring semester.

Last year, as part of a larger project to explore the development of a GPS - Loran-C integrated navigation system, another engineering team I was on investigated the viability and characteristics of Loran-C (Long Range Aid to Navigation Type C) as an air-traffic navigation and positioning system.[2] My responsibilities within the four-person team were to determine and model the sources of error contributing to the relative inaccuracy of Loran-C. I assisted in experimentally testing daily and seasonal variation and the effects

---

Note how engaging this future scientist's writing is. Her enthusiasm is palpable. And she tells a story in which a professor is the hero, the source of wondrous knowledge and light. Remember who is going to read an essay like this? Exactly.

Grad school involves lots of teamwork, especially in engineering. Telling a story about a successful team project is a great idea.

#23:   "Systems Simulation"   *(continued)*

Notice how this writer differentiates her contributions from the overall project.

of earth's conductivity and terrain. Moreover, I helped develop a MATLAB model for errors due to transmitter station synchronization. For an initial guess within a 6-kilometer radius of the true position, the average absolute accuracy of the model improved from 460 meters to approximately 100 meters. This project enabled me to demonstrate my ability to maintain good working relationships with my team members and advisor. I also discovered the importance of independent motivation and drive within a team in contributing to the success of the project.

Nice, straightforward, effective discussion of leadership and service.

Working on these research projects involves organizational and leadership skills. As President of HMC's Society of Women Engineers (SWE) for three years, I head the coordination and execution of SWE's annual Women Engineers and Scientists of Tomorrow Conference. Over 160 high school girls and parents attend this one-day conference to interact with current women in the sciences and participate in workshops in engineering. The numerous accomplishments of SWE during my term, such as initiating engineering department gatherings and arranging fundraising activities, demonstrate my leadership skills and ability to plan and complete successful projects. My motivation also is evidenced by my involvement with our collegiate chapter of Tau Beta Pi (TBP). As TBP President, I organize tutoring sessions for the seven engineering core classes and participate in TBP community service.

That captivating chart that plots the complexity of systems presented in my systems simulation course symbolizes the path I hope to pursue. So far, I have managed to edge my way toward a better understanding of the dynamics of nonlinear systems; I have modeled fascinating systems ranging from the romance of two lovers to the limit cycles of oscillating chemical reactions. At Caltech, I intend to further study nonlinear systems modeling and simulation. I am especially interested in continuing my work in interdisciplinary engineering systems with applications in robotics and the automotive industry. I hope to bring my previous research modeling the Loran-C navigation system, my most recent nonlinear variable structure robust control project in systems simulation, and my experience in hands-on experimentation techniques from my wind tunnel research to the development of modeling these systems. The proximity to the charming city of Old Town Pasadena has also factored into my consideration to attend Caltech. To be in this rich environment would be a tremendous opportunity.

1. Rossmann, J. S., Hsu, Y. J., Schauer, J., and Stratton, C. "Design and Construction of a Subsonic Wind Tunnel." UC Santa Barbara: Fluids Mini-Symposium. Santa Barbara, CA.

2. Boyd, C., Ahle, K., Hsu, Y. J., and Thatte G. "Modeling the Existing Loran-C Radionavigation System." Harvey Mudd College Clinic Final Report. Claremont, CA.

ESSAY #24: "Where Drive and Talent Can Take You—The Fulbright"

Personal Statement for the Fulbright Scholarship

When I first saw a skeleton hanging on the window of a house, I shrugged and wondered what type of neighborhood my family had moved into. What else could I think? I was a recent immigrant from Israel and the concept of Halloween was one of those American cultural entities which I had yet to learn about. It was the start of several years' worth of an interplay involving mutual ignorance on my part, regarding American culture, and on my American peers' part, regarding mine.

In fact, this was not the first immigration in my family's history. Both of my parents emigrated from Romania to Israel after World War II. The consequence was that sentences in our household sometimes started in one language (e.g., Romanian), were interjected with a phrase from a second (e.g., English), before finally being terminated in a third (e.g., Hebrew).

When I arrived to the United States (where I was later naturalized), I was "fluent" in only one word in English (the word "no"), inappropriately clothed (with respect to the fashion of the time), and culturally inept. Thus, I was cast out by many of my classmates as an outsider at first. Through hard work and determination, I strove to excel academically and initiated extracurricular involvement as I began to overcome the language barrier. With time, I believe my classmates also learned a lot about me and my previous country's culture.

Based on my experiences, I realized that the most effective way to rid oneself of ignorance of other nations (and to learn from them) is via complete immersion in the foreign culture. This is why I am so excited about the Fulbright program's general premise. How else can we gain each other's trust to the extent that we can collaborate on ideas and projects that will shape our future?

My experiences have left me with as many questions as answers. I now wonder which traits are innate to humans and which are cultural. For example, while a kiss signifies love in one country, it can serve as the equivalent of a handshake in another. Winking is considered rather impolite in some non-Western cultures. If such seemingly innate nonverbal forms of communication are interpreted differently, then certainly there must be many other differences that we can learn about.

As an individual who has seen two very different cultural worlds, I feel that I am in a position to better understand such cultural issues. It will be especially interesting for me to explore Canada, where I can see a culture that is not as different from America as that of my native land. Even though it has fewer cultural differences vis-à-vis the United States than more distant countries do, I have already witnessed several of them firsthand on a couple of trips to Canada, including a visit to the University of Toronto. It will be interesting to see how American and Canadian cultures retained some characteristics and yet differentiated in others as they split from their original British roots.

Every candidate faces many choices when writing an application essay. These next two essays were written by the same candidate, who did win the Fulbright and then took a deferral on his Ph.D. studies. The point is: You also can write a more or a less personal essay, a more or a less technical essay. This candidate's prudent choices resulted in success in two very different directions. Had he switched his essays, it's possible that neither would have been effective. You might try more than one approach to your essay before choosing the one you think will serve you best. You may have one background, but you have many stories to tell and many ways you can tell each story.

#24: "The Fulbright"	*(continued)*

Every point in this essay is chosen for its relevance to the published scholarship criteria.

I think that a Fulbright experience will help me as I look toward the future. My career goal is to apply computer and engineering methods to biology (specifically biochemistry), in order to facilitate the design of better drugs. I would also like to encourage governments to provide cooperative research funding opportunities for drug design efforts. Such opportunities would divide the cost of researching new drugs among North American companies and the government and involve North American academic institutions in the research process. Working together across national and commercial/academia boundaries would be especially rewarding in this field. Drug research is expensive, yet people all over the world realize immense benefits from each new type of drug that becomes available, no matter what country it originates from. I hope that I can be a part of the process that improves the quality of life for citizens everywhere. For, while we may be different in how we communicate and in the traditions we cherish, surely we are all made of the same "stuff of life," as the late Carl Sagan once put it.

ESSAY #25: "Where Drive and Talent Can Take You— Biomedical Engineering"

Molecular Biophysics Essay

Ever since I was young, I have wanted to understand not just how the body solved complex engineering problems, but also how these mechanisms worked at a fundamental level. In particular, I am interested in applying computer and experimental techniques to biological problems (and vice versa). Of particular interest is the use of computational tools in analyzing issues relating to sequence analysis/protein engineering, protein folding (and the reverse problem).

I think this is why I find the pursuit of a Ph.D. almost a necessity, given my need to satiate my mind's curiosity for seeking deeper knowledge in this area. In fact, I think this methodology has been reflected throughout my life, as I have always strived to challenge myself to find answers and overcome various obstacles. When I arrived in the United States, I knew only one word in English (the word "no"). Yet, I was determined to work hard in order to catch up. Graduating valedictorian of my class in high school and serving as co-president of Science Olympiad proved that it could be done.

I went on to Carnegie Mellon University, not just because of the merit-based scholarships, but also because I wanted to gain deeper understanding of computer techniques and their applications in biology/medicine. While I majored in electrical and computer engineering with a minor in biomedical engineering, I took as many relevant biology and chemistry courses as I could within the curriculum, including advanced courses like 03-510 (Computational Biology) and 42-680 (Bioinstrumentation). This spring, I am scheduled to take a biochemistry and second organic chemistry class. I expect to have the necessary prerequisites for advanced biochemistry study by graduation.

I am confident that I will succeed in advanced courses given my background. I also feel that I have some rather unique advantages as a non-biology major. Having a heterogeneous entering class composed not only of biology/biochemistry majors allows for more diversity in thought processes. Having undergone a similar curriculum with similar experiences, biology majors will likely have similar perspectives when encountering a novel problem. In contrast, an individual like myself may have a unique, novel contribution. Many of the breakthroughs in the past have come from interdisciplinary study resulting in a link between two previously unknown areas which went on to serve as the basis for an invention (and a new area for research). Two recent examples include the invention of DNA-based computers and biochips. In each case, a biologist or an electrical/computer engineer working alone could not have carried the project to fruition.

I have always strived to complement my education/experiences in computational approaches with fundamental biology. I have gained experience with biology both at the molecular level and at the systems level which allows me to see the big picture. When chosen by the Ohio governor to represent the state, I went to the Lawrence Berkeley Laboratory for a program on "Life Sciences and Biotechnology." Here, I attended both lectures and

This essay was written by the same person as the last one. Although there is a modicum of overlap, notice how different this presentation is from the prior example.

#25:   "Biomedical Engineering"   *(continued)*

---

did lab work involving biotechnology. Professors included Dr. Marian Diamond, Nobel Prize winner Dr. Glenn Seaborg, Dr. Sylvia Spenger (on the Human Genome Project), Dr. Mina Bissell, and Dr. Jeff O'Neil (Calgene). At a summer course at Case Western Reserve University entitled "Biotechnology and Genetic Engineering," I gained additional knowledge in experimental techniques.

From the aforementioned programs, I have gained experience with such biological techniques as electrophoresis, Southern blots, transformations, recombinant DNA techniques, PCR, chromatography, and sequence analysis. Through class/lab work and various programs, I have become knowledgeable in computer techniques used in biology such as coding region identification (via base composition, codon bias/preference, etc.), BLAST/FASTA algorithms for sequence match scoring methods, multiple sequence alignment, general similarity and homology methods (e.g., dynamic programming, dot-matrix methods, usage of hashing), secondary structure prediction (methods like Chou-Fasman, Garnier-Osguthorpe-Robson, SOPMA, etc.), and hydophobicity analysis.

In terms of bioinstrumentation, I have learned about NMR, IR, and techniques for novel instrumentation design. This past summer, I worked on a signal processing project in the Tachycardia Research group of St. Jude Medical's Pacesetter (a company formerly owned by Siemens). I designed and built a stimulus waveform generator. Then, I initiated a research study with the group's manager involving pain thresholds (in over 30 individuals) and co-authored "Sural Nerve Sensory Thresholds of Defibrillation Waveforms" which has been submitted and accepted. It will be presented at the next American College of Cardiology Scientific Session and published in the organization's peer-reviewed *Journal of the American College of Cardiology.*

One example where I applied computational/engineering techniques to biology (as I hope to do in my career) goes back to the first semester of my freshman year. I independently wrote my own grant proposal based on an idea I thought of while at the Lawrence Berkeley Lab which involved application of neural networks to the classification of DNA fingerprints. When my proposal won a SURG grant, I carried out the project independently under mentor Prof. Jose Moura, editor-in-chief of *IEEE Transactions on Signal Processing.* This endeavor, combined with academic achievements, resulted in my recognition via honorable mention as part of the all-USA College Academic Team competition (published in *USA Today.*) Only one Carnegie Mellon student is known to have ever been recognized in this competition. Since it involved novel coding techniques deployed on a PC and supercomputing environment, the work also led to an article (which I wrote) in the "Cross Platform Strategies" section in five magazines in 82 countries.

For the past several semesters, I have been working on a research project on the "system level" at the University of Pittsburgh Medical Center. It involves analysis of EEG signals from brain waves and design of a barbiturate drug infusion system with Dr. Marc Bloom, the director of neuroanesthesia at the University of Pittsburgh's medical center. The results

---

Name your advisers.

Make a laundry list of laboratory skills. Don't assume your reader will know what you can do.

Trace the history of your interest. This applicant is able to trace this particular idea back to freshman year.

#25: "Biomedical Engineering"   *(continued)*

---

of my project are rather exciting. The control system was tested on a live rhesus monkey and later revised. We are currently discovering and classifying relations between various patient variables and the sedative state and already have some interesting correlations. As we approach the next phase, this information will be combined "to establish an entirely new approach to patient modeling and the use of control in bioengineering systems" (as originally stated in the NSF grant from a group of three professors which I helped to form last semester).

I believe I can make a significant contribution to the current literature during graduate school and eventually lead efforts in innovation upon graduating from the University of Pennsylvania. I think the result from my experience at Motorola's Speech Technology Laboratory is an example of such an endeavor. Not only did I put forth a new idea, I also implemented it in a prototype and wrote the first draft of the patent (which I presented to the other co-inventors for input). The patent was submitted to the patent office in July after approval by the Motorola review committee.

I also have experience in writing, a skill which is obviously imperative for researchers who wish to communicate their findings with others. As a writer for several newspapers, I have had the chance to interview people such as Ohio's governor, a U.S. Congressman, a CEO (FORE Systems), three current and past presidents of Carnegie Mellon, and a managing editor from *U.S. News & World Report.*

I have found several faculty that share my interests at the University of Pennsylvania. In Prof. Lewis's lab, I am interested in the work going on related to computational methods used for studying protein-nucleic acid complexes. Papers from Prof. Sharp's research in structure of protein at the molecular level (using computational techniques as an option) also piqued my interest. I see a possible match with Prof. Wroblewski's work involving image processing and protein structure. I am open to working in other labs involving a combination of computational and experimental techniques in biochemistry as well.

Address the question, "Why here?" This candidate wrote different, and successful, applications to Caltech, Stanford, MIT, Berkeley, and others. Customize, customize, customize! Of course, it helps to be as accomplished as this scholar.

ESSAY #26:   "Bringing Politics to Life"

Personal Statement

This understated essay reveals a highly accomplished candidate, with considerable post-undergraduate education and experience relevant to this application. The writer reveals a life steeped in academia, and this next program is but a logical next step. The tone is confident but respectful, which is a very good choice for an application essay. Also, this essay is fairly short. One gets the impression that other complete essays could be written about items selected from any paragraph.

As the United States launched yet another small war in a distant corner of the globe, Senator Everett McKinley Dirksen returned to life and captivated a hometown audience in Pekin, Illinois, with the folksy eloquence that made him nationally famous. Unlike Thucydides, George Washington, and Theodore Roosevelt, who all proclaimed that the best preparation for peace is war, Dirksen (performed by local journalist and actor Dave Watters) spoke to a group of teachers and community leaders about the power of words to assuage conflict, whether on the floor of the Senate or in the conduct of American foreign policy. The relevance of Dirksen's speech to the approaching war was a gratifying coincidence; indeed, his reflections on *spoken* language seemed deliberately ironic as our country began bombing near the birthplace of *written* language. But for me the greatest pleasure of the evening was playing resurrection-man to the senator, selecting and arranging the findings of my archival research and then watching it unveiled in an educational dramatic monologue. That night I witnessed the power of the scholar to breathe life into the historical record.

The invention of the Dirksen persona, now used as an educational tool at schools and community festivals throughout central Illinois, was just one of the many Dirksen Center projects I worked on intending to educate the public about the history and legislative procedures of Congress (see attached résumé). During my three-year tenure, I researched and wrote dramatic monologues for portrayals of Abraham Lincoln and John F. Kennedy; co-wrote an essay presented at an historical conference on civil rights; and helped write a syllabus and plan readings for an advanced college seminar on the U.S. Senate. Although the Dirksen Center had previously awarded me fellowships for study in Washington, D.C., and at the Institute of International Affairs at Bradley University, I believe there was one other factor that especially prepared me for research at a nonprofit educational institution. While in college, I joined the forensics team, the national speaking champions for the last sixteen consecutive years. As an extemporaneous and impromptu speaker, traveling to weekly competitions all over the country, I followed current events daily and read and filed dozens of publications every week in order to speak on any foreign or domestic policy question that I might draw. I thus acquired an active comprehension of world affairs that extended far beyond the college classroom. But my earliest knowledge of international affairs began as a child when my parents would recount the many years they spent abroad in the Peace Corps and working for a Greek import/export company. From my parents I also learned that my grandfather was one of three Greek citizens granted transportation contracts to help fortify the Greek-Bulgarian border against Nazi invasion during World War II. I have consequently remained fascinated with modern Greek history and U.S. foreign policy toward postwar Europe.

As a makeweight to my daily absorption in public policy at Bradley, my intellectual curiosity began to broaden while encompassing politics in ever more subtle ways. In the course of reading about Italian fascism during World War II, I became intrigued with the

---

#26:   "Bringing Politics to Life"   *(continued)*

---

polemics and poetry of Ezra Pound and grew puzzled at the relationship between the literary avant-garde and reactionary politics in Italy, France, and Germany. This interest led me to leave Bradley for the intense scholarly environment of the University of Chicago, where I wrote an honors thesis on Ezra Pound's *Cantos* that synthesized poetic analysis with history of religions methodology and inquiry into the antidemocratic politics of literary modernism. Because I studied religion as much as politics during the course of my research, and because I thought that further religious study would assist me in the revision of my thesis for publication, I decided to attend the University of Chicago Divinity School to study Greek religion, sacrifice, and ritual theory, an academic opportunity I had never previously envisioned. As a student at the University of Chicago, I was also able to study educational public policy with literary critic Gerald Graff and to conduct research and write monograph chapters for a World Health Organization study on international oral health care policy.

I am applying to the Fletcher School because I hope eventually to work for a government or nonprofit institution (such as the U.S. Senate, National Endowment for the Humanities, or the Dirksen Congressional Center) where I can integrate my public policy research with my scholarly training in the humanities. Of the international affairs programs that I have researched, Tuft's offerings in U.S. foreign/diplomatic policy and political theory seem especially strong, and I am specifically looking forward to courses on U.S. foreign relations since 1917, American Constitutional history, and the development of political theory, which should allow me to build upon my already considerable knowledge of scholarship on political leadership and archival sources for U.S. legislative history. Tuft's curriculum is also very appealing to me because of its emphasis on economics and quantitative methods in the social sciences, two areas in which I would like to receive more training before beginning a public policy career. Given my experience as a lecturer at Bradley, Vassar College, and the George School in Philadelphia, I also hope to teach one day.

Working at an educational research institution such as the Dirksen Center has shown me that ideas can be put into action, a notion expressed in ancient Greek as *paideuma,* coincidentally the title of the journal in which my Pound essay will soon be published. However, it was Senator Dirksen rather than Ezra Pound who persuaded me that reverence for study and civic responsibility are compatible goals. Bringing the senator back to life on that January eve of war gave him the voice to do so.

> If you cannot name specific professors you are attracted to, then mention specific classes or areas of study in which you know the program excels.

> Be sure to mention pending or submitted publications, as well as those already released.

This essay is attractive because it reads so well. It may not be as flashy as some, but it is a clean, efficient presentation of a serious and thoughtful candidate. If you want a teaching assistantship, as does this candidate, be sure to discuss your teaching, tutoring, and proctoring background.

Use your essay to explain your decision-making processes, to tie all your other experiences together, and to "make sense" of data that may also be provided on a C.V. or other parts of your application. This candidate's background might have seemed disjointed, running from academe to government and back again, but this explication of his intentions lays such concerns to rest.

ESSAY #27: "To Be a College Professor"

Statement of Purpose, Combined Application for Assistantship and Doctoral Program

I had never had the opportunity to teach before; graduate assistants at Baylor rarely teach, and so I was still quite nervous and unsure of myself when I stepped to the lectern that first night at Ouachita Technical College as the new adjunct political science instructor. I had prepared my lecture; I knew my subject; I certainly had the desire to teach, but until that moment I still didn't know if I had what it would take to be a college professor. When the class ended three hours later, I knew.

Ever since I left Baylor with my master's, I have known that I eventually would return to graduate school to continue my work toward a doctorate. I have always considered my time in the "real world" to be a preparation for this return to graduate school, an opportunity to mature and to broaden my experience in government and politics beyond the theoretical and the textbook.

Toward this end, I have spent the past three years with the Arkansas Historic Preservation Program, a state government agency charged with the implementation and enforcement of the National Historic Preservation Act of 1966. I was initially hired to oversee the development and publication of *A Foundation for the Future: The Arkansas Historic Preservation Plan,* a comprehensive statement of the agency's mission, goals and objectives over the next five years. On the completion of this project, I was asked to stay on as the agency's staff planner. This has been a most valuable experience for a student of government and politics, a chance to apply my education and skills in a public policy area with national, state and local implications.

Over the past three years, I have had the opportunity to work on a number of interesting and diverse projects with federal agencies including the National Park Service and the United States Postal Service, with other state historic preservation offices, with state and national historic preservation interest groups, and with city and county government officials all over Arkansas. I have researched and written on numerous historic preservation public policy issues, including an intensive study on the effects of post office relocation policies on historic downtowns that resulted in a U.S. Senate Subcommittee hearing here in Little Rock. My efforts at developing comprehensive preservation plans and land protection strategies for Arkansas's Civil War battlefields through the Secretary of the Interior's American Battlefield Protection Program have been commended by officials of the National Park Service.

My time in state government has been an invaluable experience. I have witnessed firsthand the interactions and relationships among federal, state, and local governments; I have developed a better understanding of the intricacies of government bureaucracies; and I have broadened my education through extensive research and writing on Arkansas's political and social history. Through my professional connections, I had the opportunity to serve as a regional campaign manager for a gubernatorial campaign, and I was also active in the last presidential campaign; these experiences have given me valuable insights into modern political campaigning and the electoral process. I believe that these experiences have served to complement the very fine education that I received at Baylor and to strengthen my fascination with government and politics.

#27: "To Be a College Professor" *(continued)*

In August of this year, I accepted a part-time position with Henderson State University as adjunct political science instructor at Ouachita Technical College in Malvern, Arkansas; my experiences teaching "American National Government" to a class of thirteen nontraditional students have been very rewarding. This experience, more than any other, has forced a personal reassessment of my goals and strengthened my resolve to leave a position that I have found both professionally challenging and personally rewarding, and to return now to graduate school to earn a doctorate and to pursue an academic career.

For the past two years, I have collected information from a variety of Ph.D. programs in the southeastern United States, and I have slowly narrowed my choices to a handful of schools. I visited Vanderbilt and the Department of Political Science last summer, and was impressed with the friendly faculty and their willingness to speak with me about my educational interests and goals. I was already familiar with Vanderbilt's excellent reputation, but I felt that I should experience the program firsthand before I applied for admission. Academically, I feel that I am better suited to a smaller, more intimate educational environment. It was this atmosphere that I found so rewarding at Baylor, and its absence led me to leave the University of Virginia. Based on my discussions with Drs. Gare, Bennett, and Halestrap, I hope that I have found it again at Vanderbilt.

The entire remainder of this essay explains why the candidate chose this particular graduate program.

At Vanderbilt, I hope to pursue a course of study involving the nature, formulation, and implementation of American foreign policy, specifically toward Europe and the former Soviet Union. The abatement of East-West confrontationalism and the emergence of new democracies in Eastern Europe and the former Soviet Union represent unparalleled opportunities and challenges for American policy makers to encourage the growth and maturation of these new political systems. While the East-West rapprochement has not resulted in a cessation of regional conflict altogether, it has clearly altered the international political dynamics of such conflicts. Meanwhile, a number of international public policy issues will continue to demand attention from American policy makers: the environment, economic interdependence and free trade, refugeeism, and the continuing political and economic instability in the developing world. How will these issues play out in the American political process, how will the president and the Congress address these foreign policy concerns, and what factors and pressures will influence their decisions? These are the issues that I hope to address in my studies at Vanderbilt.

I am therefore applying for admission to Vanderbilt University's Department of Political Science doctoral program with the teaching assistantship option. The experience, the education, and the degree that I hope to earn at Vanderbilt will enable me to pursue a career in teaching and research at the university level, and to make a lasting contribution to this fascinating discipline. I am confident that my academic and professional experiences have imbued me with the depth and maturity that your program demands, and that, given the opportunity, I could be a valuable asset to your department. I hope that you will seriously consider my qualifications and arrive at the same conclusion.

ESSAY #28: "Solo Journey"

Statement of Purpose — Master's in Public Administration

I just spent the last year traveling throughout the United States. I am 24, a female, and I traveled alone. I have been to most of the major cities in the U.S. I have talked to Americans in Louisiana, Oregon, and Maryland. I have been to the Alamo and contemplated what decision I would have made had the fate of the soldiers protecting that fort been in my hands. I have spoken to five young men in Bellingham, Washington, as they tried to secure positions on Alaskan fishing boats, an adventure that statistically claims one out of nine fishermen. All but one held college degrees, yet they are seeking the job that eluded them in their home cities and a way to get rich on the last American frontier. I have been to Los Angeles where the homeless sleep on beaches next to 70,000-dollar cars while the cars' wealthy owners enjoy a jog in the early morning light. I have been to Boston in search of a historical city that was elementary in the "tug of war" with the English for our freedom, and I found an international mecca and the vestiges of that historical era reduced to paint on pavement called The Freedom Trail. In the Midwestern cities of Chicago and Detroit I have seen the industrial graveyards left from the decline of the Industrial Age. I have been to Washington, D.C. Walking through the monuments, I have rubbed the name of my father's best friend off of The Wall. I have also fit my face between the iron bars surrounding the White House and gawked while trying to prevent myself from getting mugged. Finally, while walking through the halls of the Capitol building I reflected upon my ability to make decisions that could affect our nation. In Washington my traveling came to an end. I am ready now to affect history, these places I have traveled, these lives whose paths I have crossed, this future of which I will be a part.

Wait. Before the national anthem starts emanating from the brass band precariously huddled over there in the corner, let me explain that I am not serenading you with patriotism in order to get into a program that prepares people for careers in various parts of the government. I am not any more patriotic than most Americans. I see the United States making mistakes. I disagree often and wholeheartedly with some of the decisions that are made in and out of official offices. I understand that there is a bureaucracy, and not only a bureaucracy, but layers upon layers of city, county, state and national bureaucracies all working simultaneously with and against each other (inadvertently or not). I understand that bureaucracy has an inherent connotation that screams "red tape" and that working in or for a bureaucracy takes political skills as well as professional expertise. I understand all of this and I am more determined than ever to become a part of an organization that works with the government.

At Western Michigan University I engineered my own curriculum. Five years later I graduated, completing majors in philosophy, communications, and political science and two graduate political science classes. I accomplished this despite it being necessary to work 20 to 40 hours per week—severely limiting the amount of time available to me. These achievements are representative of my success as a student. My majors and the classes I chose

This wide-ranging essay has had a deep impact on several people who read it. One said, "This woman is my hero. I'd love to take a solo trip like that." Notice that the candidate pursues her interests in and out of the academy, which puts her in a different category than what administrators call "a nine-to-five" student. She is consumed by her interests, and that is very attractive to professors who are also consumed by theirs.

This is a fairly informal style, but this applicant pulls it off.

Be sure to mention if you carried a heavy work load combined with a heavy course load.

#28: "Solo Journey" (continued)

---

within them were oriented toward working for the public in an organizational manner. They prepared me for a future in which I will actively study public administration and eventually work for the government.

The study of ethics has interested me like no other aspect of my philosophical studies. Its teachings are applicable to the reality today's society faces. Prior to studying ethics I had not analyzed my penchant for championing causes, for volunteering my time, for speaking honestly without sophistry, for wanting to positively affect the negative realities of people's lives instead of dreaming about the way their lives should be. Examining and questioning ethical concepts has given me a heightened awareness of public needs, as well as an avid interest in seeing those needs met. My ethical causes have varied over the years. I volunteered at the local humane society caring for cats and dogs that were no longer wanted. I walked miles to raise money for Alzheimer's disease. When I was traveling I stopped in Portland, Oregon, and instead of viewing the nationally renowned rose gardens I sponsored a rubber duck in the annual river race for a drug and alcohol outreach program. In my home town I helped organize a silent auction for the local Planned Parenthood. With the insight studying ethics has given me, I realize not everyone feels as strongly committed to the public as I do. By studying I gained the ability to assess professional situations in public affairs with ethical imperatives.

The basic skills predominant to the study of philosophy, such as logical reasoning and examining data analytically in relation to both its form and context, are intrinsic to public leadership. Studying philosophy also taught me to listen to an argument, internalize it, and then react to it with understanding instead of competitive one-upmanship. These skills will serve me well both as a graduate student and eventually as someone who is involved in a public management position. I am a responsible person whose attraction to American government is strengthened by her intellectual interest in providing substantive policies which will benefit the American public.

Studying communications came naturally to me. In high school I debated varsity for three years, participated in student government, thrived on Model United Nations conferences and was (ironically) voted class politician at my senior class mock elections. While I was never afraid to verbally champion causes or go head-to-head with someone on an important issue, I wanted to further develop my skills as both an orator and an effective organizational leader. I instinctively knew the fundamentals of leadership and management and was astonished to see my own common sense as the focus of serious studies, books, and papers. Studying communications gave me more confidence by grounding my natural abilities in fact. Later these skills came in handy when I worked on a campaign for a woman running for Michigan's state legislature (see enclosed campaign materials). Excellent negotiation skills, creative problem solving, and proactive leadership are a part of what I bring to the public administration field to help solve the approaching policy decisions and interactions that challenge public administrators.

Refer to supporting documentation in your essay, to remind the reader that there is even more to you than will fit in this format.

#28: "Solo Journey" *(continued)*

Studying political science has made me aware of the problems administrators must face. When I started at the university I had a shining vision of democracy given to me by my high school government teacher and the glorified way in which American history is taught. Throughout my years as an undergraduate that vision underwent a metamorphosis. I gained an understanding of how our system is supposed to work and how it does work given the various pressures and influences that act upon it. At the end of my years at Western, the concepts of democracy and government in America had, to me, become entirely different animals. In my administrative and constitutional law classes I learned about federal administrative agencies and the Supreme Court, those parts of the government that are not under direct public accountability. I was horrified and set out on paper and verbally to challenge their right to exist with any real power over the people of the U.S. Through my research I came to understand why these agencies exist and how they are necessary to maintain the balance of power between the governmental branches. I now realize the need our country has for people like myself who can be successful ethical organized leaders who genuinely care about the public in a nonjudgmental fashion.

By my senior year I had finished all of my undergraduate classes except for an independent research paper. Because I was required to stay in Kalamazoo for several more months and I planned to go to graduate school in the near future, I enrolled myself as a dual enrollee into Western Michigan University's master of political science program. Taking two of the core classes required for a master's in political science was eye-opening for me. I realized that while I was interested in learning more about "Modern Democratic Theory," it would not give me the power or knowledge I would need to manage information, personnel, and a budget in a public organization. I would not learn how to make the internal dynamics of such an organization run smoothly nor how to direct activities in both the short and long term to maximize the potential action of the organization. After talking to several of my mentors and doing some investigative research, I was ecstatic to find that the public administration field prepares people for management opportunities in the public, quasi-public, and nonprofit sectors. I realized that I need to attend a university with a program that will actively prepare me to work for, or become directly involved in, a governmental or nonprofit organization.

Washington, D.C., is a citadel of power that to many Americans is a symbol of hope. I ended my travels in Washington, D.C., because after seeing America at both its best and worst I wished to reaffirm that hope within myself. While traveling, I experienced first-hand the problems the people of this country face each day: lack of health care, lack of education, over-developed urban areas, privatization verses public works, pollution, drugs, crime, poverty, and homelessness. I have seen a lack of community and cohesion, and an inability to deal with these worries, especially in our large cities where they are the worst. Having seen and experienced these obstacles I wish to immerse myself in American University's master of public administration program. My goal is clear: to become a leader effective in creating

The candidate points out a perfect alignment between her interests and this graduate program.

#28: "Solo Journey"	*(continued)*

community and in implementing policies capable of evolving and alleviating the problems the American public faces every day. I see American University's M.P.A. program—with its proximity to the national capital—as an excellent place to do just that. With its active participant values and management-oriented curriculum the graduate school is exactly matched to my needs and background. This program's preparatory curriculum combined with my leadership skills and desire to succeed as a public administrator will give me the power and knowledge I need to accomplish my goals in working for the public. That is my goal and my calling: to work for the public.

ESSAY #29: "Children's Television"

Statement of Purpose — Developmental Psychology

"I want to be a Sesame Street Muppeteer and never have to grow up." I uttered those words not when I was eight, or twelve, but seventeen. I was convinced that I had found my calling as the personality behind a furry puppet, even though I had yet to formulate a plan to get myself halfway around the world to where Sesame Street was being produced. As I delved deeper into this peculiar ambition, I came to realize that it was not only the fun and creativity that enticed me; it was also the prospect of engaging children, of capturing their imaginations, of making them laugh and educating them, all at the same time.

Between the completion of my A Level examinations and matriculation to Davidson College, I worked for six months at a child care center in Singapore. There, I witnessed the influence of television on children as young as three years of age. As my charges pranced around mimicking the Power Rangers, I was amazed to find that television programs found expression in their behavior so effortlessly, even though they had only minimal understanding of what they watched. Realizing this, I began to pay more attention to children's television as I continued to work with young children. But as I looked more closely at many children's programs, I realized how many of them were unproductive—if not detrimental—for children.

At Davidson, I continued to pursue my interest in child development through courses in developmental psychology, child development, and an advanced seminar on children and television. The latter was pivotal in providing me with knowledge of key research issues and a true awareness of the power that television wielded over our perception and our attitudes. I found a mentor in Dr. Earl Plummer, who offered unflagging support for my interest. I applied for an internship with the Children's Television Workshop. How wonderfully odd that I did end up at the place that was responsible for my teenage Muppeteering dreams! The internship experience was invaluable. At Program Development, I gained insight into the decision processes involved in making a successful children's program. The process was far more complicated and daunting than I had imagined, but it fueled rather than dampened my enthusiasm for this field.

In combining my interests, I would like to pursue a graduate degree in developmental psychology with an emphasis on children and media and the applications of developmental psychology to education. Graduate study would not only provide me with specialized understanding of developmental psychology, it would also offer research opportunities that are simply unavailable at an undergraduate level. There are many research areas that intrigue me: cross-cultural developmental psychology, educational children's programming across Asian and Western cultures, and the influence of interactive technology on children's learning.

I hope to eventually conduct research in the educational children's television industry, evaluate the appropriateness and effectiveness of children's television, and develop educational

---

Note this arresting opening line. Imagine sitting down to read dozens of essays, all full of psycho-jargon, and then you get to this one. How refreshing. However, this opening only works because this person is, in fact, a serious and well-prepared candidate.

Sometimes a candidate's ultimate career interest is the prime motivation for graduate studies. Here, the candidate's interest in improving children's television in Asia is the entire reason for pursuing graduate education in child and developmental psychology. This woman is on a mission, and her education is merely a tool to be used for that end. She exemplifies the type of candidate who is going to succeed whether she is admitted to this particular graduate program or not.

#29: "Children's Television" *(continued)*

content. I want to apply such expertise not only in the United States, but also in Asia, with culture-appropriate material.

Even as a child in Singapore, I saw little Asian material in educational children's programs. When there were local efforts to develop culturally relevant content, quality was often compromised. Enhancing children's learning through educational television has not been an objective in most Asian cultures, and I would like to rectify that. During my internship with the Children's Television Workshop, I came to realize that I would not realistically be able to exert an influence in these areas with merely an undergraduate degree. As my professional goals have been clarified in my own mind, it has become apparent that the means by which I wish to contribute to child development requires graduate study.

Yale's developmental psychology program is one of the finest and most well-respected in the country. Through the course of my readings, I often came across key research articles by Yale's Family Television Research Center. Being a graduate student at Yale would offer exceptional opportunities to work at the center under the direction of such distinguished researchers as Dr. Gerald Snyder. Furthermore, the emphasis on direct research involvement in the program suits my intellectual and professional interests. Because my research interests can potentially cross several disciplinary boundaries, it is especially important for me to be able to create the program of study that best satisfies my needs. Yale's program offers such flexibility. I have also heard much about Yale's commitment to its graduate students through a Davidson psychology professor and Yale alumnus, Dr. Marconi. In short, Yale's program offers everything that I am looking for.

> Demonstrate that you've researched the targeted graduate program, as does this candidate.

Despite my efforts to ensure a sound background for graduate study, there remain some weaknesses in my preparation. Due in large part to the limited size, resources, and research opportunities at Davidson College, I have not been able to acquire formal experience as a research assistant to a faculty member. In considering my qualifications to be a teaching assistant, I concede that I lack experience in teaching psychology. However, I do serve as a teaching assistant for introductory economics and beginning Chinese. In addition, because of scheduling conflicts (particularly as a double major), I was not able to take such psychology courses as personality, learning, and cognition. I will take cognitive psychology this summer and have had solid exposure to personality and educational psychology in other courses.

> Be sure to describe academic preparation that will take place between the time you apply and the beginning of your graduate program.

Also, I believe that my field accomplishments more than compensate for any curricular weaknesses. I have worked formally and informally with young children in both the United States and Singapore. At Davidson, I have volunteered at the local daycare center, tutored first graders at the community center, and am currently a First Day School helper at the Friends Meeting. In addition, I was a waiting room volunteer at the Lakeside Family Center, an agency that works to prevent child abuse and neglect. I have had contact with children from diverse backgrounds and am convinced that I want to pursue a career that benefits children.

#29:   "Children's Television"   *(continued)*

To make up for the lack of formal research experience, I served as research assistant on a thesis study on computer-mediated communication. As a confederate, I was an integral part of the experiment. I also assisted in literature review, the sampling of participants, and data rating and analysis. This semester, I am involved in my own honors thesis, which will involve a literature survey, methodology, development, and data collection and analysis. My interest in children, educational television, and cross-cultural studies will converge in a project examining differences in content emphasis between the American and Chinese-adapted versions of Sesame Street and the extent to which the differences reflect core values in each culture. Refining methodology has been an interesting challenge as I strive to define culture and the behavioral expression of cultural values in a quantifiable way. The firsthand experience in planning, executing, and analyzing such a study will serve me well in a graduate setting.

Perhaps the most important aspects of my preparation for graduate study are non-academic. I take greatest pride in the fact that I have accepted all the challenges that have come my way in the last four years. As an international student on substantial financial aid, I work three jobs for over twenty hours a week, volunteer in service activities, and still meet Davidson's and my personal high academic standards. I have developed maturity and tenacity that surpass many others my age, and I believe that such qualities are ultimately the most indicative of my ability to succeed at a graduate level.

ESSAY #30: "Table Topic"

The Synthesis of Thiaporphyrins as Possible Photodynamic Cancer Therapy (PDT) Agents

Amy L. Gryshuk*, Dawn Cox*, Ryan J. Howard*, Lynn E. Maelia#, Edward P. Zovinka*
*Dept. of Chem., Math & Phys. Sci., Saint Francis College, Loretto, PA 15940 & #Div. of Natural Sci., Mount Saint Mary College, Newburgh, N.Y. 12550

I. ABSTRACT   The study of thiaporphyrins is of interest because of their potential use as Photodynamic Therapy (PDT) agents for cancer treatment. When light activated, the photosensitizer excites the oxygen in the cell to its toxic singlet state which kills the cancer. Prior experimentation on the insertion of molybdenum into a thiaporphyrin ligand has shown bands at 717 nm which is in the desired red region (630–800 nm).[1]

The goal of this project is to efficiently and affordably synthesize thiaporphyrins according to a "3+1" Synthesis of a thiotripyrrane dicarboxylic acid with 1-H-pyrrole-2,5-dicarboxaldehyde. The thiotripyrrane has been successfully synthesized according to ^{1}H NMR data and we are currently preparing 1-H-pyrrole-2,5-dicarboxaldehyde.

II. INTRODUCTION: WHAT ARE THIAPORPHYRINS?

Unlike the porphyrin, the thiaporphyrin (SPH) consists of 3 bridging pyrroles and one thiophene ring. The dithiaporphyrin (S_2P) consists of 2 bridging pyrroles and 2 thiophen rings. The addition of the S atom to the macrocycle core is of particular interest because the core modified porphyrins are a relatively untapped resource. The core size is smaller in comparison to the normal porphyrin and the aromatic character is modified due to non-planarity of the macrocycle.[2] The N⋯N distance is 4.383 Å in tetraphenylporphyrin, the S⋯N distance is 3.585 Å in thiaporphyrin, and the S⋯S distance is 3.069 Å in dithiaporphyrin.[3]

Our current research includes inserting early transition metals since metals later in the transition series, such as Cu, Fe, and Ni, have been previously studied with the SPH ligand. While the structural and reactivity changes brought about by modification of the core may be of interest for catalytic uses, the main purpose of this research project is to study metallothiaporphyrins for possible use as Photodynamic Therapy (PDT) agents for cancer.

PORPHYRIN   THIAPORPHYRIN   DITHIAPORPHYRIN

WHAT IS PHOTODYNAMIC THERAPY (PDT)?   PDT is a medical treatment for solid cancers in which photosensitizing agents such as porphyrins are administered and then activated with light (630-800 nm).[1] It is a safe, non-invasive treatment for cancer that is based on the "phototoxicity of photosensitizing agents like porphyrins which are the

---

#30: "Table Topic" *(continued)*

When submitting
work samples, be
sure to comply with
these two rules:
Work samples must
be very, very good,
and they need to be
directly related
to the targeted area
of graduate study.
You should have a
professor review
any work sample
you plan to submit,
both to review the
quality of the work
and to assess the
appropriateness of
the submission. This
one's a winner.

natural precursors of hemoglobin."[4] Porphyrins have been chosen because of their similarity to hemoglobin, which carries oxygen in red blood cells throughout the body including to the cancerous regions.

The photosensitizer is inserted into the body where it accumulates near cancer cells. In the ground state, the oxygen present in the cells is in the triplet state. When light-activated, the porphyrin excites the oxygen in the cell to its toxic singlet state which kills the cancer. Light with wavelength in the 650–800 nm range is preferred because of its ability to penetrate up to 3.0 cm (over 1⅛ inch) deep into human tissues.[4]

PDT eliminates the need for surgical procedures because of the possibility of irradiating the tumor through the skin, through topical applications of porphyrins, or through endoscopic laser therapy.

The Basic Idea of Tumor Phototherapy Is to:[5]

1. Select a good photosensitizer with selectivity for photodamage to tumor tissue.

2. Inject the photosensitizer and wait until the tumor region fluoresces to denote the presence of porphyrin.

3. Irradiate the tumor with the visible light (650–800 nm).

PDT[5]

Advantages

- Painless

- Non-invasive

- Able to treat multiple lesions with topical porphyrins in one sitting

- Good patient acceptance

- Good cosmetic results

- Not cytotoxic unless irradiated with light

- Can be repeated as often as necessary without damaging healthy tissue

Disadvantages

- Impure compounds currently in use

- Compounds remain in the skin for 4–6 weeks, causing cutaneous sensitivity

- Still experimental—research is continuing

PRELIMINARY EVIDENCE According to Marcinkowska, et al., "Modification of the core of porphyrins, by the introduction of various heteroatoms in place of one or two

---

#30: "Table Topic"   *(continued)*

---

pyrolle-NH groups, allows preparation of new heterocycles that show interesting properties in terms of their aromatic porphyrin-like character and the marked difference in the electronic spectra."[6]

Following this suggestion, we have prepared thiaporphyrin (SPH) and have inserted a molybdenum atom into its core. The electronic spectrum of this molybdenum thiaporphyrin (MoSPH) shows the absorption of light at 717 nm.[7] This is in the target 650–800 nm wavelength range for PDT use.

III. EXPERIMENTAL

Step 1: Synthesis of 2,5–Acetoxymethyl–thiophene

Reference: Griffing, J.M.; Salisbury, L.F. *J. Am. Chem. Soc.*, 1948, 3417.

Step 2: Synthesis of Thiotripyrrane

Reference : Boudif, A.; Momenteau, M. *J. Chem. Soc., Perkin Trans. I*, 1996, 1240.

1. LiOH

Reference : Sessler, J.L.; Cry, M.J. Burrell, A.K. *Synlett* 1991, 127.

Step 3: Synthesis of 2,5–pyrrole–Dicarbaldehyde

Reference : Boudif, A.; Momenteau, M. *J. Chem. Soc., Perkin Trans. I*, 1996, 1239.

#30: "Table Topic" *(continued)*

Step 4: Synthesis of Thiaporphyrins

Reference : Boudif, A.; Momenteau, M. *J. Chem. Soc., Perkin Trans. 1*, 1996, 1241 &
Broadhurst, M.J.; Grigg R.; Johnson, A.W. *J. Chem. Soc. (C)*, 1971, 3689.

Synthesis 2,5-bis-chloromethyl-thiophene

Reference: Griffing, J.M.; Salisbury, L.F. *J. Am. Chem. Soc.* Vol. 70, 1948, 3417.

To a 3-neck 500 mL flask with stir bar and thermometer was added 45.0 mL 37% CH_2O and 11.5 mL conc. HCl. HCl gas was bubbled through the stirring solution for 2 hours until a specific gravity was reached, 1.1797 g/mL (literature suggested 1.185 g/mL). After 2 hrs. bubbling was stopped and an ice/water bath was added to cool the 3-neck flask (kept stirring). Distilled thiophene (15.0 mL) was added dropwise at 1 drop/sec. The temperature remained between 30°C and 0°C. After the thiophene was completely added the yellowish solution was stirred for an additional 20–30 minutes. After 20–30 minutes, the stirring was stopped to allow the solution to settle into 3 layers (keep on ice/water bath). Three layers were visible: top—cream/white; middle—light yellow; bottom—larger dark-gold yellow (oil). The 3-neck flask remained on ICE at ALL TIMES (polymerizes at R.T.). The lower oily layer was siphoned off, placed into a separatory funnel, and rinsed twice with ~25.0 mL COLD distilled water. The oily layer was extracted into a 100 mL r.b. to refrigerate overnight to form crystals.

2,5-bis-chloromethyl-thiophene oil polymerizes at R.T. so it was kept on ICE at ALL times. Next day, noticed a lower dark oily layer and light golden water layer with possible para-formaldehyde solid. The flask and glass frit used for vacuum filtration were chilled. The filtrate flask was placed into an ice bath while filtrating. Solid golden para-formaldehyde was present on frit surface (discarded). Water globules present in filtrate were siphoned off and discarded. The oil filtrate was pipeted into a 25.0 mL r.b. and refrigerated.

#30: "Table Topic"   *(continued)*

Synthesis 2,5-bis-acetoxymethyl-thiophene

Reference: Griffing, J.M.; Salisbury, L.F. J. Am. Chem. Soc. Vol. 70, 1948, 3417.

Transferred 49.0 mL glacial HOAc into 100 mL r.b. Measured out 13.8053 g NaOAc and added to stirring HOAc. The solution started to solidify so a glass stirring rod was used to break up the solid chunks. Slowly 14.09 g 2,5-bis-chloromethyl-thiophene was added to the stirred suspension (kept 2,5-bis-chloromethyl-thiophene r.b on ice while waiting to add—polymerizes at R.T.). The temperature was kept steady at ~60°C. The golden yellow slurry was stirred for 5 hours. After 5 hours, the solution was cooled at R.T. for 16 hrs. to form two layers. Two layers were present: top—brown/rust clear liquid; bottom—yellow solution w/white solid on bottom. Next day, oil settled out (¾ maroon oil on top & ¼ yellow on bottom). After 16 hrs. the solution was vacuum filtrated. A white solid remained on glass frit. The white solid was tested for solubility and presence of chloride ions. The rich, brown oil filtrate was transferred to a 100 mL r.b. via pipet. The r.b. was rotovapored on a hot water bath.

After being rotovaporated a chunky, crispy, golden-orange caramel solid with white chunks remained. COLD Na_2CO_3 was added to 100 mL r.b. to neutralize. The white solid settled on the bottom leaving the brown oil layer on top. Excess Na_2CO_3 was added. The contents were transferred to a beaker where excess distilled water and ethyl ether were added. Then, the solution was placed into separatory funnel and the oil layer was extracted into a 50.0 mL r.b. (dark brown oil). The r.b. was not capped to allow the ethyl ether to evaporate off.

Synthesis of Thiotripyrrane

Reference: Boudif, A.; Momenteau, M. *J. Chem. Soc., Perkin Trans.* 1, 1996, 1240.

Added 0.9541 g distilled (Fraction #3) 2,5-bis-acetoxymethyl-thiophene to 100 mL Schlenk flask. While stirring and under nitrogen, 1.2883 g ethyl pyrrole-2-carboxylate was added to flask. Approximately 30.0 mL denatured ethanol to golden, clear solution was slowly added. Lastly, 0.1663 g p-Toluenesulfonic acid was added to the stirred solution. At first the solution was pale yellow and/or slightly cloudy. For 7 hours the mixture was refluxed under nitrogen

---

#30:   "Table Topic"   *(continued)*

---

to produce a dark, golden/tan solution. Nitrogen was blown over the top of the flask while cooling. Once cooled, the flask was placed in the refrigerator overnight.

The next day there was a clear brown liquid above a dark "caramel" oil. The clear brown liquid was decanted to evaporate off the EtOH. CH_2Cl_2 was added to the Schlenk flask to dissolve the dark "caramel" oil. Oil was transferred into large glass vial and weighed. An IR (salt plate) of the thiotripyrrane oil and EtOH oil from thiotripyrrane were taken.

The crude thiotripyrrane oil was columned using silica gel and eluted with CH_2Cl_2.

Synthesis of Thiotripyrrane-dicarboxylic acid

10.0 mL of 1.0M NaOH in water and 5 mL of absolute ethanol were added to 0.2130 g of thiotripyrrane-ethyl ester with stirring. After 22 hours of stirring at room temperature, the solution was refluxed for 4 hours. The solution was allowed to stir for another 18 hours at room temperature. Unreacted starting material was extracted into 10 mL CH_2Cl_2, the NaOH solution was neutralized with 1.0 M HCl, and the resulting carboxylic acid was extracted into CH_2Cl_2 (3 X 10 mL). This was dried over $MgSO_4$ and filtered into a round bottom without purification for further reaction to the dithiaporphyrin.

Synthesis of 2.5-pyrrole-dicarbaldehyde

Reference: Boudif, A.; Momenteau, M. *J. Chem. Soc., Perkin Trans.* 1, 1996, 1239.

Carefully weighed out 0.515 g $Pb(OAc)_4$ and 1.0476 g PbO_2 into 100 mL r.b. Approximately 30.0 mL HOAc was added to the r.b. Originally the stirred solution was black. To a 50.0 mL beaker was added 0.5166 g 2,5-dimethylpyrrole. HOAc (16.5 mL) was added to the beaker to make a slurry. When the slurry was added to the stirred solution of HOAc, $Pb(OAc)_4$, and PbO_2 the color turned to dark brown/coffee. The solution was stirred for 3 hours at R.T. and capped with a stopper. After 3 hours 20.0 mL distilled water was added to the r.b. The mixture was refluxed for 30 minutes and allowed to cool (kept stirring).

Distilled water (100 mL) was added to the r.b. and placed into 500 mL separatory funnel. The r.b. was rinsed with 100 mL CH_2Cl_2 and added to funnel. A dissecting light was used to distinguish 2 layers: top—dark maroon water; bottom—CH_2Cl_2 dark/light red-maroon layer. The CH_2Cl_2 layer was extracted into a 250 mL erlenmeyer flask. Water layer was

#30: "Table Topic"	*(continued)*

rinsed with CH_2Cl_2. CH_2Cl_2 layer was transferred back into separatory funnel and 10.0 mL Na_2CO_3 was added. CH_2Cl_2 layer was extracted into a 500 mL erlenmeyer flask. The dark, plum, maroon colored sol'n was transferred back into the separatory funnel and rinsed with 100 mL distilled water (3 times). The CH_2Cl_2 layer was extracted into a 500 mL flask and dried over Na_2SO_4. The liquid was decanted off into a 500 mL r.b. and rotovapored on hot water bath.

The crude 2,5-pyrrole-dicarbaldehyde residue was columned on 3.0 cm diameter Silica Gel and eluted with $ChCl_3$. Fractions #1–10 were collected in 50.0 mL integrals. TLC plates and IR were taken.

IV. DISCUSSION

Literature procedures were followed for the synthesis of 2,5-bis-chloromethyl-thiophen (41.4% yield), 2,5-bis-acetoxymethyl-thiphene (61.8% yield), thiotripyrrane (33.6% yield), thiotripyrrane-dicarboxylic acid (??), and 2,5-pyrrole-dicarboxaldehyde (3.4%). Step 1 (2,5-bis-chloromethyl-thiophene) and Step 2 (2,5-bis-acetoxymethyl-thiophene) were successfully synthesized while Step 3 (2,5-pyrrole-dicarboxaldehyde) is still being studied. All materials were characterized by IR and/or ^{1}H NMR spectra.

V. FUTURE PLANS

Future research will involve the synthesis of thiaporphyrins (SPH) and dithiaporphyrins (S_2P) according to the "3+1" Synthesis. Once successfully synthesized, early transition metal thiaporphyrin complexes of SPH and S_2P that absorb in the desired 630–800 nm wavelength range will be prepared. These compounds can then be used in studies as possible PDT photosensitizers for cancer.

The last few weeks of summer research will focus on the synthesis of dithiaporphyrin, followed by the thiaporphyrin. The dithiaporphyrin can be synthesized more easily because the thiotripyrrane-dicarboxylic acid can react with the commercially available 2,5-thiophene-dicarboxaldehyde. Once the 2,5-pyrrole-dicarboxaldehyde is purified, the SPH reaction can be attempted.

Once S_2P and SPH are synthesized on a small scale, they can then be attempted on larger scales. Our focus will then be on inserting molybdenum and/or tungsten into the S_2P and SPH ligands.

VI. RESOURCES

1. Pandey, R.K.; Ressler, M.M. "Creating New Photosensitizers for Cancer Therapy." *Chemtech* March 1998, 35.

2. Lato-Grazynski, L.; Lisowski, J.; Olmstead, M.M.; Balch, A.L. "The First Structural Characterization of a Nickel (I) Macrocyclic System: Structure of Nickel (I) Diphenyldi-p-tolyl-21-Thiaporphyrin." *Inorganic Chem.* 1989, 23, 1183–1188.

#30: "Table Topic"	(continued)

3. Lato-Grazynski, L.; Lisowski, J.; Olmstead, M.M.; Balch, A.L. "21-Thiatetra-p-tolylporphyrin and Its Copper (II) Bicarbonate Complex. Structural Effects of Copper-Thiophene Binding." *J. Am. Chem. Soc.* 1987, 109, 4428–4429.

4. Luma Care. Http://www.lumacare.com/ 1997 MGB Technologies.

5. Bonnet, R. "Photosensitizers of the Phorphyrin and Phthalocyanine Series for Photodynamic Therapy." *Chemical Society Reviews* 1995, 19.

6. Chmielewski, P.; Lato-Grazynski, L.; Marcinkowska, E.; Pacholska, E.; Radzikowki, C.S.; Ziolkowski, P. "The New Sensitizing Agents for Photodynamic Therapy: 21-Selenaporphyrin and 21-Thiaporphyrin." *Anticancer Research* Vol. 17, 1997, 3313–3314.

7. Zovinka, E. P.; Howard, R. J. Unpublished data on MoSPH, 1997–98.

ACKNOWLEDGMENTS   Donors of the Petroleum Research Fund, administered by the American Chemical Society (ACS) for partial support of this research; the following institutions:

Mount Saint Mary College
Saint Francis College
United States Military Academy at West Point

ESSAY #31: "The Midnight Run"

Dave McDonald
Statement of Purpose
University of California, San Francisco
Family Nurse Practitioner Program

With his only hand, Manuela's husband passed his machete up to the front of the pickup that I was driving. "Here," he said to Carlo, "take this, you might need it." Manuela was sitting between Carlo and me with a B/P of 90/40, a miscarriage causing her to bleed excessively. It was one o'clock in the morning and we were driving from the farm cooperative to the hospital in Jiquilisco. There were reports of armed gangs on the roads, so taking her to the hospital at night was a risk, but Manuela couldn't wait.

I asked myself what I was doing there and discovered that this was exactly where I wanted to be. Not necessarily on a dangerous road in El Salvador, but working in a rural community providing nursing care to the people who need it the most.

I decided to become a nurse when I was seventeen, after traveling through rural Mexico and witnessing a developing nation for the first time. This experience became a catalyst for me. Since then I have worked with a variety of underserved populations. At Northeastern University, I chose rotations in emergency rooms in the inner city and on an Indian reservation. These experiences created an interest in cardiac care. After graduation I began working on a cardiac step-down unit. Then I traveled to El Salvador during a civil war. I was strongly influenced by what I saw there and was reminded of my original interest in nursing. I decided to acquire the skills valuable to a war-torn country and began working at the hospital's rehabilitation center.

Within a year I had raised funds through an Ultimate Frisbee tournament and returned to El Salvador. Using my experience in rehabilitation, I moved to the farm cooperative and set up a clinic for disabled veterans and their families. Over the following years I visited El Salvador frequently, working with people who were developing ideas from within the community and building a medical delivery system with local resources. I became interested in how these appropriate "technologies" could be used to make health care more accessible.

Activating the Ultimate Frisbee community, I developed the tournament into an annual event raising over $10,000 a year. Funds were used for a variety of appropriate technology projects, including a prosthetics workshop run by disabled veterans and a natural medicine pharmacy. Tournament proceeds, combined with a grant I requested from the Presbyterian Hunger Program, were used to buy fifteen acres of farmland for an indigenous community.

My work with Spanish-speaking populations led to two summers with the Colorado Migrant Health Program. While setting up a school-based clinic for migrant kids in Head Start through the ninth grade, I had the opportunity to work with a family nurse practitioner. Seeing that his skills were what were most needed in rural health care, I began to prepare for graduate school. While working with adult migrants, I noticed the similarities between

Here's an arresting opening paragraph. The reader will have to know more, will have to read on . . .

This is a fascinating essay and assuredly unlike any others that may arrive in the same year. The candidate does a wonderful job of drawing the reader into an event—an emergency no less—and uses that as an intro into the bigger picture of his academic interests and how they are aligned with his sense of mission to serve others.

#31: "The Midnight Run"   (continued)

A consistent, long-term history of service is required to impress medical admissions professionals. Any last-minute conversions of the "Ohmagod, I forgot I'm supposed to be a giving person" type will be seen for what they are. This candidate has years of volunteer work to discuss.

Salvadoran and North American farmworkers. I became curious how migrant workers could benefit from appropriate technology. Specifically, I am interested in how family caregivers can combine traditional health care and Western medicine to provide greater continuity of care while traveling through migrant social systems. I hope to study this further as part of a thesis project.

Drawn by the large Central American and migrant populations, I moved to California. Over the past two and a half years I have been providing services for low-income youth through the Department of Labor's Job Corps Program, an experience that has greatly prepared me for advanced practice. At the Treasure Island Center, I saw up to twenty walk-ins per day, treating a wide range of medical problems. Working independently with a set of standing orders, I coordinated care with physicians, specialists, dentists, and a mental health consultant. I developed the department to include a referral process, wellness programs, drug and alcohol counseling, a computerized database, and Medi-Cal enrollment. While at Sacramento Center, I managed the nursing staff and coordinated care for over four hundred students. My development of new systems for charting and health care delivery has resulted in improved services for the students.

Entering an advanced practice program will be my next step to attaining greater independence and expertise in community health. Being a nurse practitioner will enhance my ability to provide nursing care to farmworker families. Working more independently and with a larger scope of practice will enable me to provide more of the services that are needed in rural areas.

I am attracted to the UCSF program for its focus on cross-cultural and international nursing. On completion of the program I will continue to provide care for Spanish-speaking and migrant families in California. I hope to continue my work in El Salvador, facilitating the exchange of appropriate technology between the two regions and using it to provide low cost care.

Again I ask myself what it is that I want to do and I go back to that night in El Salvador. As a nurse practitioner, I would have been better prepared to take care of Manuela in the clinic on the ranch. We went back to Jiquilisco a few days later, this time in the daylight, to bring her home. I was glad to have been able to help her. Next time I can do more.

I look forward to the challenges ahead and hope I am given the opportunity to contribute to your program.

Notice how neatly he draws his theme back into the wrap-up for the essay.

ESSAY #32: "Ranch Realities"

Personal Statement for Veterinary School

As I was growing up our house was always filled with an assortment of animals—dogs, cats, birds, and reptiles. In the summers I worked on my grandparents' cattle ranch in central Oregon, and there I participated in the planting, irrigating, and haying operations. My true preference, however, was working with the livestock. I rode on the cattle drives and helped in the brandings (which included dehorning, vaccinating, and castrating). Through these experiences I came to understand the relationship between rancher and livestock, and the often harsh reality of animal husbandry.

At my grandparents', too, I became interested in horses. My first horse was an unbroken quarter horse, who quickly educated me on the trials of owning a large animal. I have owned two other horses, both thoroughbreds, which I trained, showed, and later sold. As a horse owner I have experienced my share of colics, wire cuts, and mysterious lameness, as well as learned how to handle and cajole an animal that weighs eight to ten times more than I do. I have taught English and Western lessons, anatomy, general horsemanship, and first aid to Sierra Club members and summer camp children, and have been responsible for the care of fifteen lesson horses. No matter what the experience, the companionship, enjoyment, and sense of responsibility I have gained from growing up around animals has convinced me that veterinary medicine offers me a way to combine my love for animals with my interest in biological science.

More recent events have also directed me toward a career in veterinary medicine. After graduating from Duke with a bachelor's degree in biology, I accepted a four-month internship near Naples, Florida, working at a wild animal rehabilitation clinic. In contrast to my experiences with domesticated animals, the wild animals I encountered did everything in their power to flee or fight their way to freedom. We worked in cooperation with local veterinarians to provide emergency care to injured wildlife, nursing care to convalescing animals, and physical therapy to animals that were potentially releasable. I participated in all aspects of these procedures and gained invaluable experience handling raptors, seabirds, and other native species. My daily responsibilities included medicating, weighing, rescuing, and providing emergency care, as well as preparing food, cleaning cages, and answering public inquiries.

My internship ended in January and I moved back to Seattle, where I was hired by a major dog and cat hospital. The hospital provides general and specialized veterinary services, employing an oncologist, a neurologist, a radiologist, and an internist. When I started at the clinic my responsibilities included restraining animals during procedures, cleaning cages, and medicating hospitalized cases. I now am the technician to Dr. Verna Petrakis, the neurology specialist (see letter of recommendation), and my duties include placing IV catheters, drawing blood, monitoring animals under anesthesia, and preparing for joint/spinal taps and myelograms. In addition, I have been trained to operate a CAT scan, which the hospital is fortunate enough to own.

This essay is simple and direct. In its own style, it is overwhelmingly articulate. It reveals that rarest of creatures, an idealistic candidate devoid of naiveté.

Notice the straightforward expository style. It is easy to read, and the words don't distract at all from the message.

#32: "Ranch Realities" *(continued)*

In my present position I am not only learning new procedures and techniques, but also I am gaining experience in seeing how a veterinary clinic operates. I realize that in order to maintain high professional standards it takes solid managerial and financial skill. The hospital runs smoothly only when inventory is well stocked, kennels well maintained, and a positive rapport exists between the clinic and clientele. Based upon conversations I have had with veterinarians and on my own observations, I sense that the profession of veterinary medicine is undergoing rapid change. Advancements (in both human and animal medicine) have created new dilemmas for veterinarian and client. While care has improved and previously incurable conditions can now be treated, the costs for such procedures can be prohibitive. I believe veterinarians must approach their clients honestly when discussing the benefits and costs of treatments and offer alternatives to the client whenever possible.

After working in several areas of the animal care industry, I have begun to narrow down my potential career goals. While I enjoy working with small animals, my interests really lie with large ones. My experiences working in central Oregon have enforced my desire to work in a rural area and treat livestock. I am also interested in wildlife and marine mammal medicine. In addition to my work in the small animal clinic, I work as an ecology teacher on a research vessel on Puget Sound. This experience has reinforced my commitment to environmental issues. Wildlife veterinary medicine seems to me to offer a way I can help preserve wildlife and fulfill my own professional goals.

Having a clear interest in a niche implies maturity and a sophisticated understanding of your future profession. However, it will increase your chances of admission only if the program you have targeted has some special expertise in that area.

ESSAY #33: "Socrates Goes Inner City"

Application Essay for Rhodes Scholarship

In Plato's *Protagoras,* Socrates begins his interrogation of Hippocrates with the question: "What will you become?" Socrates repeats this question with increasing fury as he rebukes Hippocrates for planning to become wise by listening to the sophist Protagoras. Socrates does not care that Hippocrates will waste money on a few lectures, but instead that he will "risk his greatest treasure" by entrusting the training of his soul to a teacher skilled in speaking rather than in wisdom. Socrates's breathtaking vision of the human potential at stake in education has inspired my commitment to work in public education as well as politics. My study of philosophy began with the Greeks, and I since have found no other thinkers who so profoundly struggle with the issues of education, politics, and their relation to human potential. As I struggle with what I will become, I think the most valuable training would be an intense engagement with the texts of Plato and Aristotle in the classics program at Oxford.

When I began studying philosophy, I was shocked at Plato's devastating critique of competitive debating, the activity which had dominated my experience through high school. In the *Republic,* Plato argues that such debate suffocates constructive dialogue because it aims at conquest rather than truth. Socrates's final description of the just individual as one who would "participate in the political affairs of the ideal city but not any other [city]" forced me to reassess not only my past debating but my political aspirations.

With Socrates's words in mind, I avoided the debates of the political organizations on campus, and during my sophomore year I became a tutor for a student struggling with English at Hillhouse High School. After a semester, I guest-taught poetry to a class of inner-city students. We discussed the poem "Dream Deferred," in which Langston Hughes compares a languishing dream to a raisin which dries in the sun. At the end of the class, I asked whether the poem would have been different if Hughes had chosen a plum rather than a raisin. "It would be completely different," a student answered, "because if a raisin dries up, there's nothing, but if a plum dries up, there's a seed; there's hope."

That answer nourished new dreams, and I decided to teach English in a summer program for economically disadvantaged New Haven students. After the first day of class, I was disheartened because my tenth-grade students angrily resisted reading the *Iliad* on the grounds that it had no relation to their lives as African-Americans. I first tried to argue that Homer was worth reading, which only caused more resentment. When I told my fellow teachers about the problem, many urged me to use stricter discipline to quiet the students' complaints and to proceed with the *Iliad.* But my recent study of Rousseau had convinced me that the excitement I wanted the students to experience could only occur in an atmosphere of freedom. The problem was not only the students' lack of discipline, but the failure of my efforts to respond to their difficulties in reading and enjoying the text. I found that by reading aloud diverse scenes from the *Iliad,* the students could more readily experience the variety of life Homer describes. One student was so moved by Hector's farewell to his wife and child that

The Rhodes scholarship is reserved for those students who demonstrate excellence in a combination of academics, community service, and sports. This essayist does not mention his participation in sports, but you can be assured that somewhere else in his application he makes ample mention of his accomplishments in this area.

This candidate writes about Greco-European thinkers with great familiarity and ease, as though they were his best friends or last semester's roommates.

#33: "Socrates Goes Inner City"   *(continued)*

---

he later wrote an essay which retold the *Iliad* from Hector's perspective. Another student, who initially felt the most oppressed by the class, decided that "Achilles was cool" and wrote in his evaluation: "This was my favorite class because I felt I had some freedom."

While Rousseau's ideas on education influenced how I taught, his political thought influenced how I responded to the community at Yale. His vision of an active citizenry which contributes to a common goal offered an alternative to the fragmented community I saw outside of class. The challenge remained of how to organize students with diverse interests to contribute to the public good.

At the beginning of my junior year, I started the Branch program, which organized Yale students to share their interests with public high school students. By the end of that year, one hundred and fifty Yale students were working together with students at Hillhouse High School in programs such as art, drama, writing, recycling, and journalism. Yale students who had earlier passed by more general community service posters found a particular excitement in sharing their enthusiasm for what they loved to do. This enthusiasm was often cut short however, when Hillhouse students did not show up for their appointed meetings. The problems of the inner city can undermine the program by suffocating the high school students' sense of responsibility and their hope. This year Branch has restructured its programs to make them sufficiently reliable and engaging to encourage students to deepen their commitments and their aspirations.

As I try to respond to problems which can seem overwhelming, I often draw on the philosophy of Immanuel Kant. Kant's conviction that there are no absolute limits on our freedom to change ourselves or others provides grounds for hope. His categorical imperative challenges us to consider ourselves as architects who build a world when we act. Kant's ambitious model of our shared duty to build our society provides a foundation for Rousseau's conception of the active citizen. In my senior thesis, I will continue to explore what I see as the potentially revolutionary power of Kant's vision to respond to the inequalities that ravage our society.

Kant's vision, however, raises many questions that have urged me to return to a study of the Greeks. Plato and Aristotle's discussion of education and politics would deeply enrich my understanding of what might be done to enable people to realize their freedom. Since Oxford's program in classics is known for integrating a close study of ancient and modern philosophical texts, there would be no more exciting place to explore the relationship between ancient thought and Kant's philosophy.

Socrates's question—"What will you become?"—expresses a combination of urgency and hope that underlies my view of politics and education. I share his fury at the reckless devastation of human potential, and also his hope that we can build what we will become. In pursuit of that hope, I plan first to teach in public high school and then to work on local education policy. By the end of my course of study at Oxford, I hope to understand more fully what is at stake in Socrates's question, and be better prepared to respond to it.

Right here idealism meets reality, and yet survives. Being blindly optimistic and upbeat is often not as impressive as being committed in the face of frankly daunting circumstances.

This is a nice summation, drawing all the parts of the essay together.

ESSAY #34: "A Happy Childhood—Then Architecture"

Autobiography for School of Architecture

I was born in Port Harcourt, Nigeria, to a middle-class African family. I feel fortunate to have had a beautiful early childhood. I attribute most of my success as a adult to a strong foundation made in early life by a warm and loving family which provided nurture, guided direction, enforced discipline, inspired excellence, established norms and value systems that were ethical and humane, and instilled a good sense of judgment. Above all, there was endless love. On the other hand, though, the school (elementary, high school through college) was a big partner in this enterprise. They reinforced and complemented some of these efforts. And for me, it was a pleasure to seek, wonder, and learn, combined with the splendor of meeting new friends, each of whom had a meaningful significance in my life. Subsequently, I developed a very good social, moral, and intellectual base that enhanced my capacity to succeed in a competitive and dynamic society.

As time evolved, my decision to attend undergraduate school in the United States was a major one. First, there was the thrill of adventure, the joy and excitement of discovering the "New World," the United States of America, and the enthusiasm to begin college work. America has fascinated me, especially as portrayed by Mark Twain, Ernest Hemingway, Emily Dickinson, and depicted in the paintings of Norman Rockwell. Of course I was also aware of the superior design education available in the United States. After graduation, I emigrated to the U.S. to study architecture, attending Hampton University in Hampton, Virginia, a beautiful college by the sea with a committed and informed faculty, rich in resources.

Architecture was a challenging and demanding major; however, my interest to seek involvement in building human habitation and improving the quality of the environment was a strong one. In addition, it is my nature to accomplish and excel. I have particularly liked the works of valued, appreciated architecture, an architecture that makes impression and quality statements, that provides refinement and distinction. To this effect, quintessence and excellence in design leadership reinforced my inspiration and commitment to the study of architecture.

At Hampton, I completed a rigorous five-year program that emphasized concept development and design. I graduated top in my class with the first professional degree, bachelor of architecture (B.Arch.), three years ago last May. I was elected chairman of the Design Council by my fellow students of architecture and was appointed to the visiting lectures committee by the student body president. I was elected president of the International Students Association, was initiated into Alpha Kappa Mu honor society for distinguished scholars, and served as a peer counselor and a mentor to architecture majors. I was the director of the visual aids department within the university's architecture department, including supervision of work-study students, and by invitation of the professor, served as a teaching assistant for "Architectural History," for which I also gave lectures on African art, architecture, and aesthetic influences.

If you read a lot of admissions essays, you get a little tired of the "victim mentality" of applicants. I've read essays from candidates who claimed they were victimized because their parents were middle class, because their pet bird died, or because they had to ("Gasp!") like, you know, work while they went to school. This is not impressive to adult admissions readers. Strife is when your mom dies in your arms from a horrific and excruciatingly painful disease the day of your comprehensive exams. Strife is when you are so poor that you can't afford to buy postage stamps, much less something so expensive as food. Strife is when you grow up in an active war zone where attending school is an act of insane bravery. That's strife.

#34: "A Happy Childhood—Then Architecture" *(continued)*

This essay is an absolute slap of fresh air. This candidate had a happy childhood, is well adjusted, and promises to bring this optimism with him to graduate school. Wow!

During this period, I was recipient of distinguished academic and professional awards, including (a) The American Institute of Architects' Scholastic Award: The Certificate of Merit for Excellence in the Study of Architecture, (b) the Virginia Foundation for Architectural Education's O'Pendleton Wright Scholarship to a Distinguished Architecture Student in Advanced Standing, two years in a row, and (c) the Adrian Freeman Scholarship prize and citation awarded by the Hampton University President to the "Outstanding Graduating Senior who has shown Excellence and Promise."

During my college years, I also came to appreciate coffee instead of tea, discovered the hamburger, learned to play golf, played on the varsity table tennis team (competing in an ad hoc mid-Atlantic conference), and continued to pursue my interests in photography, nature, fishing, sailing, and surfing. Hampton is well situated for such sports, as it is at the mouth of Chesapeake Bay. During the summers I traveled extensively throughout the United States, and attended summer sessions at Virginia Tech and the University of Texas at Arlington.

Autobiographies should focus on your life experiences that molded you into a good candidate for the targeted graduate program. Be honest and forthcoming, certainly, but don't forget that this, too, is an admissions document.

In professional practice, my involvement evolved from working as a junior gofer and plan check corrections personnel through assisting in various efforts of the design and working drawing process to leading the production crew, interfacing with principals and consultants, and agency coordination for reputable design firms in the Los Angeles area. I last worked as project manager with the R.L. Atkins Company, a Beverly Hills–based design-build land development company.

Even though my career was advancing rapidly, I felt the need for continued, specialized education to achieve my ultimate goals. I left practice to pursue the second professional degree, the master of architecture degree (M.Arch.) at UC Berkeley, which I selected for its preeminence in design leadership and with the recommendations of my professors from Hampton and my mentors from my professional career. At Berkeley I am doing quite well, currently ranking a 3.88 GPA, and expecting to graduate with high honors.

Upon completion of my current studies, I hope to begin study immediately with the Ph.D. program. During the course of my experience of architecture, both as a student and as a professional in practice, I have considered the terminal degree as an appealing option, both to achieve the fulfillment of my intellectual interests and to serve as the foundation of my later career. My objective is to serve the practice of architecture in a leadership role and ultimately to contribute to research and education in my chosen field.

ESSAY #35: "Ireland and King Coal"

Autobiography for Law School
"Tell us about your childhood and upbringing, and relate it to your interest in a career in the law."

I loved Williamson, West Virginia, with its exciting Little League program and the King Coal Festival in the fall. I grew up happy and content in the rich coalfields of southwestern West Virginia. That is, until the economy began to falter. The failing coal industry took its toll on Williamson and my joy slowly turned into disappointment. Businesses in town closed, families began to leave at an alarming rate, Little League became obsolete, and overall morale in the little town of 4400 became as depressing as the economy. My idealistic notion of Williamson was gone; the King Coal Festival no longer gave me joy and pride but a sense of shame. To compensate for my feelings, my attitude about Williamson turned from content to a longing to get out. I did not want to live there; I was embarrassed, and I was going to prove myself better than where I had come from. My mission was set: I was going to leave Williamson, leave my past behind, and conquer the world.

I was fortunate enough to attend a small, liberal arts university in another state. The first couple years were tough; I had kept my attitude about my hometown and focused my attentions solely on proving myself better than my roots. But something happened in my college career that changed my view of my world. My junior year at Transylvania, I received the opportunity to study abroad at University College Dublin in Ireland. I was thrilled and nervous at the same time. This was really the first time that I had ever left any "comfort" zone alone. However, when I arrived in Ireland and settled in, I got more out of the experience than I could have ever hoped or imagined.

While in Ireland, I became completely immersed in Irish culture. I lived with Irish women, went to school with 18,000 Irish students, ate Irish food, and followed their lead. Becoming familiar with their tradition and values, I began to reflect upon my own. My college experience, coupled with my study abroad experience allowed me to meet individuals who were proud of who they were, where they had come from, and what they stood for. The Irish showed me the strength of tradition in facing both bad and good times, whether the country was in a time of strife like the Potato Famine or on its way to economic stability. Regardless of the circumstances, the Irish never forgot their heritage and that made an enormous impact on me. Thus, I began to realize the attitude and feelings that I had toward my origins in Williamson were not necessarily wrong, but definitely not right. The mission I had geared myself toward was not the way to handle those experiences. My "roots" were an integral part of my ever-evolving character.

My return from Ireland has left me with the realization that I must re-orient my attitude about my roots and heritage as well as my goals in life. I now see that I can never get away from my origins, and Williamson is actually a large part of who I am today. I feel that there is more that I need and can do in this situation. There are individuals out there who become

Here is another autobiography for a school of professional studies. This one follows a well-established theme in the history of literature—that is, going on a trip to discover that one's home is not so bad after all. This essay demonstrates a depth of thought and maturity that is attractive to graduate programs, which is why they solicit essays like this. (In their continuing quest to get original work from candidates, graduate programs are always reworking their queries. One of the popular ones from a few years ago was this: "If you were stranded on Mars for three years, what book, what item, and what person would you want along for the wait?")

#35: "Ireland and King Coal" *(continued)*

---

trapped in the exact same way of thinking and lifestyle I found myself to be encompassed. Unfortunately, many are not afforded the opportunities that I have been. Therefore, I feel compelled to try to change the situation for others who have had the same experience. The best way I believe I can make a difference is by obtaining a legal education. Through law school, I hope to acquire the tools and resources needed to help change economically depressed areas.

Beyond a constructive legal practice, I hope to use my skills to found and operate a children's advocacy nonprofit. So many children get trapped in the same depressed mind-set I found myself in, but they do not possess the resources to find a way out. I hope that through obtaining a quality legal education, I can help children from disadvantaged areas like mine or even from disadvantaged urban areas overcome the negative attitudes toward positive outcomes, and to let them know that they do matter. I want to help others learn, as I have, that their heritage and upbringing are integral parts of who they are, even if that means there are things about it that need fixing—something that took me 21 years to finally figure out.

Be cautious about mentioning a distracting goal near the end of your essay. This one works, but just barely.

ESSAY #36: "Cosmopolite"

Robert Lewis
Statement of Motivation — Peace Corps
"Of Bedouins and Bulgarian Circuses"

Like many people who are both idealistic and practical, I sometimes have struggled with my goals, my intentions, with the very heart of the question, "What is important to me?" So for many years, I mixed occasional traveling and trekking with a career in the financial services industry. In one world I am a tough negotiator, able to iron out operations problems in an environment where many thousands of dollars are involved in every transaction. I consume and synthesize a massive amount of data, facilitating the profit motive of others. Sometimes it is like consuming sand.

In the other world I always feel I am the guest, the one whose invitation is a gift, the one who strives to learn the house rules and be the ideal visitor. My tough veneer is left behind (except for solving crises), and I am a student in a classroom without walls. It is clear to me that this is better living, and this is what I want to do for years at a stretch, rather than just months.

Traveling runs in my family. My ancestors were barrel makers from a village near Tokaj, Hungary, before they came to the United States early in the last century. One of my sisters married a Swede and lived in Sweden for three years. Another is a photographer, who often works and lives abroad as well. I have lived in England for six months, in Rome for ten weeks, and have traveled throughout Europe, Africa, and the Middle East. Wherever I go and no matter how short the stay, I tend to put down roots almost immediately. I learn the local grocer's name. I discover the intricacies of the town, the hidden nooks and shops the locals use, who knows the best gossip, how to get fresh fruit, and so on.

I have worked in almost every country I have been to, also. Jobs I have held have mostly been manual labor, the sort of jobs that people get when they have no papers: apple picker, waiter, tomato picker, dishwasher, gardener, cook, painter. Some of the jobs have been quite interesting, however, such as staff at a popular night club. Of course, I have taught English on several continents. Ironically, in London I even tutored the English on British English. I taught American English to Russian immigrants in Israel. I really enjoy this type of work and find it to be an ideal way to become really well acquainted with locals.

In southern Egypt, I passed from Bedouin tribe to Bedouin tribe like a token for four bizarre and yet serene months. I took to the nomadic life rather well, but I preferred riding a horse to riding a camel. After months of seeing no one from my own century, I crossed the Nile and entered Sudan.

Once while waiting to use an international phone in Israel, I listened while an acrobat from the Bulgarian Circus tried to get a connection to Sofia. His Russian was not very good to begin with, and it was clear that the operators were totally at a loss. I stepped forward and offered my services as a translator, and speaking Russia to the acrobat and English to the

This is an essay submitted as part of an application to the Peace Corps. The applicant is already an accomplished and widely traveled citizen of the world. This type of candidate is more common than the average academic adviser might believe, setting a high bar for acceptance.

Being willing to work is good. Being willing to work with your hands may be better. Having skills related to growing food or building or mechanical equipment repair may be best of all.

The Peace Corps has many different assignments and is subject to trends in its selection criteria. Ask around before you apply, to see if you can discover what they're most interested in this year.

Bulgarian Circus? Nothing could be better.

#36: "Cosmopolite" *(continued)*

operator, I got the call put through. This led to several weeks in which the Bulgarian Circus provided me with room and board—not to mention lots of entertainment—and carried me around with them in return for translating and dealing with local authorities.

Although it is great to have adventures, I do not want to misrepresent my interest in the Peace Corps. I could easily just continue my double life of travel and work, but my main interest is to combine these two lives, to bring my work in line with my true interests. I believe that helping others is the root of all true meaning in life, and I want to help others in an endeavor more meaningful than increasing the wealth of the wealthy. I grew up in a small town of 6000, mostly "gentlemen farmers," where the center of town was literally a combined general store and post office. I would be comfortable anywhere you may wish to assign me, and I look forward to any assignment. I am experienced, and I think skilled, at teaching English, but I would be happy to pursue agricultural or development projects as well. I have no preference as to geography, either. I am interested in Poland, Hungary, and the rest of Eastern Europe, because I believe history is in the making there, but I would most certainly welcome an assignment anywhere in the world.

As to my future after the Peace Corps, I would want to incorporate my Peace Corps experience in a new career in the United States, or perhaps with an international development or international aid organization. Career possibilities include teaching, social services, or perhaps serving a development organization with my financial skills. I look forward to these new directions with eagerness and the certainty that my future holds a more integrated life, with work and leisure, heart and mind, involved in all my endeavors.

Here's the rationale that reveals the candidate to be a serious and thoughtful person, not just an adventure seeker.

ESSAY #37: "Blue Collar to Psych Scholar"

Statement of Purpose—Ph.D. in Psychology

Following nearly ten years of employment as an aircraft mechanic, I took a hard look at where my life was going. Although I was responsible for important work, requiring extensive technical knowledge and mechanical skills in manufacturing and maintaining aircraft—I felt compelled to include myself in a larger arena. Each airplane that I repaired and that flew away was a poignant reminder that I was standing still. Consigned to the tedium of long commutes and time clocks—my daily routine was empty of genuine enthusiasm and curiosity. Predictable, the content of my days offered little beyond another paycheck, another weekend, another Monday. I realized that in order to redirect my life and fully experience the world, I would have to confront the uncertainties that change would bring.

My first step was to face an embarrassing truth and reenrolling at the age of thirty, I earned my high school diploma. I could have forgone this step of earning a diploma but I was compelled to alter how I approached my past and in doing so, how I would meet my future. Resigning as an aircraft mechanic and enrolling full time at my local community college I attained my associate of arts degree. Unquestionably, these initial accomplishments contributed to my deep-rooted curiosity about human behavior and motivation. Focusing my academic direction I then earned a bachelor of arts degree in psychology from California State University San Bernardino (CSUSB). While working part time and attending college full time proved exhausting and at times frightening, nevertheless, the decision to change my life was revealing itself as the correct path. In preparing for a career within psychology, I recognized that a doctorate in this field would be essential. With this goal in mind, I resolved to strengthen my academic and practical background by entering the master's program in general/experimental psychology at CSUSB.

Having proposed my master's thesis on the perception of family resources and the psychological adjustment of parents caring for a child with autism, I expect to defend by October and earn my master's degree. Data collection for my thesis topic was based on protocols created during my work as a research assistant at the University Center for Developmental Disabilities (UCDD) at CSUSB. The UCDD has over 120 families with developmentally disabled children who receive behavioral treatments and family services. The opportunity to work directly with these families was sobering when considering factors affecting family dynamics. However, it offered practical as well as conceptual understanding within this area. Additionally, involvement with the UCDD was fundamental in understanding the steps of setting up a research investigation from its earliest stages. During my time there, I was able to: research literature related to the field of autism and developmental disabilities, evaluate measures used for test construction, write test items, pilot test questions and testing administration procedures, and interview parents and siblings for data collection. Seeking to expand my research experience I also participated in a study investigating the effects of amphetamine on glial cells. This study, utilizing an animal model, offered the chance

This man is matter-of-fact about having made a major error in his first career choice. His bravery in returning to school is admirable.

Be sure to run laundry lists of skills, techniques, and even equipment you can operate, as this writer does here and on the next page.

#37: "Blue Collar to Psych Scholar"   *(continued)*

to learn laboratory techniques related to: handling, injecting, surgery, profusions, cryostat brain slicing, slide mounting, and finally digital microscopic cell counting. This study will be published this year.

Eager to compliment my basic course requirements for the master's program, I have completed two extra upper-level statistics courses (multivariate and structural equation modeling) as well as two additional clinical courses (family dynamics and pervasive developmental disorders). Moreover, having been selected from among many candidates to instruct an introductory experimental course, I have just completed a full academic year instructing a laboratory section. My responsibilities included facilitating experiments and teaching the associated APA writing style and content format to upper-level psychology students. Additionally, following my teaching assistantship, I was hired as a writing consultant for my university's McNair Scholars Program. As a writing consultant, I am responsible for reviewing students' research content and writing styles across a range of disciplines including: physics, economics, geology, as well as diverse subjects within psychology. Though these opportunities to interact and advise undergraduate students require long hours of detailed review—I found them extremely rewarding and they have made me, I feel, a more well-rounded person.

To understand the application of psychology, I have sought out volunteer opportunities as well. As a crisis counselor for a local suicide/crisis hotline, for over three years, I have assisted individuals who are overwhelmed by the burdens of stress. In addition, as an unpaid assistant at Patton State Hospital, a state forensic treatment facility, I assisted staff in reintegrating patients for release into community halfway programs after many years isolated from society. Currently, I have begun training to volunteer at a rape crisis center that will require that I meet with victims and act as an advocate and assistant during their initial hospital and police investigation. Moreover, employing my expertise as a photographer, I have documented artwork and activities at a local museum.

In changing the direction of my life, I also decided to reenlist in the United States Air Force Reserves. Reenlisting as a photographer rather than in my previous military career as an aircraft mechanic has opened an esthetic outlet fostering creativity and even fun. As a supervisor in a combat photography unit tasked with visual documentation of worldwide military activities, I have been able to pursue my interest in people and travel through a medium that integrates aspects of both psychology and art—a rare opportunity in the military. The experiences and paths I have led are diverse; adopted as a child from Korea, living and working in Europe, traveling around the world, as well as the life of a student have all etched their marks within me. I believe the breath and depth of my life experiences are my best qualities. Through them I can appreciate how perspectives are influenced through ethnicity, culture, geography, and even history. My competence in the laboratory, as a teaching assistant, as a researcher for the UCDD, as a paid writing consultant for the

This student is establishing teaching, writing, and statistical skills, virtually assuring that he will get an assistantship. Teaching, writing, and statistical skills are the trifecta for graduate assistants.

Combat photography? Wow. That's a conversation item.

Notice how he mentions this adoption bombshell in passing, without elaborating at all. Another great example of how sometimes less is more.

#37: "Blue Collar to Psych Scholar" *(continued)*

McNair Scholars Program, volunteer efforts helping people during crises, and even my work as a photographer with the USAF have solidified my dedication to the field of psychology as a career choice. My goal is to complete a clinical Ph.D. program, commit my life to the field of psychology and learning, and be of service to others.

I am highly interested in the topic of psychotherapy and anxiety and would be excited to work under the direction of Dr. Tehanson. Additionally, Dr. Lehman's work with anxiety and depression would be particularly interesting. I would be an enthusiastic member of either one of these professor's research teams.

This essay needs more "why here" than this. Strive in your essays to make a close connection to faculty, especially research faculty. The general rule is to identify three or more with whom you have affinity.

ESSAY #38:   "Underwater Archaeology"

Personal Statement for Doctoral Program in Anthropology (Archaeology)

The peculiar fact that archaeology is both a social and physical science forms the basis of my attraction to the study. The process whereby information gained from chemistry and geology is transformed into statements about human culture and society fascinates me. I have chosen to study archaeology because it is one of the few fields I have found which demands a knowledge of metallurgy in order to make statements about trade networks, or of religious forms to understand settlement patterning—in short, an open and enquiring mind into all aspects of the past and present world as a basis for an understanding of humankind. I am applying to Brown University because my investigations have led me to believe that I will find an atmosphere of intellectual interest and diversity in faculty, students, and course work paralleling those I would like to see in myself.

An overworked catechism among marine archaeologists is that "there is no such thing as marine archaeology, only archaeology under water," but after four years of exposure to the field I am skeptical. The dichotomy in archaeology between technique and technology on the one hand, and the questions of human social processes which these try to answer, is not fully appreciated by many. My experiences on projects in Jamaica, Bermuda, and Italy, and my personal research into the matter, has led me to believe that technique exists in marine archaeology apart from any humanistic component and that most researchers follow the Gary Cooper school of "shoot first, ask questions later." Even after thirty years, most of its intellectual parameters continue to be defined not by the archaeologists, but by the artifacts themselves. Although there is no doubt that other institutions in the United States and abroad offer fine education in the techniques of marine archaeology, techniques, in and of themselves, hold little interest for me. These techniques should only be a means, and my studies at Brown will be directed toward understanding and defining an end.

In general, therefore, what I would like to do while at Brown is to examine the nature of the interaction between human social processes and the maritime environment and to see what light marine archaeology can throw on existing questions of human culture change. On a more specific level I am currently interested in the following questions: Did the deforestation of Crete lead to the decline of the Minoan civilization as a sea-power; was the site of Troy an inevitability given the nature of the Hellespont and the abilities of Bronze Age shipping; and at what point in time, if at all, were the Mycenaeans able to penetrate the Black Sea to the Danube, perhaps for tin from Bohemia?

Given the nature of these questions it seems logical that I should stay at Oxford. My professors are pleased with my work to date and have asked me to stay on to complete a D.Phi. There are two reasons for which I have chosen to apply to Brown instead of staying on. On a pragmatic level I have financed my year here without any financial aid by working for two years; I am unwilling to spend the equivalent of a small condominium or two BMWs for three more years. Money aside, I enjoy teaching and intend to make a career of

This candidate is clearly going to be an asset to any department he might join. In the second paragraph he has articulated his reasons for selecting a school stronger in archaeology than in marine archaeology, and it would seem that any school would be interested in his affiliation with Oxford's Marine Archaeological Research Expedition (M.A.R.E.). This is another example of a student who is going to excel regardless of whether he is admitted to any particular program.

A student who brings intellectual queries with him is more interesting than one who expects to be told what to investigate.

Of course Brown would love to be told why it is a better choice than Oxford.

#38: "Underwater Archaeology" *(continued)*

---

it at the university level. Oxford does not emphasize teaching for its graduate students, and I feel that an important part of my education is lacking. Although I will be leaving Oxford I will maintain my ties here and I expect that my involvement with M.A.R.E. (the Marine Archaeological Research Expedition) will continue, allowing both myself, and hopefully other students at Brown, an opportunity to do marine archaeology in the Mediterranean.

In conclusion, I would like to say that given my interests and concerns, I feel Brown is the very best place for me to be. The facilities, scholarship, and traditions of the institution, combined with the calibre of the student body, make me confident that I will be stimulated throughout the course of my studies. I feel confident of my ability to succeed and hope that I have demonstrated a commitment to, and some ability in, the study of archaeology.

ESSAY #39: "Advanced Nursing"

Goals Statement for Advanced Program in Nursing

This next essay starts off with a bold and challenging statement that is bound to alert the reader. The rest of the essay is an excellent example of clear and concise writing. The reader is carried along by the text, and the points are made so smoothly that anyone would have to agree with the last line. With the ascendance of advanced nursing and physician assistant specialties, it is important to note that the top-ranked nurses are earning more than the bottom-ranked doctors, and it's cheaper, faster, and easier to become a top-ranked nurse.

Pursuing a few courses specifically related to your graduate interest is very persuasive to admissions professionals. This is especially important if you've been out of school for some →

When my sister Michelle first told me of her anticipated career choice, I was less than enthusiastic. "Nursing," I said with typical teenage disdain. "Why would someone as intelligent as you want to change bedpans for a living?" My image of nurses was one formed by television. Those sweet, heavy-on-the-mascara fluffers of pillows and minions of doctors were on display in the programs of my youth. Such TV nurses were merely filler for dramatic scenes of doctors making profound observations and brilliant diagnoses. However, nursing as a profession and I as a person have grown a lot over the past decade. I now see that the options for nurses are as diverse as the healthcare system itself and that nurses are finally being given the credibility and respect they have earned.

As an early college undergraduate, I put aside my original ambitions in art and literature to explore a burgeoning interest in life sciences and psychology. I was fascinated by the intricacies of the human brain. I anticipated graduate study in neuropsychology and perhaps a career in research. However, I realized that a life spent in a research lab, however edifying, was not for me. I knew that I would sorely miss human interaction.

Upon graduating *summa cum laude* with a degree in psychology, I took a position as a resident adviser in a group home for developmentally disabled adults. The clients were considered profoundly retarded with severe cerebral palsy and a host of other health problems. It was difficult at first, both emotionally and physically. But in two years I learned a lot about health care, nurturing, and empowerment. Over the past six years, I have worked and volunteered in a variety of social service positions (see enclosed curriculum vitae). I am currently employed as a family counselor at a homeless multi-service center which caters mostly to the mentally disabled. However, as a social worker one is often frustrated by the many limitations of an overburdened, inefficient system. I find nursing appealing in that it provides more concrete, tangible aid. Nursing skills are generally specific, and results more directly observable. In addition, I have retained an avid interest in the life sciences and have been taking science courses for the past three semesters to give myself a firm grounding for graduate study. (See NYU transcript.)

I would like advanced specialty preparation so that as a nurse practitioner I will have more autonomy to make decisions about a patient or a program as a whole. I'd also like to have the option to teach, both in-service at a medical center and at the college level. Working closely with the nurse practitioner who heads the mobile clinic which attends to the health problems of our clients at the Homeless Project, I have had an excellent opportunity to observe her role and responsibilities (see letter of recommendation). This observation has solidified my career objective.

My projected specialty is adult primary care with a minor in mental health nursing. This appeals to my keen interest in community health issues, as well as my belief in the value of preventive health education and pre-screening programs. I see a strong need for more health education in the population that I work with; specifically alarming is the lack of

#39: "Advanced Nursing"   *(continued)*

knowledge on such basic issues as birth control, AIDS, and nutrition. I feel that as a nurse practitioner, I would have greater impact on an economically disadvantaged community. A mental health minor would allow me to deal in a more holistic fashion with the complex problems of this population. Upon graduation from this program, I would like to use my nurse practitioner license to practice in a clinic which provides both on-site services and outreach care. This may include home or shelter visits, or school and community health education seminars.

I am enthusiastic about your Masters Entry Program because it is the ideal way to achieve my goals. I feel the accelerated pace is appropriate to my level of preparation and ability to perform. I feel confident that my academic and practical background would allow me to excel in the program.

time. It can also help you overcome any prior grade liabilities. A handful of recent A's may overcome any problems from the past.

Refer to supporting documentation, as this candidate does, which reminds the reader there's more to you than would fit in an essay.

ESSAY #40: "Multifunctional Enzymes"

Research Summary in Application to Doctoral Program in Chemistry

This is an example of a highly technical essay detailing research projects in chemistry. The reader will be a specialist in this area of chemistry. Note the total lack of personal information.

My first research project involved determining whether the enzyme Uridylate Synthase "channels" the intermediate Orotidine 5'-mono-phosphate. This is a multifunctional enzyme and explanations for the evolution of this multifunctionality have been somewhat widespread throughout the literature. This project then questioned the basis of these explanations and offered new hypotheses as to why such multifunctional proteins have evolved. I wrote the computer modelling programs which integrated, through recursion, all of the relevant Michaelis-Menton rate equations. This analysis proved that a channelling argument was unnecessary to explain the available experimental evidence. I also performed some related enzyme assays in order to check several related hypotheses developed by Dr. McClard and myself.

Last summer I worked on an organic synthesis project which involved synthesis of one interesting analogue of a potent, possibly the most potent, regulator of the gluconeogenesis glycolysis pathways fructose 2,5-bisphosphate. The key to the synthesis of the analogue shown below is control of the stereochemistry of the previously anomeric carbon. My work was involved in the reactions with I_2 and Br_2 and creation of the "halogenonium" ion of the Wittig product from the starting protected arabinofructoside sugar, also shown below.

Analog

Fru 2.6 bisphosphate

My current research project, my senior thesis, is related to the one I was involved in during the summer. In this case I am attempting to synthesize an analogue of phosphoribosylpyrophosphate (PRPP) which is the molecule which provides the sugar portion in the *de novo* pathway of pyrimidine biosynthesis. This work utilizes the same synthetic scheme as shown above with the exception of starting with the ribose sugar and several changes

#40: "Multifunctional Enzymes" *(continued)*

in the phosphorous portion of the molecule. The synthetic scheme below shows the route I hope to exploit in synthesizing the target molecule. These projects were all carried out with Prof. McClard at Reed College.

ESSAY #41:   "Latino Scholar Sets Pace"

Autobiography—Law School

The adversity frequently associated with growing up Latino in an American society has left an indelible mark on me. Fortunately, I have been equal to the challenges and have learned, as well as prospered from the obstacles I have overcome.

My mother migrated from Colombia so that I, her only child, would be born American. To stay here, she entered into an ill-fated marriage. The inevitable divorce forced her to clean people's homes while stretching her limited resources. I became compelled to assume, at a young age, significant household and family responsibilities. I supplemented the family income, cared for my mother during frequent illnesses, served as her advocate during battles with landlords, and taught her English. Thanks, in part, to my assistance, my mother is now an American citizen.

Following the divorce, we were required to move to a predominantly white neighborhood and the transition proved difficult. In high school, my ethnicity and social origin made me different, as teachers and classmates were quick to point out. Rather than ignore their narrow-mindedness, I became profoundly introverted and my self-esteem plummeted. I lost complete regard for my well-being, began overeating, and watched my weight skyrocket. I fled school, vowing never to return.

I spent one year working before beginning my life anew. I earned an equivalency diploma and entered a local college. To restore my health, I began jogging and eating sensibly. I lost thirty pounds and my physical endurance, as well as my mental stamina, soared. Since then, I have followed a sound fitness regimen.

My undergraduate years have been instrumental to my intellectual development. Early on, I tapped my latent academic prowess and, as a result, excelled in and out of the classroom. I also learned to broaden my horizons through academia. Freshman year, I registered for a class unaware that the professor, Dr. Adam Levine, an excellent educator, was H.I.V. positive. Dr. Levine's struggle inspired me to attack my curriculum with unflagging zeal. This experience culminated in my writing an "A+" term paper, "Attitudes Toward H.I.V. in the College Community," for Dr. Levine, a noted authority on A.I.D.S., and earning an "A+" for the semester.

I built on this success by engaging professors in rich dialogue. One professor, an African-American, suggested I read *Dusk of Dawn* by W.E.B. DuBois or *Cheer the Lonesome Traveler* by Leslie Alexander Lacy. I read them both. They opened new realms and helped foster my thirst for reading more works like this. I found Dr. DuBois's work on race relations fascinating. When his heritage made him self-conscious at Harvard, he did not drop out. On the contrary, he overwhelmed his classmates with the strength of his acumen. I took to heart his notion that educated minorities can and should use their talent to uplift their communities.

These lessons manifested themselves as I hit my academic stride. I began helping my peers, both non-white and white. I tutored students and was chosen to mentor underclass-

This scholar overcomes many challenges to set a high academic standard for himself and others. His "life crisis" could have had many outcomes, but he triumphs over a rough beginning and finds mentors in W.E.B. DuBois and a considerate professor. This essay exemplifies the rules for mentioning adversity: It must be in the past, it must be resolved, and it must be unlikely to recur. This particular presentation won admission to a top-ten law school.

Usually adversity should be kept to a paragraph or so, but this candidate has a compelling story and tells more.

When a particular professor has been a hero to you, a catalyst in your development, or a pivotal force in your academic career, he belongs in your essay.

#41: "Latino Scholar Sets Pace"   *(continued)*

---

men while assisting the administration in its attempts to increase the school's retention rate of minority males. Also, the Educational Opportunity Fund (E.O.F.) hired me to tutor and counsel inner-city students. Working with E.O.F. was particularly valuable in that it helped fill a void by introducing me to positive Latino role models like Jeanne Habib, a Deputy Attorney General and E.O.F. alumna.

My Latino heritage has undoubtedly motivated me to transform myself into an effective role model for future generations. *Growing Up Latino,* a remarkable anthology, and Earl Shorris's *Latinos: A Biography of the People* illustrate the pride I wish to convey. These books and others have helped me to realize that it is time to offset negative images of the Latino community with more constructive and accurate representations of what Latinos can offer society. By successfully preparing to practice law, I hope to embody these more positive realities.

Tutoring and community service are always well regarded.

> ### ESSAY #42: "Child and Adolescent Clinical Psychology"
>
> Statement of Purpose, Martina Greene
> Question: "What influences in children result in happy adults?"
>
> In my experiences as a preprofessional psychological worker, I have adopted a working hypothesis that the majority of outpatient-treatable mental health problems stem from negative childhood experiences. These negative experiences are overwhelmingly traceable to influential adults in the patient's past, primarily parental figures and teachers.
>
> When we were children my father used to get my sister and me to stand in front of a mirror and say positive things to ourselves. It didn't matter what we said, as long as it was positive. He did not make us stand in front of the mirror and say nice things to ourselves; he jumped around and coached us and encouraged us until we did this almost every morning as a matter of getting up. My family provided warmth, fair and consistent discipline, and a true feeling of secure, inclusive boundaries separating us (the family) from the greater society in which we lived.
>
> Due to the juxtaposition of my own experiences and the experiences of others, I have long been quite interested in familial and educational influences on the development of children's adjustment. Although it has faced some public ridicule in the past, my own area of greatest interest is self-esteem: Where does it come from? How do we get it? How can we repair it after assaults against the factors that engender it?
>
> I am particularly interested in the development of self-esteem in late childhood, puberty and adolescence. I have always been interested in children, and I have consistently and diligently prepared myself to become a specialist in child and adolescent clinical psychology. In addition to the details in my c.v., I would like to address three major influences on my career direction:
>
> (1) When I was at the University of Massachusetts-Amherst (U. Mass.), I had the good fortune to work with Dr. Morgan Burke, dean of social sciences and founder and executive director of The Farm School. Dr. Burke is an inspiring professor, and he encouraged me to pursue my interest in the internal and external influences on socio-emotional development. He accepted a proposal of mine to launch an experimental class at The Farm School to test teaching techniques. The program had the working title of "Testing Models of Self-esteem Training in an Elementary Class of Girls and Boys: Toward Developing Applied Techniques for Teachers." I was the teacher, with free rein to develop and run the class.
>
> (2) As a psychological worker with Boston Free Psychological Services, I was intake counselor for a very diverse and multicultural incoming patient population. In this position I was the very first contact many self-referrals had with a mental health services organization. I got a feel for my clinical aptitude, and how I might enjoy clinical services. I was able to establish a quick rapport with patients, and gain their trust and cooperation. I was lauded by the staff psychologists for my skills in triage and assessment, and my ability to get an accurate and complete psychological history from patients. My success with and enjoyment

Clinical psychology programs are extremely competitive. Many are statistically much harder to get into than your average medical school. The programs look for psychology research and any kind of experience in a mental health clinical setting. Often an interim degree, such as a master's in developmental or child or counseling psychology, is the key. This candidate did everything right, and then wrote about it well.

Be sure to mention key professors by name.

#42: "Child and Adolescent Clinical Psychology" *(cont.)*

of this position was a major influence on my resolve to pursue clinical psychology concurrent with my interest in developmental psychology.

(3) While I have always respected the integrity of psychology as a science, I must credit Dr. Kowalski of the graduate program in psychology at Boston University (B.U.) for giving me a solid grounding in experimental methodology. Although I had a working knowledge of experimental methodology, and I had certainly designed and executed a number of experiments in psychology, over the last two years I have developed a passion for correct methodology. In my clinical career I may not have to design many original research projects, but my increased understanding of methodology has influenced all my thinking about psychology and has especially improved my ability to critique the research I read in journals.

Finally, I would like to address the issue of my academic career. As you have my transcripts, you can clearly see that I was not especially serious in my first few years as an undergraduate at U. Mass., and you can also see that I have improved dramatically. I have done quite well in my master's program here at B.U., and I expect to continue or exceed this performance in your program.

My eventual goals are to divide my time between (a) clinical outpatient treatment of children and adolescent patients, (b) program development and consulting with schools and institutions on self-esteem, specifically development of teaching methodologies that enhance it, and development of treatment programs that repair it, and (c) teaching at the university level on developmental and clinical psychology areas.

I am confident of my ability to excel in your program academically, and to be an effective and valuable clinical psychologist both in practice and in consulting roles. I would like to think that I am the type of candidate that would be a good representative of your program.

This is a good way to deal with a rough start to an academic career. Let the reader know that the grades that count are good, and explain your rationale.

This is an excellent example of reductionism.

Predict your own success, as a graduate student and as a practicing professional.

The following essay illustrates several of the principles espoused in this book. It has a great opening. It provides a rationale for the applicant's candidacy, and it demonstrates the candidate's strong dedication to his goals. It says a great deal about his personality without using any phrases that begin with "I am a _____." Most important of all, it allows the admissions reader to make sense of the entire applica-tion; it ties the other elements—grades, recommendations, test scores—together into a coherent whole. One warning: It has something of an ethnocentric point of view. This might be ill advised for graduate programs in anthropology, but it is just fine for business school.

ESSAY #43: "Business Lessons from Africa"

Statement of Purpose for Graduate School of Business

Alhaji Sannoh's tear-filled eyes, his embarrassed smile, and his small, wrinkled, yet firm hand shaking mine symbolize the successful culmination of a two-year-long international partnership. I was an agricultural consultant for the U.S. Peace Corps, assigned to Firawa, a small remote village in Sierra Leone, West Africa. Alhaji Sannoh was a Firawa farmer who planted rice just as his father and grandfather before him, by burning virgin, hillside forests and scattering seeds. Every week for an entire year I trekked out to Alhaji Sannoh's farm where we discussed the advantages of planting rice in swamp paddies. I emphasized that heavy rains wash nutrients from the hillside soils into the swamps. It is advantageous, therefore, to plant rice in swamps where crop yields are easily doubled.

We became friends, but eventually it struck me—a painful realization—that my ideas and suggestions were not materializing. My ideas were logical in my own mind, yet Alhaji Sannoh's planting techniques remained the same. Where was the key?

I decided on a new approach. I leased an acre of Alhaji Sannoh's farm and hired two men. In just two months we produced a fantastic crop of rice. Alhaji Sannoh came to me and said, "If you can plant such fine rice on this land, so can I!" Alhaji Sannoh harvested rice twice that year and quadrupled his yearly rice yield. The key had been his witnessing firsthand what I had tried to convey only in words.

Two years have elapsed since I returned from Africa and first applied to Wharton. The vivid images of palm trees silhouetted against a crimson sky, and of children's laughter emanating from tiny mud huts, have faded. I have recognized the true worth of my experience not from a romantic perspective, but from a pragmatic one. In my reapplication to Wharton, I cannot emphasize enough the importance my Peace Corps experience has played in the realization of my personal strengths and in the formation of my career goals.

My greatest strength, perseverance, has propelled me through an array of challenges. While working with men like Alhaji Sannoh, I encountered an initial rejection, a mistrust in my sincerity and skills, a language barrier, and cross-cultural embarrassment. While coordinating shipments of food aid and agricultural products from the coast to my remote village, I encountered a dilapidated infrastructure, corrupt officials, black market prices, and nearly impassable road conditions. After numerous delays, I traveled to the capital to discover that the village food aid had been sitting on the docks for three months. Instead of reproaching the local project managers, I found a truck driver and bought him a meal. The shipment arrived the following week.

Because of endemic economic malaise, Lesser Developed Countries have been abandon-ing new investments to cope with their increasing debt burdens and depressed commodity prices. In order to be self-sufficient, these nations have to realize the importance of small- and medium-scale enterprises in meeting their domestic demands for manufactured products. They must also exploit openings in niche export markets. In Sierra Leone it really disturbed me to see idle lathes and mills. I often passed one modern jelly/marmalade producing facility that

---

#43: "Business Lessons from Africa" *(continued)*

---

was shut down due to a lack of technical and managerial expertise. Sierra Leone, as well as other Lesser Developed Countries, must set up a national forum to encourage entrepreneurial activity. I want to help make that happen by promoting manufacturing enterprises in West African nations, and by facilitating foreign investments in these ventures.

Two years ago my Wharton interviewer, as well as managers of international development organizations, suggested that my lack of manufacturing experience would limit my effectiveness. At the time I disagreed, but I set out to address this deficiency nonetheless. I left Washington, D.C., to seek pertinent employment. Within one month, I joined a start-up company in California's Silicon Valley as a mechanical/manufacturing engineer. At [name withheld], we design and manufacture an improved intravenous catheter. I have been heavily involved in the growth of our company, from the introduction of a new manufacturing process to the current production rate of 5000 devices per week. Because of the small size of our company, my position has enabled me to implement my own decisions. I have improved our designs and processes and have helped to bring down the cost of goods by a more efficient use of company resources. (See enclosed letter of recommendation.) I take a hands-on approach. I am seldom at my desk, but often on the production floor, troubleshooting machinery, streamlining workstations, coordinating the activities of our six-person assembly crew, and providing technical feedback to our design engineers. Working at a start-up company has exposed me to valuable experiences that I could not have gotten at a larger company.

My preparation for a career in international development has not been confined to the workplace. Twice a week I practice French with a tutor so that I can more successfully operate in the business environment of West Africa. I want to be as fluent in French as I am in West African Krio, and, incidentally, Hungarian.

Upon graduating from your program, a variety of options are available for pursuing my objectives. The United Nations Industrialization Development Organization's primary objective is the promotion of industrial development in developing countries. Development Alternatives, Inc., and Transcentury Corporation are just two of the numerous profit and nonprofit organizations that encourage economic development by promoting entrepreneurial activity. Whatever path I choose to follow, I will concentrate my operations in the countries of West Africa and make every effort to encourage their self-sufficiency and active participation in the global economy.

The last two years have enabled me to view my Peace Corps experience from a different perspective and to gain additional experience in the challenging environment of a start-up manufacturing company. I think that I can now make a unique contribution to your program, and look forward to the opportunity to do so.

If you don't get into a graduate program on your first attempt, try again after improving your skills. This candidate was successful on round two.

Detail your compliance with any advice or suggestions from your first application.

If you claim that you are going to business school for any reason other than to make a lot of money for you and your employer, better be ready to back it up with evidence, not intent. This candidate passes the test.

ESSAY #44: "Otolaryngology"

Personal Statement for Residency in Otolaryngology

Otolaryngology attracted me for three main reasons. First, my father recently retired as director of the Boston Center for Hearing and Speech. Through his involvement in speech pathology and audiology, I've been exposed to some aspects of otolaryngology all my life. Second, I'm interested in the opportunity to practice with all ages of patients, from children to the elderly. Third, I am drawn by the combination of medical and surgical practice.

I've done very well in school, both as an undergraduate at M.I.T. and as a medical student at [name withheld]. Last year I was awarded one of the two Lange Book awards for outstanding scholastic achievement. I also have significant undergraduate awards for scholarship.

Research is an aspect of graduate medical training for which I have both an interest and a sound background. This summer I was a research assistant to Drs. S. McQuown and T. A. Cook in a study on the effects of liposuction on porcine fat cell populations. While at M.I.T. I learned well the investigative thinking of basic research, with extensive experience in biochemistry, cell biology, and histology. During my last year I completed a senior honors thesis involving the laboratory investigation of protein-folding mechanisms: *Deamidation of Glutamine and Asparagine Residues: An Approach to the Study of Protein Folding.*

I find working with my hands quite satisfying. For the last seven years I have supported myself in part by cleaning and repairing microscopes at colleges, universities, and research centers throughout the greater metropolitan area. During my surgical rotation at Good Samaritan Hospital, I was encouraged by two of the attending surgeons, who remarked that I showed surprising facility for surgery for one so early in a medical career (see letters of recommendation).

In addition to these technical and academic facilities, I am able to interact with and enjoy a great spectrum of people; this is one of my strongest personality traits.

On the personal side, my wife Heather and I have been married for two years and have future plans for children. She is attending university for a teaching degree and will graduate next spring.

I believe I have the skills (academic, social, and manual), and the interest to excel in the field of otolaryngology. The time ahead of me will be exciting. I look forward to the discovery and the challenge of my chosen career.

You may think that once you get into medical school your career is set. Not so. Medical doctors must compete vigorously for internships, residencies, and fellowships. This essay was used as part of a successful application for a residency in otolaryngology, at *fifty-to-one odds.*

When professors or other mentors have encouraged you or commended your skills, be sure to mention them. Also, refer to supporting documentation submitted with your application.

Predict your own success. This is not bragging. It's confidence based on self-knowledge and an understanding of the challenges ahead.

ESSAY #45: "Watson Traveler"

Personal Statement for the Watson Fellowship

After high school I took a job as one of the first females on a 20-person forest fire–fighting crew. In the autumn I attended [name withheld] University where I became disillusioned with college life. After another summer on the fire crew, I spent my earnings overseas.

Shortly after my nineteenth birthday, I hitchhiked through the South Pacific and Indonesia with a friend. We did a lot of hiking and worked in several towns. I gained independence and strength; I came to appreciate a tremendous diversity of people.

I returned home and transferred to another college. That winter I started a women's soccer team, began writing poetry and prose, tutored foreign students, and held a depressing but eye-opening job in a nursing home. The following summer I returned to the fire crew, was promoted to foreman, and earned enough money to plan an extensive trip through Asia and the Orient.

As I traveled through Asia, I grappled with difficult ethical questions. People cheated me; I was plagued by questions, beggars, and propositions. I wanted to experience Asian ways and leave Western values and habits behind. I felt that an open mind would enhance the experience of travel. But in the poor countries of Asia, blonde hair and light skin spell "rich tourist." I found this stereotype and the accompanying behaviors difficult to deal with.

I also had to deal with the draining effects of illness in remote areas while trekking hundreds of miles over an 18,000-foot pass in the Himalayas. I learned to deal with language barriers, with the frustrations of appealing to legal systems that seemed incapable of adjusting to foreigners. Especially in India, I learned perseverance and patience.

In the Orient I came to know the Chinese people; I was amazed and saddened that what little I had learned in school about the green- and blue-clothed, bicycle-riding citizens of China, their culture and their land, was labeled under "Communism." I was enthralled with the quiet, unpretentious Chinese people and their vast country.

In China I met a traveler who had snuck into Tibet when the borders were still closed. My affection for the Chinese people, and this traveler's hate for Chinese rule in Tibet, stimulated my interest in Tibetan Buddhism and the recent changes in Tibet. I was frustrated that I could not visit Tibet.

After almost a year abroad, I returned home and joined a friend for a car trip to Baja California. Inside a car, I missed interacting with the native people; I learned that traveling by foot or bicycle from village to village is the best way for me to experience different cultures.

For the next two summers I was employed as a forest worker, working and living independently in the wilderness. In my time off, I took up rock climbing, mountaineering, and snorkeling. In the winter I attended and graduated from a junior college. Then I began a year-long internship in Alaska, where I worked as a health education intern. I also worked in cold storage, on a fishing boat, and as recreation coordinator in a health camp set up for Tlingit Indian youths with alcoholic parents. Among the Alaskan natives I had my first

If it were not for the unusual nature of the experiences and the personality revealed little by little with each passing paragraph, this next essay would run the risk of being a list of activities. As a travelogue in application for a grant to travel, however, it works rather well. By the end of the material, the reader has a great deal of confidence in the candidate as a traveler and as a scholar with integrity.

#45: "Watson Traveler"   *(continued)*

good look at a group of people who were on the fringes of health and stability in my own wealthy society.

Between camp sessions I began cycle-touring with a 350-mile, two-week trip from Haines to Skagway. Then the following spring I invited a young friend to join me to cycle up the Alcan Highway from Seattle to Alaska; we took two months to traverse the roughly 2000 miles. Besides looking out for my seventeen-year-old companion, I was challenged with frostbite, desolate stretches of road, and a snow-bound 7000-foot pass in the Rocky Mountains. But I met many wonderful people and enjoyed desolate and beautiful parts of North America.

I also embarked on two month-long kayak trips along the coast of Southeast Alaska. On one trip I tried living off the land; I carried only one sack of rice in case of an emergency. I was often hungry, but I found interesting things to eat—even more interesting than some of the dishes I sampled in Hong Kong.

That fall I entered Reed College, majoring in international studies. My extracurricular activities have been performing as a folk musician, playing soccer, cycling, marketing my poetry and prose, and continuing to meet interesting people from all walks of life. This year I am also a house adviser, jointly responsible for 24 students, over half of which are in their first year of college life.

Reed has been a perfect school for me, and my former reservations toward formalized education have been erased. Academically, I am focusing on China; I am studying late traditional China, modern China, and Chinese history, culture, and government. I am especially interested in policies and ideologies concerning China's interactions with Tibet, the demise of Tibetan Buddhism, and recent rebellions in Tibet. My thesis will be on Tibetan Buddhism and the problem of Chinese rule in Tibet with regard to justice and international law.

All the religions of China hold special interest for me. I have been interested in religions since grade school. It has continued to fascinate me that religious beliefs are so powerful and influential, yet so diverse and mutually exclusive. While traveling, I read books about the religions of each country I visited; Buddhism in India especially interested me. I have studied the sociology of religions and the economics of religion, including Confucianism and Tibetan Buddhism. I have become interested in the tendency of governments to deliberately destroy religions of subjugated peoples, as has occurred in Tibet.

I hope to teach overseas in the near future while continuing to study different nations—their cultures, histories, and languages. I would like to somehow bring the world closer together, and I believe that I can best do this by gaining expertise in one area and sharing my understanding with others through writing and teaching.

My proposed project under the fellowship involves cycling from Beijing to Guangzhou to Lhasa. My route passes through the most important religious sites in China, and my mode of travel allows me to interact with people from all over China—not just those of the largest

#45: "Watson Traveler" (continued)

cities or those who live near tourist attractions. While cycling seems ideal because it would offer maximum exposure to the land and people of China, the same journey could be done by train and bus if necessary due to unexpected changes in Chinese tourism policies. The logistics, contingencies and other details of this trip are covered in Part II of this essay.

Like essay #44, this is a residency essay. It helps to have a combination of outstanding academic preparation and clinical skill.

ESSAY #46: "Cardiology"

Statement of Purpose, Cardiology Residency

I am currently completing my third-year residency program at Presbyterian Hospital, where I have been exposed to their cardiology service. This of course includes experience with critically ill patients, and also includes a transplant service. We have referrals of patients with all types of chronic heart conditions, and we have addressed the moral and therapeutic problems associated with critical organ transplant cases.

My first interest in cardiology results from my assessment that it is a "rational" sub-specialty. I have always enjoyed the classical "hard" sciences such as physics and physiology because they make sense to me. These principles apply directly to cardiology. What appeals to me is the excitement of working in this area, with an opportunity to make rapid decisions according to specifiable formulae, with a critical impact on a patient's status. Needless to say, it is quite satisfying to see observable improvement as a result of one's actions.

My second interest in the sub-specialty comes from my appreciation of the diversity of cases and treatments available. I have always been good with my hands, including success in trades work (carpentry and amateur auto mechanics). I feel I could deliver the reason, diagnostic sense, and mechanical finesse required to excel in the field. I would relish the opportunity to use such a collection of diverse skills in one disciplinary area.

Thirdly, I have been particularly impressed by the versatility demonstrated by the cardiologists whom I have met to date. They were skillful not only in a broad variety of cardiac problems, but also in all their responsibilities as internists. The high degree of acumen and skill which I have witnessed in the cardiology staff suggests to me that a special type of person is attracted to this field and that their training must shape these individuals into highly skilled medical professionals.

Finally, I view cardiology as one of the more vital sub-specialties (no pun intended). I feel that we are poised for a period of continuing rapid advancement in both diagnostic and therapeutic methods. So far I am particularly interested in invasive treatments, e.g., thrombolytic therapy, coronary angioplasty, and valvuloplasty. Whether or not invasive treatments continue their great advances, the field will continue to have a bright future, and will continue to be the preferred area for those of us who want to continue to advance our knowledge and skills throughout our careers.

I complete my internal medicine residency in June. In the meantime, the Technical University Berlin has awarded me a stipend to perform clinical research on ischemic mitral insufficiency at the German Heart Center in West Berlin. I expect to have the opportunity to become involved in clinical drug trials as well. I strongly believe in the importance of research, not only to investigate specific problems and questions, but to become a more well-rounded professional.

I previously had the opportunity to complete an elective at the German Heart Center. I have found that the exchange of experience with colleagues abroad demands that one

It doesn't hurt to know the latest trend in your specialty and to be laudatory about the field's professionals.

#46: "Cardiology"   *(continued)*

reexamine one's experiences closely. Cross-cultural study of medicine remains a strong interest of mine.

My immediate goals are to complete a fellowship in an academically stimulating environment, to be able to participate in the ongoing development of the science of cardiology, and to gain experience in clinical management.

My medium-term goal is to combine clinical practice with research and to teach at a medical center affiliated with a medical school. I know from experience that the best way to learn and keep learning is to teach as well.

My long-term goal is to contribute directly to the advance of cardiology as a clinical science for the ultimate benefit and well-being of patients.

I appreciate your considering this application, and I hope this statement has helped you to make your decision about the fit between my background and this medical and academic speciality. I look forward to visiting your program and meeting you personally.

This is the magic trilogy: practice, research, teach.

ESSAY #47:   "Chaos Theory, Biodynamics, and the Law of Unintended Consequences"

Statement of Purpose—Alan Williams

This is an excellent example of an essay organized around a theme. The result is an idea (chaos theory) and a story (injury and then triumph) interwoven into an interesting whole.

This scholar brings a rigorous approach to methodology in an area with "a paucity of research," always a promising combination.

Chaos theory suggests that tiny, imperceptible events, over time, are responsible for extraordinary changes that otherwise would never occur. It seems incomprehensible that a single sentence, muttered eight years ago by an unknown bystander watching me run laps to improve my faltering P.E. grade, could have such a profound impact on my life. As I loped by this ancient man sitting on the cold concrete steps for perhaps the tenth time that lonely morning, I caught what I interpreted as, "You are a natural runner." Short, sweet, and barely audible, those "chaotic" words were a blessing to me, inspiring me to achieve at something of which I had no prior conception.

The definitive role running has assumed in my life has instilled within me the ability to endure, in both a physiological and a psychological context. It has given me an appreciation for the human body, from both a scientific and an aesthetic frame of reference. Driven by the popular contention that the human species seeks to avoid discomfort, running has given me a confidence that I am able to do something most people cannot. Most important, running has introduced me to the field of human biodynamics, intriguing me to participate at a rigorous level in the discovery and teaching of new methods leading to increased human performance.

Biomechanists love running for the very same reason I do. In its apparent simplicity, there is a wealth of knowledge to be learned from watching running, analyzing its component pieces, and experiencing it. Running is remarkable in that humans have it so deeply ingrained in their neuromuscular pathways that the combined motion of individual body segments succeeds in orchestrating a smoothly coordinated whole, with relatively little conscious thought.

I majored in kinesiology because I found its interdisciplinary analysis of the human mind and body to be both fascinating and useful. I have had the opportunity as an athlete to apply the integration of these concepts to my own athletic venue, so that I may improve and help others improve as well. Presently, in response to a paucity of cross-training research and the debate over whether American running is experiencing a "downfall" as a result of reduced running mileage, I am conducting a study that seeks to address the question of specificity of training in distance running, in particular whether cross-country skiing is an adequate supplement to a distance running training program. Through an electromyographic and kinematic comparison I hope to quantify the differences and similarities between key neuromuscular recruitment patterns in both modes of exercise.

My own running was the inspiration for this research. Over the years, eleven thousand miles of pounding pavement were not without a price to pay. Once, a severe inflammation of the tendons sweeping over my feet forced me to the sidelines just as I was experiencing a great deal of success in running. I had no choice but to adjust my training to accommodate the injury.

#47: "Chaos Theory, Biodynamics . . ."   *(continued)*

Transplanted into an entirely unfamiliar medium, I skied, swam, cycled, and attacked my studies. From this new perspective, one without the overwhelming emphasis placed on running, I saw myself shifting first from athlete to scholar, and finally to scholar-athlete. I began to realize that the two were not mutually exclusive. Driven by a newfound stimulus, one more thoughtful and well-rounded, I taught myself to persist as a person, not just as an athlete. Simultaneously, my running began to surpass what I had ever run before. Any preconceived path I had expected to take toward success as an athlete was forever changed. Had I been forewarned, I would have never conceived it possible to achieve All-America status in the two consecutive years following the injury.

As a goal-oriented individual capable of overcoming unforeseen barriers, I envision myself as a motivator and an innovator. I look forward to the challenge of ultimately earning a doctoral degree in human biodynamics with an emphasis in locomotory biomechanics. As far as long-term plans, I see a natural marriage between my experiences and the teaching of the philosophy and physiology of human movement. I view the pursuit of a higher degree in this field as an extension of what I have already learned from the sport of running and the undergraduate classroom, as well as an opportunity to enjoy a lifelong career. Somehow, I doubt the old man on the concrete steps could ever imagine the ramifications of his simple passing thoughts.

Essay #48 "African Kashmiri"

Letter of Interest—African American Studies

I was born in Arusha, Tanzania, on the slopes of Mt. Kilimanjaro. My father was a son of a Kashmiri immigrant. My grandfather came to Tanzania as a cheap laborer for the British colony. My mother is a daughter of a Segeju woman (Tanzania coastal indigenous group). As a child of these two great parents, I had an interesting childhood that continues to inform my personal and academic life. The union of my parents, my mother having being an "African," caused a split in my father's family. Furthermore, in school and public areas, my fellow Tanzanians called me a "Hindu," while I am an African and a Muslim. And the Indian Diaspora community derogatorily referred to us as "half castes." As a child I could not grasp these racial and identity issues; it is only when I came to America that I seriously began analyzing and questioning my childhood experience. I have learned that the African American experience in North America is an heroic narrative that speaks of similar quests for identity, belonging, and ownership for the past five hundred years. This is one of the many reasons I want to pursue a graduate course in the African and African American Studies Department at Harvard. The African American experience, past and present, is a useful model in explaining a wide array of issues such as identity, politics, and ownership in other countries of the world. Harvard's African and African American Studies Department is an environment that can personally empower me to explain my social and historical bits and pieces through the study of the black experience.

My life experience as a person belonging to either the African or Kashmiri side has offered me a unique perspective to life. Therefore, I am endowed, or have developed through no particular effort of my own, the ability to look at issues in many different perspectives. I can be neutral (invoking neither African nor Kashmiri side), I can take a side (invoking African, Segeju, Kashmiri, or the Muslim side, etc.), and I can also employ the meshed perspective (invoking all the parts). The permutations of my perspectives are endless as they are continuously enriched through similar experiences and age. For example, I grew up with an exiled Black Panther community in Arusha, Tanzania, where I learned about American history and its people away from America and especially from an exiled American/minority point of view. This ability of employing multiple perspectives on issues resembles the call in academic settings for a multidisciplinary approach. I am interested to join African and African American Studies at Harvard because it has a long tradition of scholarship and research on issues of culture and race that I am interested to explore. W.E.B. DuBois, who was also of mixed ancestry such as mine and whose life reflects some of my own experiences, was educated at Harvard. Training at Harvard will equip me with tools and training that will transform my experiences and passion into practical and tangible outcomes such as research skills, networks, and resources.

Harvard has a lot to offer in raising my intellectual capacity as a critical scholar of African culture and experience through analytical training, research, and networking with like-minded scholars. While at Harvard, I would like explore the evolution of a poetic

---

It is important to know the level of competition you are facing when applying to elite programs. This young student has more accomplishments than most of us could fit into a lifetime.

Being a unique candidate always garners interest from reviewers. So many candidates seem all the same to admissions readers. But not this one.

#48   "African Kashmiri"   (continued)

performance called *Mashairi ya Kuimbana* (poetic form of criticism) practiced in the 1940s in Tanga, into a newer form known as *Mipasho,* practiced in commercial centers such as Dar es Salaam. Specifically, I would like to analyze the performance of two female artists[1], who are one of the contemporary exponents of this form in Tanzania. This exploration will also look at how Mipasho embodies social and political criticism. The research will analyze both the poetic texts and performance aspects of Mipasho to paint a coherent picture of this dynamic cultural form. Lastly, I would like to make a comparative analysis between Hip Hop's "dissing" and "beef" phenomena with Mipasho. I believe the faculty, peers and resources at Harvard are best equipped to transform my interest into an exciting and rewarding research experience. While at Harvard, I would like to work with Prof. William Julius, who is an expert on youth culture and politics of race. Working with Prof. Francis Irele, known and respected expert on post-colonialism and cultural renaissance, will guide my research with appropriate theoretical tools. Additionally, I would like to seek the guidance of Prof. Marla Fredrick; her expertise on religion, culture and gender issues will be crucial in giving my research the appropriate academic nuances. A diverse and resourceful faculty body at the African and African American Studies Department will provide me the right place to shape and nurture my intellectual faculties. At Harvard, I expect to learn a lot from students and faculty members and at the same time, I hope to share some of my own experiences.

I have been fortunate to conduct research under the guidance of Dr. Aileen Julien, funded by the project on African Expressive Traditions Grant on Mashairi ya Kuimbana (mentioned above). The research entailed the audio-video recording of the poetics texts as recalled by few remaining exponents of the form. In addition to the earlier research which was well received by faculty and my fellow researcher, I conducted additional research on Mipasho, a contemporary form of poetic criticism practiced in urban centers of East Africa. Specifically, the research looked at the enduring relevancy of poetic criticism forms in airing grievances. This research was guided by Prof. Adesokan and generously funded by the Ronald E. McNair Scholars program at Indiana University, Bloomington. The research was presented at numerous academic meetings and conferences (see attached C.V. for complete list).

It is not enough for me to be purely a scholar, with no direct impact on this world. I have put my background and interests into action when I co-founded Aang Serian, a global NGO that works on preservation of indigenous knowledge. Aang Serian is of diverse ethnic, gender, religious, and international composition and works in mainly three areas of development: appropriate education, audio-video recording studio, and fair-trade initiatives. Aang Serian's education program, which currently runs a secondary school in Masailand, Tanzania, has created a unique and innovative educational model for the indigenous communities of Tanzania. This model was cited by UNEP[2] as a model for Africa as it combines Tanzania's

1.   Hadija Kopa and Nasma Khamis are thought to be bitter enemies.
2.   See www.UNEP.org/CBD/WG8J/3/INF/3, page 53.

Note how he mentions specific professors he would like to work with, and shows that he has more than passing knowledge of their areas of expertise.

This candidate uses footnotes appropriately, which means sparingly and only to keep citations from disturbing the flow of the narrative.

#48 "African Kashmiri" *(continued)*

---

national syllabus with Aang Serian's indigenous knowledge curriculum. This educational model aims to address these communities' immediate needs, systematically record the indigenous knowledge, and instill confidence and identity among the indigenous youth. I intend to interest Harvard's faculty and student body to volunteer and conduct research in Tanzania, an engagement that will enrich and impact the lives of both parties, I am hoping.

Besides the preservation of indigenous knowledge through creation of an innovative model, I helped co-found a community recording studio (now a radio station[3] in Arusha, Tanzania) and a media centre[4]. The objectives of the recording studio and the media centre are to encourage Tanzanian youth to use media technology to voice, critique, store, and disseminate their cultural heritage and personal voices. The community recording studio, a space for underrepresented youths, has been an enormous success. Some of the members of our media and recording studio have attained international reputation such as the Xplastaz[5], a music group that fuses Hip Hop with Swahili/Masai tribal chants. A graduate of our media centre won a National Geographic grant to create a documentary on the disappearing rock paintings of central Tanzania. I had an opportunity to speak about my experiences and projects at Harvard last May and received positive feedback from students and faculty members. I kept my connections with Harvard ever since working with the project on African Hip Hop as an adviser and contributor of audio-visual resources. These are some of the experiences and projects that I would like to continue.

Harvard's innovative teaching experience and research facilities offer me an unparalleled academic and personal opportunity. Attaining an education at Harvard will not only answer some of my fundamental personal questions but will offer me an opportunity to serve my people who have invested so much in me. In addition, I am looking forward to being in the Cambridge area to reunite with friends and colleagues. After my education, I intend to return to Tanzania to work as a professor, lecturer, consultant, and as a professional writer.

Thank you for your attention to this material, and I am deeply grateful for your consideration.

---

3. Provided by generous assistance from Prometheus Radio Project at: www.prometheusradio.org.
4. See www.asdrum.org for further details on the project.
5. See www.xplastaz.com for further details on the music group.

ESSAY #49: "The Radio Lady"

Statement of Purpose for Graduate School of Business

Radio has been my passion for as long as I can remember. I was one of those high school kids who sat by the radio waiting for the magic touch tones to dial in and win; my fascination with the medium was kindled.

My college radio station, WXXX at [major university], actually let me on the air. I'd get up for my 3 a.m. shift to play the immortal Dead Kennedys to insomniacs in the greater metro area. An internship at a "real world" station substituted for my senior thesis, and launched me into professional radio.

In the seven-plus years that I've been out in the working world, my objective has not changed: I want to own my own radio station. Maybe a station group, even a network.

I often try to analyze what it is about this medium that excites me so much. The immediacy of it. The power to reach people, relay a message, get under people's skins. As a work environment, I adore the wacky people attracted to radio. The casual type of workplace. The fact that a station is a small business where creativity can flourish, and one person can make an impact. And as an institution, a radio station can and should be an integral part of its community. Its voice, its friend.

And despite all the predictions to the contrary, radio is still alive and well. Prices of stations remain sky high. Radio is omnipresent. As an industry, there is a lot of action—more and more stations are becoming increasingly specialized—all-talk, all-sports, all Elvis? Is AM stereo going to take over the world? Is satellite ever going to reach its promise? Will a new administration change the joint ownership laws? What is the future of AM radio as young people grow up listening only to FM? There are so many questions, and in my mind, a lot of opportunity for bold thinkers—who have the knowledge to make their ideas into reality.

Recently I made a decisive move toward attaining my goal. I became an account executive for a major market station. I knew that unless I could effectively sell radio, I'd never be able to successfully run a station. Sales is the traditional route to advancement in radio: good salespeople become sales managers who become general managers. I know that if I stick with it, I can rise to the top via this route.

The truth is, I've worked for a good number of general managers who rose through the ranks through the sales department, and frankly, I am not impressed.

This business requires more knowledge than one can acquire by simply climbing the sales ladder. I need to know accounting and finance. If I don't know how to put together a deal, who's going to bankroll my first acquisition? With an increasingly media-intensive market, how can I strategically position my station to garner its share of the ad dollars? With all the diverse personalities and egos in a "showbiz" enterprise like a radio station, being a good people manager is essential, but so is knowing how to utilize resources and how to streamline an organization. These are just a few of my goals for business school.

The student who wrote this next essay told me she thought she came across to the admissions counselors as "that crazy radio lady." She said she earned an interview with this essay, and she won over the committee with her sense of purpose to an unusual goal. Once again, admissions counselors are drawn to people who they think will succeed whether they are admitted or not. This candidate certainly leaves that impression.

#49: "The Radio Lady" *(continued)*

I am very impressed by Columbia's diverse offerings in all these areas. I will learn the entrepreneurial skills I need, while having the opportunity to interact with leaders and top students, with interests both similar to and diverse from my own. I hope to take advantage of some of the Graduate School of Journalism's offerings as well. And by staying in New York City, I hope to keep up with my valuable contacts, developed in my years already in this business.

ESSAY #50: "Strip Club Culture"

The bouncers at the strip club are beginning to recognize me. I am the woman who comes in with a notepad asking questions but is not interested in a job. I am intrigued by the small but significant population of dancers who use stripping as an economic means of supporting their higher education. They contradict stereotypes regarding both dancers and educated women. These dancers and their ever-increasing business- and professional-class clientele affirm the success of the upscaling campaign that the "Gentlemen's Club" industry has implemented over the past decade. These upscaled strip clubs play out socially relevant concepts such as power, gender, and class in a unusual arena that commodifies sexuality in an increasingly acceptable forum.

I find efforts to alleviate the stigma that has been traditionally associated with patronage and employment in these cultural meeting spaces to be engaging. Gentlemen's clubs are increasingly prominent in the media, primarily for their novelty value. They raise interesting historical questions regarding their forerunners in the sex industry (such as the burlesque theater) and regarding American culture as well. Ethnographic interview and historical research methods form the basis of my American civilizations honors thesis project (to be completed for presentation this spring).

My American civilizations major has provided me with a versatile background for intellectual inquiry. Since high school, American cultural history has been a substantial part of my intellectual life. My long-standing interest in this field led me to consider becoming a historian. However, I wanted a broad-based foundation in American culture for my undergraduate studies. Therefore, I chose a major with a multidisciplinary approach to American culture. My undergraduate training as an American culturalist has been in historical fields and in diverse subjects such as material culture, historical archaeology, anthropology, sociology, women's studies, and American literature.

The transition from American culturalist to American cultural historian became logical to me as I realized both the importance of concentrating upon one discipline, and that many history programs have embraced a myriad of cultural studies. I will bring my versatile American civilizations training to both the study of American cultural history and to a future career as a professor and researcher. One program that has sparked my interest is the American cultural history program at Johns Hopkins University.

I am very impressed by the helpfulness and enthusiasm of the several professors who spoke with me regarding their own work and the work of other members of the department. Professor Ronald Walters described his work and the work of several of his students in 20th-century popular culture. Having a multidisciplinary background in American culture, I was delighted to learn that the department's approach to courses of study is, as Professor Walters phrased it, "driven by problems rather than by rigid fields. . . ." Professor Walters also discussed with me the graduate history program's unique mentorship system.

I feel that it is important to develop one's academic career in an environment that has visible and accessible mentors. I greatly value independent research and independent

This scholar designed her own undergraduate research project in an environment where field studies might seem daunting. Then, she researched graduate programs well enough to identify a program with a bias toward students with undergraduate field studies experience. This is the epitome of a smart application to graduate school. Her interest is not simply admission, but admission to a program where she can excel and gain maximum benefit.

Feel free to quote professors, as long as you do it accurately. Note that the entire rest of the essay deals with the alignment of the targeted graduate program with this candidate's interests.

#50: "Strip Club Culture"	(continued)

thought—my undergraduate work and the structure of my major coursework attest to this bias. Nevertheless, I feel fortunate to have had close interactions with several professors—all of whom I would consider academic role models—who helped me to critically evaluate my ideas and my work. I believe that such relationships become even more essential in a doctoral program as one's chosen discipline becomes increasingly specific. My understanding of Johns Hopkins' graduate history program is that these relationships are not only encouraged but also fostered by the department.

Johns Hopkins' history program is known for its rigorous course of study and for its ready inclusion of graduate students into its intellectual community. I think that a strong society of peers is essential in developing one's academic career. All of the professors with whom I spoke described the departmental graduate seminars as engaging forums of intellectual exchange in which both students and faculty participate. Structurally, Johns Hopkins' history program seems to benefit from a close mentorship system and an interactive community of scholarship. I welcome such a learning environment.

Substantively and temporally, my interests in American history have generally led me to the industrial and post-industrial eras. I plan to study cultural history in general and women's history specifically. For these reasons, I particularly look forward to the opportunity to study with Profs. Ronald Walters and JoAnne Brown for their work in 20th-century topics of political and popular cultural history, respectively, and with Prof. Toby Ditz, who discussed with me her work in women's and family history and in cultural history.

My undergraduate work in American civilizations has allowed me to explore my many interests in American culture. I look forward to defining my research and intellectual paths in a more rigorous historical framework. I hope that the committee views my credentials and my interests to be complementary with Johns Hopkins' resources, professors and focus.

9

Letters of Recommendation

Your grades, your test scores, your essay, and your letters of recommendation make up the entire body of evidence upon which the admissions committee will base its decision. Each admissions counselor will weigh these factors differently, but no matter how they view them, letters of recommendation are one of only four sources of information about you, and thus are vitally important.

Interestingly enough, the more competitive the program, the more the letters count in the final decision-making process. All the finalists for these programs will have outstanding grades, academic preparation, and test scores; the committee will decide based on the essay and letters of recommendation. The less competitive the program, the more likely it is that the committee will be able to make sufficient differentiation from quantitative measures such as grades and scores. In either case, if you are a borderline candidate, your essay and letters of recommendation become even more important. Even one well-thought-out and laudatory letter of recommendation can push you into the admit category, while a handful of lukewarm endorsements can leave you to languish on the wait list or be rejected as nobody special.

There are several strategies for ensuring that your letters of recommendation are outstanding. Look again at the handout on pages 36–37, "Getting Fantastic Letters of Recommendation." The first and most obvious strategy is to approach your letter writers at the earliest possible moment. These are busy people; you must be considerate of their other time commitments. Be very clear about when you are going to apply, but try not to mention the deadline; let them know that you would appreciate it if they would send in the letter as soon as possible. Always provide neatly preaddressed and prestamped envelopes for their convenience.

It is your job to prompt your letter writers to actually write and post the letters on time. Prompt them at least once a week. Many professors try to catch up on their work during long weekends and holidays, so it is a good idea to put a little extra pressure on them right before such breaks. Be sure to let a letter writer know if his letter is the last item you need—many schools will not review your application file until it is complete, so turning in your essay and application three months early is of little use if your last letter of recommendation arrives after the deadline.

It is a good idea to solicit at least one more letter of recommendation than the target school or program requires. Some schools issue stern warnings—"Do not submit additional letters of recommendation; they will not be considered"—but you can disregard them. These warnings are designed not to keep you from sending one extra letter, but to prevent the onslaught of meaningless endorsements some candidates forward. One admissions officer received some twenty letters in favor of one candidate, including one from his pediatrician. "You could tell from the letter," the admissions officer recalled, "that the pediatrician didn't have any better idea why he was writing that letter than we did." But one extra letter is okay, and requesting one allows you to forward all your materials as soon as you collect the minimum number.

•   •   •

You should select your letter writers carefully, using three criteria: Do they know you well enough to write about you in a detailed and persuasive manner? Will they say wonderful things about you? Are they reliable enough to write and post your recommendation in a timely manner? Most schools don't require that all your letter writers be professors; read and follow the school's requirements carefully.

Although it may be hard to resist, avoid those celebrity letter writers who offer letters of recommendation to all comers. For example, a certain politician who lives in San Francisco will write a letter for practically any nonincarcerated Democrat. These letters work better the farther from San Francisco you are, but in California they are viewed with snickers. (For one thing, they are all virtually identical.) Every state has politicians like this, who write such letters on behalf of the sons and daughters of friends and benefactors.

Schools usually prefer that you have letters of recommendation written by employers and professors who have the most intimate knowledge of your work and study habits. A specific letter from your immediate supervisor will carry more weight than a vague letter from someone higher up in the organization who obviously does not know you very well. Some letters may have two signatories, such as a full professor and a teaching assistant, or the president of the company and the vice president of sales.

Of course, you should select letter writers who will say the most wonderful things about you. Some professors are known for writing letters of recommendation that are timely, well wrought, and successful; you should ask around and discover who they are. Do not assume just because someone is friendly with you that she will write a good letter for you. A professor or supervisor who respects you, no matter how she feels about you personally, is probably the best bet.

Finally, keep in mind that the admissions committee will expect letters from certain key people. If you conducted a senior research project or wrote an honors thesis, the committee will expect a letter from your faculty adviser. If you reported directly to the president at your last company, the committee will expect a letter from that president. However, you may have a good reason to intentionally fail to solicit a letter from one of these people.

When you have your list of preferred writers, ask each of them to tell you honestly what they could say about you in a letter of recommendation. This can be tough, but it is far better to find out that a professor is not able to endorse your candidacy than it is to have your targeted school find this out before you. Sometimes you can negotiate with professors; for example, you might get them to agree not to mention your habit of turning in papers late, and to keep the focus of the letter on the quality of your writing and scholarship. If you feel that someone is less than thrilled to write a letter of recommendation for you, select someone else. A reluctant and tepid "endorsement" can be the kiss of death.

Should you waive your rights?

Letters of recommendation used to be secret testimony. Now, however, you have the right to review every item in your educational files—thanks to the Family Educational Rights and Privacy Act of 1974, commonly known as the Buckley Amendment. Because this student right made some professors nervous, and because some graduate schools believed that nervous professors may be less than honest and forthcoming, graduate schools have invented a waiver for those rights. On almost every application extant today, you have the opportunity to sign away your rights, or to retain them, and therein lies a dilemma: Should you, or shouldn't you?

The answer is a little complicated. First of all, you should do your best to select recommenders you can trust. You should sit down with them and ask, point blank, "What will you be able to say about me in a letter of recommendation?" Even the best letters include some little criticism; listen for the overall tone. Is this a strong endorsement you're discussing, or not?

Second, it is always the prerogative of the professor to share the letter with you—*many professors will*. This is the best of all possible worlds. Of course, some professors, as a matter of personal policy, will not ever share the contents of letters with applicants. Personally, I would think twice about using a recommender who refuses to let you know what is in the letter.

Third, graduate programs discount the recommendations—even when they are strongly laudatory—when the student retains the right to review the file. This is patently unfair, as some faculty acknowledge. One professor wrote this in response to one of my surveys on faculty attitudes about letters of recommendation: "If there is integrity in the process, professors should have the backbone to state their opinions and back them up with evidence." To paraphrase Dr. Johnson, secrecy is the first resort of scoundrels. Nevertheless, your goal is to be admitted to a challenging program. If your laudatory letters could be discounted because you choose to retain your rights, this is a concern.

I think you should waive your rights. I have seen some very strong students refuse to waive their rights. I have interviewed students who failed to get into programs because of mean and spiteful comments by professors in their letters of recommendation. It's your decision. Make it thoughtfully.

—BETTER LETTERS OF RECOMMENDATION—

a handout for faculty

1. Be sure you want to recommend this student.

    - Discuss a student's academic plans and preparation before agreeing to write a recommendation.

    - Help student choose grad programs that match interests, skills, and preparation.

    - Consider declining some so you can do a better job on others.

2. Get enough data to do your job.

    - Transcript and/or list of classes in major

    - Graded work sample: paper or lab

    - Résumé or C.V. — list of honors and awards

    - Some idea of what the student would like you to focus on

    - Letter of recommendation form from the targeted grad school

3. Assemble a laundry list of basic skills; assume nothing. For example: "_____ has command of coherent wave optics, Fourier optics, laser physics, lens design, optical metrology, optics of thin films, paraxial optics, physical optics, and all related areas of physics."

4. Describe a particularly successful project.

    - The candidate needs to be special, out of the ordinary (or, presumably, you shouldn't be recommending him/her).

    - Find one or more "above and beyond" stories to focus on.

- Mention student experience as proctor, TA, RA, tutor, other forms of departmental service.

5. Get personal when appropriate.

- Has the student overcome adversity—work, first generation, health or family, special challenges? You can be the candidate's advocate on these issues, which is more sophisticated than having the student address them.

- Do you enjoy having this student in your classes?

6. Close by predicting success, for example:

- "One of the top students I've worked with in recent years."

- "Razor-sharp mind."

- "Tremendous potential."

- "More than adequately prepared."

- "I am confident that _____ will be an outstanding graduate student and go on to make major contributions in the field through both research and teaching."

7. Abandon the form and customize.

- "See attached letter addressing these and other issues."

On the form, fill out your name and the student's, perhaps, but no more, then attach the form to your much-superior letter.

Note when the student is going to apply, not *the deadline.*

Should you use a credentials service?

Credentials services are often available from college and university career centers, and sometimes from individual departments, such as education. For such a service, you have "To Whom It May Concern" letters written by your recommenders, and they are placed in a confidential portfolio. The service then mails out this portfolio to graduate schools or, in some fields, potential employers, on a demand basis.

Although this is an efficient system, you should avoid it when you can. You may be applying to dental school and a doctoral program in physical anthropology at the same time, and the same letter of recommendation for both targets will not serve your best interests. Beg your recommenders to customize for each school. Ask them to mention any colleagues they may know at the targeted institutions, or to relate your skills specifically to what they know of the targeted program. If a professor is too busy to write individual letters for many schools you are applying to, ask if she would customize for your top three choices, and then revert to a "To Whom It May Concern" version for the remainder.

Some programs require you to collect the letters from your recommenders, possibly signed across the seal to ensure confidentiality, and forward them with the rest of your application. As mentioned earlier, this is called the "self-managed application process." Others ask the recommenders to forward the letter directly to the graduate program. Either way, you want to keep close tabs on the progress of your letter writers.

Once you have the letter or have been assured that it was forwarded to the graduate program, be sure to send a prompt and sincere thank-you card to the author. As one doctoral student wrote me, "You'll find that you use your recommenders again and again, and they'll be more inclined to help you next time if you really appreciate it this time."

By the way, if a professor is particularly enthusiastic about you, have her call up your targeted school and intercede on your behalf. This will be most effective if she knows someone where you are going, which is frequently the case. (You should note that this is how most academic *jobs* are obtained, as well, so practice getting these extra endorsements now.)

Content

An effective letter will address the candidate's intellectual capacity, work habits, social skills, and particular academic preparation. These statements need a frame of reference, so some letter authors will rank students in a greater context, such as "I find Ms. Ashton's academic performance to fall consistently in the top 10 percent of students I have ever instructed," or "Mr. Herzel is a solid student, certainly ranking in the top half of students at St. John's, but you have to take this ranking in the context that the overwhelming majority of St. John's students obtain an advanced degree within a few years of graduation, most of them from the top programs in the nation."

Some letters will describe specific academic accomplishments that illustrate the student's abilities. Such letters are usually compelling because the reader can personally judge the performance described. (This is also a particularly apt style of letter to request if you have had a spotty career. Ask your professor or employer to focus the entire letter on your most successful project.)

Authors often cite challenges the student has overcome or unusual aspects of the student's background. In order to remain believable and to demonstrate objectivity, letters of recommendation almost always contain some modicum of criticism or warn of some weakness. So, if you review your own letters and discover moderate criticism, do not despair. In an outstanding letter, of course, the weakness will be a strength in disguise, just as in the essays; for example: "If Johanna has any fault it is that she spends too much time on her extracurricular activities. However, as you can see her academic performance remains excellent."

One admissions reader told me that he is particularly impressed when a professor cites a student's contributions to her undergraduate department or school. On a similar note, one highly successful candidate told me, "The trick is to look like a rising star, somebody who is going on to do wonderful things whether you attend their school or not. Remember, in the long run *they* want to be associated with *you*." Graduate schools are seeking people who will contribute to their programs as outstanding students, who will enhance the reputation of the program by the success of their careers, and who will later on return to be involved as benefactors. A good letter of recommendation will definitely predict a bright future for the candidate, as a scholar and later as a professional with a career. This is often an effective way to close a letter of recommendation.

As you read the sample letters of recommendation in this chapter, look for these components: credentials of the writer; depth of knowledge of the candidate as a person and a scholar; testimony as to the candidate's intellectual capacity, work habits, and preparedness for graduate studies; some small fault to demonstrate the writer's objectivity; and predictions of the candidate's future career contributions.

LETTER #1: "Consolidated Letter"

Attn: Selection Committee
Maudie Jane Watkins Medical Fellowship for Women
The Watkins Family Foundation
Chicago, Illinois

Dear Selection Committee,

This is a letter of introduction for Ms. Meredith Archer of Lake City, Iowa, who is making application for the Maudie Jane Watkins Medical Fellowship for Women. Ms. Archer graduated *summa cum laude* from [school withheld] two years ago, receiving a bachelor of arts degree in anthropology with a minor in psychology. Ms. Archer completed an honors thesis, *Age and Gender Differences in Delivery of Medical Services in Afghanistan under the Taliban.* She is a member of Phi Beta Kappa and Lambda Alpha, the anthropology honors society. Ms. Archer has been accepted into the fall entering medical school class at three universities, all of which meet the criteria for the Watkins Fellowship.

It is indeed a pleasure for me to write this letter. Meredith is one of the most engaging, intelligent and talented students that I have encountered in my fifteen-plus years in higher education. Her curiosity and quest for excellence, coupled with her joie de vivre and infectious nature, make her an extraordinary student and a charismatic personality. I remember when she first came to my office to tell me that she thought that she had begun to consider medicine as her professional goal. This was three summers ago. The only premedical requirement that she had fulfilled was calculus. In her senior year she took introductory chemistry and following graduation she enrolled at the University of Iowa, where she completed the premedical requirements with a 3.89 cumulative GPA. When she took the MCAT exam last April she received a score of 34. She will shine as a medical student and walk away with prizes like the Frieman Prize she won for excellence in writing the spring of her freshman undergraduate year here.

I am certainly not the only person at [school withheld] who has been impacted by this awesome young woman. I was particularly struck by the words of her introductory chemistry professor. Meredith made one of her few B's in Prof. Blair's section. (And it is worth noting that she did make an A in the first semester of introductory chemistry.) Prof. Blair writes, "She is a unique student and person. Although she is not the most clever student I have met in 18 years of teaching, she is among the top in commitment, creativity, curiosity, energy, and love-of-life. During help sessions, she persisted (through the groans of classmates) until she understood. Often it was clear that the object of her question was not relevant to the upcoming exam (hence the groans), but that didn't stifle her. She loves to understand. I find it interesting that she made an effort to become acquainted. I was one of the few faculty who gave her a grade of B. That didn't bother her as much as her impatience with herself to learn basic chemistry. She could see its relevance, but sometimes had problems

This letter is an example of a consolidated letter of recommendation, a style sometimes used by medical school advising committees. This is a particularly rich example, showing the student as a real human being, with a personality and a unique set of experiences. Note the honest depictions of the student's academic limitations as well as her assets. This student's advisers went to a great deal of trouble to assemble this letter, and that effort alone supports the student's endeavor. Needless to say, this letter won the fellowship.

with quantitative thinking. As you study her record, you will see that her quantitative background as a student was—at the time—not as strong as it would have been had she started her studies in basic science."

Meredith took advantage of the study abroad program while she was an undergraduate here. We offer the opportunity to participate in a special program at the University of Paris (Sorbonne). Meredith studied there in the spring of her junior year. Dr. Dupree in the department of anthropology at the Sorbonne was her adviser. Dr. Dupree writes, "In terms of the combination of energy, enthusiasm and intelligence, Meredith has been one of the more exceptional students I have come across in years, and she is most suitable for medical training. In addition to being a rigorous student, extremely hard-working and diligent, she also has a strong humanistic side, is very compassionate and generous with her peers. She possesses the most important qualities required of a physician: she is wise, responsible and empathetic; these traits, combined with her resourcefulness and industriousness will prove a tremendous asset in her chosen field."

Meredith took abnormal psychology as part of her psychology minor and was taught by Prof. Andrews. Prof. Andrews was so impressed by her abilities as a student that he invited her to join a senior seminar devoted to developing in-depth psychiatric roles. He writes of her work: "What Ms. Archer had to do was master both the theoretical as well as the clinical literature about both of her assigned syndromes . . . [and] master how these particular patients would express their psychopathology in cognitive psychological tests. . . . [This] requires of the student the capacity to know herself very well, to not be frightened by another person's psychopathology, and yet to be able to put themselves into a particular patient's mind-set and to develop the subtle nuance of behavior as well as the cognitive styles reflective of the particular role assigned. Ms. Archer was so successful in playing one role (that of a borderline personality disorder who was also an incest victim), that I made a special training tape to use in future years. Her performance of this role, her profound understanding of both the theoretical and the clinical literature really represented high-level graduate work."

Meredith, as you might expect, was involved in a number of extracurricular activities. She was an active member of a social sorority and a member of the All University Choir. Her sophomore year she played the role of Emily in Thornton Wilder's *Our Town* at the university's Circle Theatre. Following that role she was nominated to compete in an acting competition of soliloquies held at Carnegie Mellon University. When she was at home in the summers, I know that she participated in a soup kitchen. Also, in the summers she waitressed thirty hours a week to earn money to help defray college expenses. Being the adventuresome soul that she is, when she studied in Paris she joined a parachute club and "dropped in" around the countryside.

Since she has been a student at [school withheld], Meredith has made a significant volunteer commitment to a free health clinic. The executive director, Laura Collins, writes,

---

#1: "Consolidated Letter"   *(continued)*

"Volunteering here requires some unique traits above and beyond the professional skills expected of most volunteers. We found that Meredith had no trouble negotiating the sometimes intimidating first few sessions here. Though she has been with us only five months, she has demonstrated a wonderful 'can-do' attitude, though not overbearing in any way. Meredith is industrious, resourceful and determined to complete any task assigned to her. In addition, she seems to possess the innate compassion and sensitivity so sorely needed in modern caregivers."

Meredith has also worked as a nurse extender at City Hospital, emptying bedpans, giving baths, changing linens, etc. This young woman is no *prima donna;* I can assure you that she did all these things with grace and good cheer.

What else can I say? Meredith is one of the jewels that we all treasure: the curious and dedicated student, the effective and committed volunteer, and the warm, sensitive and empathetic person whose enthusiasm for life is enviable. Clearly, this remarkable young woman will be a leader in her class and leave her imprint wherever she goes. She will most certainly be an excellent caregiver, as illustrated by her commitment to volunteer work and her well-thought-out choice to pursue the role of physician. It is, indeed, with great pleasure that I recommend Meredith to you with effusive enthusiasm and the utmost confidence. I envy the people who will have the pleasure of her company in the classroom, in the lab, in the clinics; they can look forward to four very rewarding years indeed. Her patients can look forward to an intelligent and caring physician who will always give the very best of herself and her knowledge.

Please give every consideration to this most remarkable young woman as you review her application for the Watkins Fellowship.

LETTER #2:   "Letter from the President of the Company for Graduate School of Business"

Dear Admissions Committee:

I am pleased to write this letter of recommendation for Shane Whittington to attend graduate school in business. I have close daily experience of Shane's work habits and contributions to this company, and I can only report that I rank him in the top 5 percent of business people I have ever had the pleasure to know.

His analytical abilities are first rate. In addition to his research and reporting work, he has designed several methodologies that are now in use throughout the company. Even more important, and perhaps harder to define, he always understands the reasoning or the goal behind any analysis that he performs. This is a rare and refreshing trait.

His interpersonal skills are one of his most outstanding traits. Everybody who knows him thinks favorably of him, and I know I can trust him to represent the company to our numerous shareholders and business associates. He is enthusiastic and optimistic in his dealings with investors, and this has been of benefit to the company. Shane's duties have included several opportunities for direct sales, and it is clear that he could have a highly successful career in this area should he choose to do so.

In short, when I give an assignment to Shane I know it will be done right, on time, and in excess of my specifications. If he has any fault, it is adding enhancements to assignments, doing more than what was asked. In summary, he is a tremendous asset to management, and will surely rise rapidly in any organization in which he is employed.

Note how this letter covers the candidate's analytical skills, interpersonal aptitude, and mental acuity in general. The letter was from the president of a finance company and was on company stationery. The details of the candidate's career are covered in his résumé and his application essay, so this letter is free to focus on the president's impressions of the candidate.

LETTER #3:   "Letter from Professor for Graduate School of English"

This letter is short, sweet, and over-whelmingly effective. I read three letters recommending this student, and each was unequivocal and unreserved in its praise. This student does not appear to have any faults, so none is mentioned. Note how the author describes the candi-date's performance in a specific class so clearly that the reader is able to think to her-self, "I want a special student like that."

Attn: Prof. Sarah M. Hardesty
Chair, English Language and Literature
St. Lawson University

Dear Dr. Hardesty:

It is a great pleasure for me to recommend Ms. Celeste Wallace for admission, and fellowship support, to graduate school in English. I first encountered her in a large lecture course I was teaching three years ago. Within days, Ms. Wallace had distinguished herself as an absolutely extraordinary student—one who could ask the most penetrating questions about the assigned reading and expound her ideas with effortless extemporaneous elegance. I soon found that in a class of 150 students, I was beginning to carry on a dialogue with just one—much to the fascination of her classmates, who seemed as awestruck as I was. Not surprisingly, Celeste's written work proved to be of the same caliber as her conversation; she received a grade of A+, and even that seemed inadequate to her accomplishment.

Since then, I have stayed in touch with Ms. Wallace and have helped to steer her toward courses worthy of her gifts. I have read four of her subsequently written papers, and have noted in them a deepening and broadening of theoretical concerns. With her boundless curiosity and energy, her wit, her good humor, and her blazing intelligence, she has all the makings of a first-rate critic and college teacher. I would rank her among the top few undergraduates I have ever taught in thirty-three years at Michigan.

LETTER #4: "Letter from Dean of School of Dentistry for Residency in Orthodontics"

To Whom It May Concern:

It is my pleasure to write a letter of recommendation on behalf of Akira Tokuyoshi in his pursuit of postdoctoral education in the field of orthodontics. I can state unequivocally that his academic and clinical skills have placed him among the top students in his class. His polite manner, his concern for his studies and his patients, and his emotional maturity are well known and respected among his peers and the faculty and staff.

His academic credentials alone qualify him for postdoctoral study and advanced training, but I can recommend this student enthusiastically for other reasons as well. He has complemented his academic schedule with leadership activities in many extracurricular areas, and has enhanced the reputation and the image of [major university] Dental School as much as a student can.

Akira was selected student editor of the [major university] Dental School's journal, *The Dental Explorer.* As such, he has worked closely with many faculty and students to put together the annual issue, which will be released soon, and which has already been highly praised by the faculty reviewers.

Akira has served (by invitation) as a preceptor in the [major university] Dental School's Summer Enrichment Program. There he taught dental morphology and head and neck anatomy to incoming dental students. Also, he has volunteered as a tutor for the preclinical laboratory classes every year since his arrival. In these capacities, his professors have rated him very highly on both communication skills and technical knowledge. His concern for his fellow students is admirable, and a credit to himself and the success of our program.

Akira's natural ability to work with and motivate others has helped him hold several offices. He is currently president of our campus chapter of Delta Sigma Delta, the international dental fraternity, and he is vice president and senior editor of our Student Research Group, an IADR affiliate to promote primary research in dental science.

Akira has also participated in research with distinguished members of our faculty and has participated in several presentations and table clinics at scientific meetings. I understand that somehow he finds time to play sports as well.

In summary, Akira distinguishes himself as an individual who exhibits an organized, scientific approach to work and an ability to plan, organize, and implement projects of varying complexity. He is a team player, who with a high degree of motivation, innovation and initiative, can accomplish his goals.

I know him to be a most personable and sincere young man, well liked and respected by those who work with him. I enthusiastically recommend this individual as an outstanding future orthodontist, and I predict he will have a bright future.

This letter is for a postdoctoral residency in orthodontics. The salutation is "To Whom It May Concern," as the candidate applied to a number of programs. Nevertheless, the letter is warm and personal, and clearly demonstrates how a student's contributions to his own school enhance his desirability as a graduate or postgraduate candidate. It is clear that this candidate provided the author of the letter with a complete list of his accomplishments and activities.

LETTER #5: "Letter from Former Employer for Fellowship Award"

Fellowships and scholarships often require letters of recommendation in addition to an essay and an application. This letter cites the author's intimate knowledge of the candidate's background, then praises her strengths in all areas necessary for success in the field in question. In addition, the author is a well-known figure to the members of the fellowship awards committee. This letter, combined with a persuasive application and a cogent essay, is worth thousands of dollars.

Dear Members of the Committee:

I worked with Maureen Daly Pascoe, an applicant for the ULI Land Use and Development Fellowship, for five years while she was employed by the East Bay Regional Park District. As a program analyst in the Land Acquisition Department, she was invaluable in a wide variety of acquisition and land planning projects. The issues that Maureen dealt with were involved, sensitive, and difficult. She proved time and again that she was capable of handling complex land use and development issues, often in the face of opposition. Many acquisitions involved developers, planners from several local governments, and a variety of community groups; she worked well with each. She was always well informed, prepared, and insightful on the range of interests represented.

I consider among Maureen's strengths her genuine enthusiasm for the subject of land use planning and development, her ability to analyze the subject at hand and cut through the mire to the essence of the situation, her attention to the necessary details (including numbers), and her intelligence. She was an outstanding employee.

Maureen Daly Pascoe is an excellent choice for this fellowship; she has my highest recommendation.

LETTER #6: "Recommendation from Professional Acquaintance"

Admissions Committee
The Accelerated Premedical Studies Program
University of New England
Biddeford, Maine

Re: Matthew M. Moffett

Dear Members of the Committee:

As a writer specializing in careers and education, I interview and write about academic and business leaders on a regular basis for the *Wall Street Journal*. I originally learned of Matthew Moffett over ten years ago through a mutual acquaintance, who told me Matt was an engineer who had never gone to college. I was fascinated to hear about this rather unusual career path and called Matt up to interview him for an article. I found him delightful and unique, and since then have written about him in several articles and mentioned him and his accomplishments in two of my books. I think Matthew Moffett's story is an inspiration to others, and I have told it many times.

Over the years I've watched Matt's development rather closely out of professional curiosity. I do not know of another person even remotely like him. Matt is really a throwback to Renaissance ideals. Who could imagine that in this day and age someone would teach himself the math and physics required to be an engineer? Who could imagine that in this day and age someone with a technical orientation would also be able to win over the management of not one but a continuing series of Fortune 500 employers? We live in a credentials-driven society, and Matthew Moffett has repeatedly used his mind as his most powerful and impressive credential. I hesitate not one bit to say that Matthew Moffett could teach himself any subject and master any profession. There is no other person I know about whom I would say this.

I've come to know Matt rather well. He met his wife at a gathering at my house, and I've served as an informal career counselor for him since we first met. I know how and why he's made each move he's made, career-wise, for the last ten years. He's given me blanket permission to share with you what I know of him. Matt has been searching for integration and purpose, and a way to use his mind in helping service to others. For some at his stage in life, entering premedical studies with the goal of pursuing a healthcare career would be imprudent. But I know that Matthew Moffett will continue to surprise us. This is a young man of seemingly unbounded potential, and any way you can assist him in his quest will be returned many times over to us all.

Please call me if you would like me to elucidate further on any point.

Most graduate schools will expect letters from professors or employers who have had direct supervisory experience over you. However, the next four letters explore some other options for recommenders, including a professional acquaintance, a colleague, a peer, and a pertinent character reference from a religious leader. This first letter is from a journalist, describing a most unusual candidate in a most persuasive way.

LETTER #7:   "Recommendation from Former Colleague"

Dear Admissions Committee:

David Arthur has asked me to write this letter of recommendation for him for the Executive MBA program at Stanford, and for the Faculty Committee Merit Scholarship, and I am honored to do so.

As I have known David Arthur for almost ten years, both professionally and personally, I feel qualified to comment on his abilities. I was his office manager when we were running Crash Marketing, a small business consulting firm, and we have remained in close contact ever since.

In fact, Mr. Arthur is the most valuable mentor I have ever had. I graduated *magna cum laude* from UCLA with an MBA, and have gone on to become a top-ranked business analyst in Taiwan, but I credit Mr. Arthur with the most important parts of my business education. He has the best business mind I have ever encountered, and I work daily with business leaders of global enterprises. Without his valuable mentorship in "the human element," I could never have achieved my goals in the corporate world.

In addition to his intelligence and insight, he is a very efficient person. I've seen him write a book on small business marketing in six weeks while running a very demanding business daily. He leads by example and was good at motivating others beyond their normal abilities. It was a very exciting company to work in while I was a business student.

Finally, I must say something about David Arthur's congeniality. People respond well to Mr. Arthur. People walked into his office and within ten minutes they were willing to tell him everything about themselves and their businesses. Launching a company can be a traumatic time in people's lives, and they always seemed to trust Mr. Arthur. They were always happy with our plans and programs, because they were happy with the experience of dealing with Mr. Arthur. Clients enthusiastically recommended our company to their friends and acquaintances. At the same time, I think it was the parade of different people who came into the office every day that excited Mr. Arthur the most about the company. People like him because he likes them, whatever their gender, race, politics, income level, or personal style. He is very much at home in a modern international, multicultural environment. And although he focused on serving an entrepreneurial and high-tech clientele, he was just as successful working with tradesmen who wanted to start their own companies, or the founders of ethnic or family businesses—if they came to our office, and they frequently did. He has an uncanny ability to establish rapport with anyone.

In closing, Mr. Arthur is one of those rare individuals who seemingly can do anything he sets out to do. He is certainly the type of person who would be a credit to a quality graduate business program. I recommend him without reservation. He will make an outstanding addition to your alumni.

Should you need any additional information, please contact me. Perhaps email is best due to the time difference between Taiwan and California.

When you own the company, or you cannot find your former bosses, or they would say awful things about you, letters from colleagues, clients, or customers may be your only option. If you solicit a colleague or customer letter, choose someone who will say wonderful things about you and say them well. Such letters need to be substantive, as this one is, or they will be discounted. Note how this recommender lays out her credentials for the reader, which lend credence to the recommendation.

LETTER #8: "Peer Letter for Medical School"

Geoffrey Savage
196 Foulswell Street, #1-B
Boston, Massachusetts 02125
(617) 555-3063

Office of Admissions and Student Affairs
University of Minnesota Medical School
Box 293 UMHC
420 Delaware Street SE
Minneapolis, Minnesota 55455-0310

September 8, 2009

Attn: Selection Committee
Contents: Letter of Evaluation from Roommate for Applicant
                Robert Savage, SS# 171-15-0029

Dear Committee:

Robert Savage has been my roommate for the last four years—he is also my brother. I am proud to have Robert as a brother. He is a person of strong ideals, he is a serious person, and he is someone on whom his friends can count. We are roommates by choice and friendship, not just because we are brothers.

As to Robert's qualifications for medical school, I know of his strong aptitude, especially in the sciences, his long intent to go to medical school, and his daily work habits.

If I were to pick a few words to describe my brother, at least from my point of view as his roommate, it would be: busy, active, efficient. Robert is someone who is always doing something. He takes on more than most people, and I have watched him effortlessly handle a very large load of commitments (classes, sports, clubs, and social activities) that would make other students fall apart.

One of the reasons Robert is able to do so much is because of his study habits. He studies every evening for one to five hours except when he has a class or lab. He plans for his tests and presentations so that he doesn't have a work "crunch" in the last few days. In addition to this, he seems to get any science subject on the first pass through. I have learned a lot from him about good study habits, mostly about planning ahead, but I know few students who "get" the material so easily. In his lab groups, many sessions of which have met here in our apartment, he is usually the natural leader, setting the strategy for the lab and the write up.

Schools occasionally ask the applicant to provide letters from peers. Professors and employers are trained professionals, practiced in the arts of innuendo and scratch-my-back-I'll-scratch-yours. Peers are more likely to be guileless, which is exactly why schools request these letters. Peers often convey more unintentionally than intentionally. A candidate's peer letters reveal a great deal about him— about the quality of his friends and his judgment—so it's important to pick your peer letter writers very carefully.

#8: "Peer Letter for Medical School"   *(continued)*

Robert is a good roommate because he never complains about anything. I enjoy his company, and we have many friends together. We are both pretty busy, actually, so it is good that we enjoy the company of each other.

Robert has many strengths—strong intellect, a level-headed personality, he knows a lot of people all over campus—but if he has any weakness it is forgetting to take the time to relax more and "smell the roses." I think his ability to focus his attentions on a goal and ignore all distractions is probably handy for medical school, though.

I recommend Robert Savage for acceptance to your medical program. I know that he will be able to excel in your program, and I know that he will be a highly professional, skilled, and compassionate physician. Besides, you should know that his nickname already is "Doc" Savage.

Thank you for this opportunity to speak up on Robert's behalf.

Sincerely yours,

Geoffrey Savage
B.A., History (History of Navigation Systems),
Boston University
Ph.D. candidate, History of Science, M.I.T.

LETTER #9: "Character Witness Letter for Medical School"

Dear Members of the Committee:

I am pleased to recommend to you Aaron [last name withheld]. It is my opinion that Aaron will make an uncommonly good medical doctor, and that he has demonstrated character traits which will ensure this. Since I have known him well over ten years, I hope my letter will have weight of consideration commensurate with that length of time.

My organization, International Organization for Sephardic Rescue (I.O.S.R.), is dedicated to rescuing Sephardic Jews from oppressive regimes, mostly in the Middle East. We brought Aaron [last name withheld] to New York City from Iran ten years ago. He was a child of eleven years when he emigrated, leaving his parents behind. It was thought at the time that they would complete some business matters and follow their son, but in fact they were detained for several years.

During this time, from when he was eleven until he was thirteen, Aaron lived under the benevolent protection of I.O.S.R. He lived in a dormitory situation, and in the homes of some of our more dedicated members. He was always a delight to us all, and his personal strength and courage were a testament to human potential. I say this not out of appreciation for his ability to carry on without his own parents, and in spite of his deep and ongoing concern for them, but because of his ability to *excel* and *thrive* in these adverse conditions.

Being of a young age, he mastered the English language and went on to study at the Talmudical Seminary here in New York, a very rigorous Orthodox Jewish high school with a national reputation. There he excelled in a program of science, religion and classical liberal arts (just for the record, all subjects except Hebrew language studies are taught in English). He was the valedictorian of his class, and he of course graduated with honors.

Then at just the moment when some students would have gone on to a carefree college experience, Aaron's parents finally arrived from Iran. I know of his dedication and his daily assistance to them. He smoothed the path for these new immigrants who were without the language and social skills he had learned so well. At the same time, he was highly active in youth programs for I.O.S.R., rising to the position of director of youth programs, including our summer program involving hundreds of students.

So you see how I have watched this young man grow and develop, and I know the tremendous focus he has upon his studies and his service to mankind. It is my firm belief that his maturity, initiative, and self-reliance could only lead to success in medical school, and that his strength of character could only lead to an outstanding contribution to humanity as a medical doctor.

I highly recommend Aaron to your school. It is my unconditional belief that he will become an ethical, compassionate and extremely competent physician.

Professors and employers are the preferred authors of letters of recommendation, but sometimes someone with a long-term personal knowledge of you can be quite persuasive. This example is a "character witness" letter. Admissions committees will not be impressed if all your letters of recommendation are of this type; however, one may be effective when submitted in addition to a full set of letters from those who know your work and study capacities. If your character witness cannot add compelling weight to your application, it may be a good idea to forgo such a letter altogether. Note how this letter is full of factual evidence for the committee's consideration.

This fine dog, Dot Snize, attended many years of graduate school. If she can do it, you can too.

Resources

This is by no means a comprehensive listing. For more books and websites about applying to graduate schools go to www.donaldasher.com/gradschool.

Books

Accounting to Zoology: Graduate Fields Defined, Amy J. Goldstein, ed., 1987.

Ace Your Case! The Essential WetFeet.com Management Consulting Case Workbook by Wet Feet Press and Gary Alpert, 1998.

Annual Register of Grant Support 2000: A Directory of Funding Sources. 33d ed., R. R. Bowker, ed.

The Associated Press Stylebook and Libel Manual, Norm Goldstein, ed., 1998.

The Chicago Manual of Style: The Essential Guide for Writers, Editors, and Publishers. 15th ed.

Dan Cassidy's Worldwide Graduate Scholarship Directory: Thousands of Top Scholarships Throughout the U.S. and Around the World. 5th ed. by Daniel J. Cassidy, 2000.

Directory of Financial Aids for Minorities, 1997–1999 by Gail Ann Schlachter (biannual).

Directory of Financial Aids for Women, 1999–2001 by Gail Ann Schlachter, 1999.

Directory of Graduate Programs in Sports Medicine and Exercise Science, The American College of Sports Medicine, 2000 (call 317-637-9200 to order directly).

Double Billing: A Young Lawyer's Tale of Greed, Sex, Lies, and the Pursuit of a Swivel Chair by Cameron Stracher, 1999.

Edit Yourself: A Manual for Everyone Who Works with Words by Bruce Ross-Larson, 1996.

Educational Rankings Annual 2000: Over 4700 Rankings and Lists on Education, Lynne C. Hattendorf Westney, ed., 1999.

The Elements of Style. 4th ed. by William Strunk Jr. and E.B. White, 1999.

Encyclopedia of Associations. 35th ed., 1999.

Essential Guide to Graduate Admissions, Council of Graduate Schools, 1992 (available from their Web site: www.cgsnet.org).

15 Questions: More Practice to Help Ace Your Consulting Case by Wet Feet Press and Gary Alpert, 1998.

Financial Aid for Study and Training Abroad, 1999–2001 by R. David Weber and Gail Ann Schlachter, 1999.

Financial Aids for Higher Education. 17th ed. by Judy K. Santamaria and Oreon Keeslar, 1993.

Financial Resources for International Study: A Guide for U.S. Students and Professionals, Institute of International Education, 1996.

Financing Graduate School: How to Get Money for Your Master's or Ph.D. 2d rev. ed. by Patricia McWade, 1996.

Foundation Grants to Individuals. 11th ed. Foundation Center, 1999.

Free Money for Graduate School, H. Holt and Co., 1993.

Free Money for Graduate School: A Guide to More Than 1,000 Grants for Graduate Study by Laurie Blum, 2000.

Full Disclosure: Do You Really Want to Be a Lawyer? compiled by Susan J. Bell for The Young Lawyers Division of the ABA.

Funding for United States Study: A Guide for International Students and Professionals, Marie O'Sullivan (ed.) and Sara Steen, 1996.

GMAT Information Bulletin. (free)

GRE: Guide to the Use of Scores, Graduate Record Examinations Board of the Educational Testing Service.

GRE Information Bulletin. (free)

Getting What You Came For: The Smart Student's Guide for Earning a Master's or a PhD by Robert L. Peters, 1997.

The Gourman Report: A Rating of Graduate and Professional Programs in American and International Universities. 8th ed. by Jack Gourman, 1997.

The Graduate Student's Complete Scholarship Book, Student Services, Inc., 1998.

Guide to Graduate Education in Speech-Language Pathology & Audiology, 1988–89, American Speech-Language Hearing Association, 1988.

Harvard College Guide to Grants by Lisa M. Muto, 1994.

The Higher Education MoneyBook for Women & Minorities: A Directory of Scholarships, Fellowships, Internships, Grants and Loans, 1996. rev. ed. by Doris M. Young and William C. Young.

MAT Candidate Information Booklet.

MLA Handbook for Writers of Research Papers. 5th ed. by Joseph Gibaldi and Phyllis Franklin, 1999.

Medical School Admission Requirements, United States and Canada, 2000–2001 by Kimberly S. Varner, Association of American Medical College.

Medical School Admissions: The Insider's Guide by John A. Zebala, Daniel B. Jones, and Stephanie B. Jones.

Miss Thistlebottom's Hobgoblins: The Careful Writer's Guide to the Taboos, Bugbears and Outmoded Rules of English Usage by Theodore M. Bernstein.

The New Fowler's Modern English Usage. 3rd ed. by H.W. Fowler and Robert Burchfield, 2000.

Nitty-Gritty Grammar: A Not-So-Serious Guide to Clear Communication by Edith Hope Fine and Judith Pinkerton Josephson, 1998.

The Official Guide for GMAT Review. 9th ed., 1997.

Official Guide to Financing Your MBA by Bart Astor, 1994.

On Writing Well: The Classic Guide to Writing Nonfiction. 6th ed. by William Zinsser, 1998.

Paying the Piper: Productivity, Incentives, and Financing in U.S. Higher Education by Michael S. McPherson, Morton Owen Shapiro, and Gordon C. Winston, 1993.

Peterson's Grants for Graduate & Postdoctoral Studies. 5th ed., 1998.

Peterson's Guide to Graduate & Professional Programs: An Overview, 1997.

Peterson's Guide to Graduate Programs in Business, Education, Health, Information Studies, Law, & Social Work, 1997.

Peterson's Guide to Graduate Programs in Engineering and Applied Sciences, 1997.

Peterson's Guide to Graduate Programs in the Biological Sciences, 1997.

Peterson's Guide to Graduate Programs in the Humanities, Arts, & Social Sciences, 1997.

Peterson's Guide to Graduate Programs in the Physical Sciences, Mathematics, & Agricultural Sciences, 1996.

Practicing to Take the GRE General Test. 9th ed. Educational Testing Service.

Practicing to Take the {subject name here} Test, Educational Testing Service.

Prentice Hall Guide to Scholarships and Fellowships for Math and Science Students, by Mark Kantrowitz and Joann P. Digennaro, 1993.

The Real Guide to Grad School: What You Better Know Before You Choose Humanities & Social Sciences, Robert E. Clark and John Palatella, eds., 1997.

Research-Doctorate Programs in the United States: Continuity and Change, Marvin L. Goldberger, ed., 1995.

Running from the Law: Why Good Lawyers Are Getting Out of the Legal Profession by Deborah L. Arron.

Scholarships, Fellowships, and Loans: 1998, Gale Research, Detroit, 1997.

The Wharton MBA Case Interview Study Guide, Volumes I and II, 1997.

Write Right! A Desktop Digest of Punctuation, Grammar, and Style. 3d ed. by Jan Venolia, 1995.

The Yale Daily News Guide to Fellowships and Grants, Justin Cohen, ed., 1999.

Web Sites

About.com's page for graduate school admissions
www.gradadmissions.about.com

All About Grad School: comprehensive directory of U.S. graduate schools
www.allaboutgradschool.com

American Dental Association
www.ada.org

Association of American Medical Colleges
www.aamc.org

Council of Graduate Schools
www.cgsnet.org

Educational Testing Organization
www.ets.org

Fast Web: large site includes scholarship and college directory
www.fastweb.com

Financial Aid
www.finaid.org

Grad Schools: directory of graduate and post-graduate programs worldwide
www.gradschools.com

Graduate Management Admissions Council
www.gmat.org

Graduate Record Examinations
www.gre.com

Kaplan Educational Centers
www.kaplan.com

Law School Admissions Council
www.lsac.org/lsat.htm

National Center for Education Statistics
www.nces.ed.gov

Online Testing Center
www.test.com

Petersons
www.petersons.com

The Princeton Review
www.review.com

The Psychological Association
www.hbtpc.com/mat/index.htm

The Psychological Corporation: Pharmacy College Admissions Test (PCAT)
www.tpcweb.com/psc/g-contsO.htm

Sallie Mae: provider of educational loans
www.salliemae.com

Ulinks: Links to major educational institutions in the U.S.
www.ulinks.com

"Vocabulary University" (test preparation site)
www.vocabulary.com

Sample Essay Index

This index covers only material included in the sample admissions essays. Be sure to also check the General Index. Whatever you do, remember this: Do not even think about modeling your essay closely on one of the examples in this book; essays in this book are provided so that you may learn how to write the best statement for your own unique background. Admissions people have also seen this book, and if you copy material, they will notice it right away.

General Index

This index does *not* include materials covered in the Sample Essays chapter. Be sure to also check the Sample Essays Index.